INTERNATIONAL BUSINESS ENVIRONMENT AND FOREIGN EXCHANGE ECONOMICS

INTERNATIONAL BUSINESS ENVIRONMENT AND FOREIGN EXCHANGE ECONOMICS

(For MBA Students of U.P. Technical University, Integral University, Lucknow University and other Indian Universities)

V.P. SINGH

M.A. (Eco.), MBA, Ph.D.
Associate Prof.
KIPM College of Management
Gorakhpur

S. SRIVASTAVA

B.Sc., B.E. (Mechanical), MBA
Amity Business School, Amity University
Lucknow

NEW AGE MANAGEMENT

An Imprint of

NEW AGE INTERNATIONAL (P) LIMITED, PUBLISHERS

New Delhi • Bangalore • Chennai • Cochin • Guwahati • Hyderabad
Jalandhar • Kolkata • Lucknow • Mumbai • Ranchi
Visit us at **www.newagepublishers.com**

Published by New Age International (P) Ltd., Publishers
First Edition: 2011
Reprint: 2014

BRANCHES

- **Bangalore** 37/10, 8th Cross (Near Hanuman Temple), Azad Nagar, Chamarajpet Bangalore-560 018, Tel.: (080) 26756823, Telefax: 26756820 **E-mail: bangalore@newagepublishers.com**
- **Chennai** 26, Damodaran Street, T. Nagar, Chennai-600 017 Tel.: (044) 24353401, Telefax: 24351463 **E-mail: chennai@newagepublishers.com**
- **Cochin** CC-39/1016, Carrier Station Road, Ernakulam South, Cochin-682 016 Tel.: (0484) 2377004, Telefax: 4051303 **E-mail: cochin@newagepublishers.com**
- **Guwahati** Hemsen Complex, Mohd. Shah Road, Paltan Bazar, Near Starline Hotel Guwahati-781 008 Tel.: (0361) 2513881, Telefax: 2543669 **E-mail: guwahati@newagepublishers.com**
- **Hyderabad** 105, 1st Floor, Madhiray Kaveri Tower, 3-2-19, Azam Jahi Road, Near Kumar Theater Nimboliadda, Kachiguda, Hyderabad-500 027, Tel.: (040) 24652456 Telefax: 24652457 **E-mail: hyderabad@newagepublishers.com**
- **Kolkata** RDB Chambers (Formerly Lotus Cinema) 106A, 1st Floor, S N Banerjee Road Kolkata-700 014 Tel.: (033) 22273773, Telefax: 22275247 **E-mail: kolkata@newagepublishers.com**
- **Lucknow** 16-A, Jopling Road, Lucknow-226 001, Tel.: (0522) 2209578, 4045297 Telefax: 2204098, **E-mail:lucknow@newagepublishers.com**
- **Mumbai** 142C, Victor House, Ground Floor, N.M. Joshi Marg, Lower Parel Mumbai-400 013, Tel.: (022) 24927869, Telefax: 24915415 **E-mail: mumbai@newagepublishers.com**
- **New Delhi** 22, Golden House, Daryaganj, New Delhi-110 002 Tel.: (011) 23262368, 23262370, Telefax: 43551305 **E-mail: sales@newagepublishers.com**

ISBN: 978-81-224-3037-0

₹ 150.00

C-14-05-7592

Printed in India at Ajit Printing Press, New Delhi.
Typeset at A.V. Compositors, Delhi.
PUBLISHING GLOBALLY
NEW AGE INTERNATIONAL (P) LIMITED, PUBLISHERS
7/30 A, Daryaganj, New Delhi - 110002
Visit us at **www.newagepublishers.com**

This Book

is

Dedicated to

Our

Parents & Family

Preface

The prime objective of this book is to provide a full and comprehensive text and contents of International Business Environment and Foreign Exchange Economics that covers the international business environment and the foreign exchange determination and functions in international business. With the day-by-day complexity of the international business and the changing scenario of the application of business in international business, this book will be helpful for teachers and students opt the papers in International Business and Foreign Exchange Management.

The contents of the book fulfill the requirement of the MBA, M.Com., M.A., BBA students. The book describe about the overviews of the international business, the changing dimensions of international business and globalization. It depicts about a details of the various theories of international trades. It also provides the depth knowledge about the foreign exchange determination, risk involves in it and different hedging techniques of avoiding risk in foreign exchange. It also shows the glimpse of the different International Institutions and Integration of different International Economics Regionals.

This book has been designed strictly according to the syllabus of U.P. Technical University, Integral University and Lucknow University for the core subject offered to the management students. The book provides a complete view about the environment of international business and economics used in foreign exchange business. There are 9 chapters in the book with comprehensive coverage, examples, diagrams and tables.

Dr. Vinitendra Pratap Singh
Er. Sachin Srivastava

Contents

CHAPTER 1

Overview of International Business

1.1 INTRODUCTION

Global economy is at crossroads. There is no single or simple answer to current economic problems. Transparency in the conduct of monetary and fiscal policies is needed to provide an anchor for expectations. Developments that seem unusual, even unbalanced, need to necessarily be judged unsustainable. For example, the potential gains offered by new technology, particularly in the production of goods and financial services, may provide a sound rationale for a number of trends that currently seem hard to explain. Yet, a starting point characterized by significant macroeconomic imbalances and major financial restructuring does not present a comforting environment for policymakers; given very low interest rates and virtual price stability in many countries, the scope for lowering real policy rates is now limited. This chapter implies a continuing need to focus on measures to strengthen the global financial system which looks to be the most vulnerable part of market-based economies.

1.2 WHAT IS A BUSINESS?

A business is an economic activity. It refers to buying and selling of goods. Today's business carries a complex area of commerce and industries which includes the activities of both production and distribution. To the enterprises business is related with the decision. What to produce? When to produce? Whom to produce? Where to produce? How much to produce? In simplest word we can say that the modern time's business is very much complex. As the environment is dynamic and changes frequently so the above questions always make the business enterprises to rethink about their business strategies.

1.3 INTERNATIONAL BUSINESS

International business means the buying and selling of the goods and services across the border. These business activities may be of government or private enterprises. Here the national border are crossed by the enterprises to expand their business activities like manufacturing, mining, construction, agriculture, banking, insurance, health, education, transportation, communication and so on.

A business enterprise who goes for international business has to take a very wide and long view before making any decision, it has to refer to social, political, historical, cultural, geographical, physical, ecological and economic aspects of the another country where it had to business.

India has managed an average economic growth rate of 6% since the 1990s. In the period 2000-2003, it averaged 5.8%. In the 1990s, the major contributors to Indian GDP have been traditional farming, modern agriculture, handicrafts, a wide range of modern industries and support services. India has a history of high inflation rates. However, in recent years it has been well under control. The RBI has been promoting liquidity in the economy since 1996. It took measures such as reducing the CRR, cutting short-term lending rates, and allowing banks to lend loans in foreign currency. The growing fiscal deficit is a macroeconomic problem the Indian economy faces. India's trade has been booming in recent years with increasing IT exports.

Brazil is the largest and the most populous country in South America. It is the 10th largest economy in the world. Brazil's economy is expected to recover in 2004 after going through a bad phase in 2003. Brazil experienced high inflation in 2002 and 2003. According to the central bank of Brazil, the fiscal deficit of the regional governments and state owned enterprises grew by 1.1% of GDP during 2003. The currency of Brazil, the real has been stable in the second half of 2003. The government does not want the currency's value to appreciate in the future as it fears that this might huit its exports.

Economic growth in China in 2004 is expected to be around 7.7 %. Despite the high level of money circulating in the economy, the People's Bank of China (PBOC), the Chinese central bank, does not favor an increase in interest rates. Government spending has been quite high in years 2002 and 2003. The current account surplus of China decreased from 2.9% of GDP in 2002 to 1.8% in the first half of 2003.

The US economy is the largest and most developed economy in the world. The economy grew at 3.3% in the second quarter of 2003. The economy posted strong growth of 8.2% in the third quarter. The inflation rate is expected to fall in 2004 due to lower food and energy prices. It is expected that the US Federal Bank will continue its low interest rate policy at least until the middle of 2004.

The US fiscal deficit is mounting. The deficit as on March 2004 was US $ 129 billion. The dollar has lost its value by as much as 21% since early 2002 period. US exports are pıcking up. But trade is not a significant contributor to growth in the US economy at present. Germany is the largest economy and the most populous country in Europe. The GDP of Germany grew by 0.4% in the first quarter of 2003. It fell by 0.7% in the second quarter. Inflation has been low in recent years.

It was 2.0% in 2001, 1.4% in 2002 and 0.7% in May 2003. Germany had an unemployment rate of 10.7% in April 2003. This is a marginal increase over the last two years (10.1% in 2002 and 9.6% in 2001). Fiscal policy was restrictive in 2003. It aimed at reducing the budget deficit. This policy is expected to continue in the next few years as well. Germany had a trade surplus of 119.2 billion Euro in 2003 compared to 124.4 billion in 2002.

To function effectively and efficiently, companies operating internationally must understand the social environment of the host countries they are operating in. Today there are thousands of MNCs which operate in many parts of the globe. Such companies should familiarize themselves with the languages, cultures and the business environments of the countries in which they are operating.

The global business environment can be defined as the environment in different sovereign countries, with factors exogenous to the home environment of the organization, influencing decision making on resource use and capabilities. This includes the social, political, economic, regulatory, tax, cultural, legal, and technological environments.

The political environment in a country influences the legislations and government rules and regulations under which a foreign firm operates. The economic environment relates to all the factors that contribute to a country's attractiveness for foreign businesses.

Every country in the world follows its own system of law. A foreign company operating in that particular country has to abide with its system of law as long as it is operating in that country. The technological environment comprises factors related to the materials and machines used in manufacturing goods and services. Receptivity of organizations to new technology and adoption of new technology by consumers influence decisions made in an organization.

As firms have no control over the external environment, their success depends upon how well they adapt to the external environment. A firm's ability to design and adjust its internal variables to take advantage of opportunities offered by the external environment and its ability to control threats posed by the same environment, determine its success.

Companies operating in international markets function in a highly competitive environment and require strategies that differentiate their products and enhance their perceived value, while reducing production costs. Traditionally, many such companies have confined much of their value adding activities to their home countries.

Alternatively, they may duplicate some value chain activities such as production and sales and service in individual countries. Companies operating internationally face conflicting pressures. They need to offer their product at competitive prices, and at the same time, tailor it to suit local needs. To bring down prices, they may be forced to standardize the product and operate from a single location.

Customization of products to suit local preferences does not allow for standardization or location of the manufacturing unit in just one region. Customization raises a firm's operating costs. To cater to specific and special needs of local customers, the firm may have to set up similar facilities in several countries and modify their product features.

Pressures from local competition for customization and price competition from international competitors with low-cost production bases pose a challenge to international companies. These companies have to choose between standardizing products, manufacturing at a low-cost location and passing the cost advantage to customers, and setting up plants in different countries for customizing products, regardless of the high costs that may be involved.

Such companies have to frame a strategy that strikes a balance between these conflicting demands. For example, when choosing a location, they have to consider various aspects like labour costs, tax rates, infrastructure, distribution systems, patent laws, suppliers and government support. They should also identify the extent to which customers are willing to pay for customization.

1.4 BUSINESS DEFINITION FOR INTERNATIONAL MANAGEMENT

- The maintenance and development of an organization's production or market interests across national borders with either local or expatriate staff.
- The process of running a multinational business made up of formerly independent organizations.
- The body of skills, knowledge and understanding required to manage cross-cultural operations.

1.5 INTERNATIONAL BUSINESS

International business is a term used to collectively describe topics relating to the operations of firms with interests in multiple countries. Such firms are sometimes called multinational corporations (MNCs). Well known MNCs include fast food companies McDonald's and Yum Brands, vehicle manufacturers such as General Motors and Toyota, consumer electronics companies like Samsung, LG and Sony, and energy companies such as Exxon Mobil and BP. Most of the largest corporations operate in multiple national markets.

Areas of study within this topic include differences in legal systems, political systems, economic policy, language, accounting standards, labor standards, living standards, environmental standards, local culture, corporate culture, foreign exchange, tariffs, import and export regulations, trade agreements, climate, education and many more topics. Each of these factors requires significant changes in how individual business units operate from one country to the next.

MNCs typically have subsidiaries or joint-ventures in each national market. How these companies are organized? How they operate?, and their lines of business are heavily influenced by socio-cultural, political, global, economic and legal environments of each country a firm does business in. The management of the parent company typically must incorporate all the legal restrictions of the home company into the management of companies based in very different legal and cultural frameworks. International treaties, such as the Basel Accords, the World Trade Organization, and the Kyoto Protocol often seek to provide a uniform framework for how business should be influenced between signatory states.

International business by its nature is a primary determinant of international trade, one of the results on the increasing success of international business ventures is globalization. Trade helps to prevent conflict. International business essentially is about trade, and when people trade they are in contact with one another. As a result, there is less isolation that countries can do. When countries begin to interact through trade, they are less likely to fight. This is also linked to the theory that democratic states are less likely to go to war with one another because they are interconnected and dependent on each others success.

1.6 DISTINGUISH BETWEEN DOMESTIC AND INTERNATIONAL BUSINESS

Trade means exchange of goods and services for the satisfaction of human wants. The process of exchange includes purchase of goods and services and their sale. The trade may take place within geographical boundaries of a countries or may be extended to across the border. When trade is confined to the geographical limits of a country, it is a *domestic* or *national trade.* In national trade both the buyer and the seller are of the same countries and they enter into trade-agreements subject to the national laws, practices and customs of trade. But *International* or *foreign trade* refers to the trade between two countries. Purchaser and seller are citizens of two different countries and are subject to International or bilateral laws of trade and tariffs.

Technically, domestic trade and International trade are more or less identical and are based on the same basic principles of trades. But practically, there are certain differences between internal and International Trade. It was on the basis of these differences that the old classical economists propounded a separate theory for international trade. The main points of difference are as follows:

1. **Difference in Currencies:** There is only one currency acceptable all over the country and therefore there is no difficulties in making payments in Internal trade. But, each country has its own monetary system which differ from others. Exchange rates between the two currencies are fixed by the monetary authorities under the rules framed by the International Monetary Fund. All payments for imports are to be made in the exporting country's currency which is not freely available in importers country. The scarcity of foreign currency may sometimes limit the size of imports from other countries.

2. **Difference in Natural and Geographical Conditions:** Natural resources like availability of raw materials, composition of soil, fertility of soil, rainfall, temperature etc. differ widely from country to country. On the basis of this speciality, countries specialise themselves in the production of certain selected commodities and therefore they produce better quality of goods at lower rates and sell them in the International market. It causes difference in domestic trade and foreign trade.
3. **Mobility of Factors of Production:** Mobility of different factors of production is less as between nations than in the country itself. However, with the advent of air transport, the mobility of labour has increased manifold. Similarly mobility of capital has increased with the development of international banking. Inspite of these developments, mobility of labour and capital is not as much as it is (found with) the country itself.
4. **Sovereign Political Entities:** Each country is an independent sovereign political entity. Different countries impose different types of restrictions on imports and exports in the national interest. The importers and exporters shall have to observe such restrictions while entering into agreement. These restrictions may be:
   (*i*) Imposition of tariffs and customs duties on imports and exports;
   (*ii*) Quantitative restrictions like quota etc.
   (*iii*) Exchange control;
   (*iv*) Imposition of more local taxes etc.

   No such restrictions are imposed on domestic trade or restrictions imposed on internal trade are quite different.
5. **Different Legal Systems:** Different legal systems are operated by different countries and they all widely differ from each other. The existence of different legal systems makes the task of businessmen more difficult as they have to follow legal provisions of the two countries as regards the particular trade.

1.7 WHY DO COUNTRIES ENTER INTO INTERNATIONAL TRADE?

Today hardly is there any country which is not engaged in International Trade. The economies of certain small countries are dependent mainly on International Trade. Here a genuine question arises as to why two countries enter into International Trade. There are a number of factors which contribute to the development of foreign trade. Most important among them are:

1. **Natural Resources and Geographical Factors:** Each country differs in natural resources and geographical distribution of various factors of production. Diversities in natural and geographical distribution of various factors of production. Diversities in natural and geographical conditions make a country more efficient in the production of one commodity and another country in some other commodity. These

countries specialise themselves in the production of such commodities and supply them to other countries in exchange for the commodities which they do not produce but other countries have specialisation in their production. For example, because of favourable natural conditions, India and Sri Lanka taken together produce 87% of the world total production of tea. Mica in India, manganese in Russia and oil in Arab countries are a few examples of this kind of specialisation.

2. **Occupation Distribution:** The population and its occupational distribution also differs from country to country. Occupational structure of its population decides the field of specialisation. For example, a large part of India's population is engaged in agriculture, hence it has specialised in the production of food grains and other agricultural products. England, on the other hand, has specialised itself in the production of Industrial goods as it has abundance of capital and scarcity of land and a large part of its population is engaged in Industries. Thus, countries specialise themselves on the basis of their occupations. Specialisation gives birth to international trade.
3. **Means of Transport:** Means and costs of transportation also contribute to the International trade. Industries using weight losing raw materials one generally localised at places near to the raw materials because the transport costs is the deciding factor. The countries where such raw materials are found in abundance, get specialised in their end-product. For example, India is a large producer of sugarcane and therefore, sugar industry is located mainly in India. At International level, the factors of production are not freely movable, because they involve high cost of transportation. Other countries, therefore cannot set up sugar industries and shall make imports of sugar from India and other sugar producing countries.
4. **Large-scale Production:** Large scale production of a commodity gives many advantages of scale. The industry of such a commodity can produce it at a lower cost because of scale economics and specialisation. After meeting the demand for the commodity in the national market, the surplus can easily be exported at a price fetching and handsome profits to the industry. For example, an industrial unit producing locomotive engines for the Indian Railways, can specialise itself in the production of locomotives. Large scale production of locomotives may enable the unit to export them to neighbouring countries.
5. **Differences in Costs:** Production costs of a commodity differ from country to country due to a number of factors:
   (*i*) Availability of natural resources and geographical conditions.
   (*ii*) Occupational structure.
   (*iii*) Large-scale production.
   (*iv*) Development in the field of science and technology etc.

   Countries having favourable conditions can produce the commodities at a lower costs and other countries at higher costs. Higher domestic costs of production shall encourage the imports of that commodity into the country and lower costs items may be exported.

6. **Degree of Self-sufficiency:** No country of the world is self-sufficient. The degree of self-sufficiency, however differs from country to country. For example the Russia imports 2% to 3% of its requirements and the USA only 4% to 5% of its total consumption. The degree of self-sufficiency is 40% to 50% in underdeveloped countries. Therefore, the countries which cannot produce at all or can produce only at a very high cost, arrange the supply of such goods through imports from other countries.

CHAPTER 2

Changing Environment of International Business

2.1 INTRODUCTION

The trade barriers are falling very much in international business which can be considered as the legal barriers and international interruption in international business.

The number of countries has more than tripled in the past 50 years. Businesses find themselves dealing with more individual countries, each with their own commercial laws and legal systems.

During the last 15 years, world exports for goods have grown on average 6% a year. Twenty years ago, people often associated business law with a particular nation. Today, they cannot afford to a variety of international trade rules and practices. The legal systems have not evolved; investors operate in a climate of uncertainty. In the last decade, many developing countries have become WTO members; yet few have ratified more than 30% of the world's 200 most important trade treaties.

All the international business enterprises know the changing environment of the legal formalities which is tough and tightly negotiated. In today's scenarios more deals means more cases are finding their way to the courts. Countries that have not invested in alternatives to court trials are seeing backlogs of cases, with associated high costs and lost business opportunities.

With different business and legal cultures and practices across the world, small firms need help to export in terms they and their foreign business partners understand. Most cannot afford lawyers. Nor can they afford to isolate themselves from international trade.

2.2 PRESENT SCENARIO IN INTERNATIONAL ECONOMIC SYSTEM

The free market economic system, as currently practiced, has been shown to promote more economic growth and prosperity than any other economic system. The international economic system has four main economic systems, two, *traditional* and *market*, are not currently practiced. A form of traditional economy may be practiced by remote tribes in New Guinea or the Amazon but of course this takes place within the sovereign territory of a recognized nation state. Pure market economies don't exist and are unlikely to as long as governments exist and special interest groups have their ear. The two systems most familiar to us from the 20th Century are planned and mixed economies. Since the collapse of the Soviet system, planned economies are not as prevalent as they once were but still exist in states like North Korea, Iran and Cuba. While the current phase of globalization has been spurred by that collapse, the negative effects of economic liberalism, particularly in emerging and less developed nations, could give rise to another era of centrally planned economies. Popular discontent with economic upheavals has been exploited recently by autocrats like Venezuela's Hugo Chavez to return his country's economic system back a more familiar command system.

2.3 GLOBALIZATION AND INTERNATIONAL BUSINESS

Perceptions about globalization and its effects vary, and have gone through a definite cycle in the past ten years or so. The upswing of the cycle occurred in the first half of the 1990s, a period characterized by a highly optimistic mood in industrialized countries. Politically, the collapse of Communism in Eastern Europe at the end of the 1980s and of the Soviet Union in 1991, and the enthusiastic adoption of democratic systems and market oriented policies by these countries, contributed to an air of triumphalism in the West. The change was viewed as epoch making, heralding what Francis Fukuyama had called the "end of history". These events coincided with the start of a prolonged boom in the U.S., which was fed by extraordinary productivity gains from new technology especially the application of IT. The benefits of globalization were expected to flow to developing countries also through access to export markets in industrialized countries and integration into global supply chains, while also promising a limitless supply of capital to all "well managed" economies.

This mood of triumphalist optimism did not last very long. The East Asian crisis towards the end of 1997 provided a rude shock and this was followed in quick succession by the currency collapse in Russia in 1998, Brazil in 1999 and Turkey and Argentina subsequently. These crises, and the severe economic downturns they caused, focused attention on the vulnerability of emerging market economies, and the risks posed by globalization, especially in the financial markets. The failure of the international financial institutions to warn about these vulnerabilities, and their subsequent failure to restore stability quickly, eroded confidence in the quality of institutional support underpinning economic integration.

The economic mood in the industrialized world also changed contributing to an evaporation of the earlier optimism. The prolonged boom in the U.S. economy ended in 2001 with the collapse of technology stocks and the downturn in economic activity. As unemployment began to increase in the industrialized world, there was a backlash against globalization in the industrialized countries and slogans of "fair trade" became common currency. The political mood also changed as the triumphalism associated with the "end of history" gave way, by the end of the 1990s, to worries about terrorism as a new and shadowy threat to democratic and open societies everywhere. These concerns were greatly magnified by the terrorist attacks of September 2001 in the United States.

Given this extreme swing in perception in the world at large, it is not surprising to the average man or woman in India is plagued by doubts about the nature of globalization, what impact it will have on ordinary people and what it implies for our policies. Before turning to these issues, we would like to emphasise that the issue is not whether one is "for" or "against" globalization. Globalization is not a specific policy, or even a defined set of policies, that one can be for or against. Rather, it is a process taking place in the world around us, driven by international developments which are largely outside our control.

Globalization has undoubtedly created a totally different external environment, and we must try to choose policies which enable us to derive the maximum benefits from it, it does not mean that dealing with the global environment must be the only, or even the central, focus of development policy. It will be better able to cope with globalization if the country have a strong economy. That is why the National Common Minimum Programme has outlined a broad objective of achieving 7-8% growth per annum. It will be our endeavor, in the Planning Commission to speak out the implications of achieving the goal.

2.4 CHANGING BUSINESS SCENARIO IN INDIA

To achieve the objective of high growth and a strong economy it is the need to focus on many areas in the domestic policy agenda which are not primarily aimed at deriving benefits from the external environment and also to devise policies to deal specifically with the external environment.

Three areas at present that are critical for the domestic agenda independent of what can be do externally are the provision of essential social services (i.e., primary education and health) the need to restore dynamism to agriculture and the need to strengthen infrastructure. All three are essential whatever approach adopt towards the globalization. The third–strengthening infrastructure – is particularly critical derive the full benefit from globalization.

Another important, and largely domestic area which demands priority attention is agriculture. The Tenth Plan GDP growth target of 8% per annum was based on the assumption that could achieve agricultural growth of around 4%. This was a reasonable target and has been achieved in many other fast growing countries in East Asia. However, a review of recent experience suggests that our country is far from achieving this target. In fact, agricultural growth, which was around 3.4% per year from 1980 upto the mid 1990s, has decelerated subsequently to around 2.0%. This deceleration is undoubtedly at the root of much of the reported dissatisfaction with the pace of progress in rural areas, and the many instances of acute distress in some areas.

Measures to restore dynamism to Indian agriculture will receive high priority in the Mid Term Appraisal. The agenda for corrective action in this area is complex. There is general agreement that it will be necessary to reverse the steady decline that has been witnessed over several years in public investment in basic rural infrastructure relevant for agriculture. It is very important to invest more in irrigation, rural roads and schemes for watershed management. It is also important to improve credit delivery in rural areas, strengthen extension services which have deteriorated almost everywhere and revitalize agricultural research.

It is also needful to evolve an agricultural strategy that would help agriculture to diversify away from an excessive reliance on food grains and towards higher value added horticultural crops. This is necessary even from a domestic perspective but it is also relevant from globalization since India could potentially become an exporter of certain fruits and vegetables. Diversification of agriculture poses its own problems some of which would be of special. Marketing of perishable horticultural produce requires very different marketing arrangements from cereals. It is needful to build a value chain from the farm to either on agro-processing industry or directly to the retail consumer and this chain must take account of the need for post harvest technology, cold chains, refrigerated transport, grading and modern marketing. This is clearly an area where there is scope for a much closer involvement of the corporate sector to provide value enhancement for the farmer through contract farming arrangements. This calls for changes in many areas including the current laws relating to the marketing of agriculture produce. It may require new form of co-operation between the corporate sector which provides the seed and technology and the extension services. A few pilot projects have shown good results, but these experiments need to be generalized and scaled up.

A third critical area constraining our growth is the quality of infrastructure. Infrastructure development is obviously important for growth in general, and it is especially important if we want to achieve competitiveness in world markets since this requires infrastructure of comparable quality. India has done much less than should have in this area, and corrective steps are urgently needed.

2.5 COMPARATIVE ANALYSIS OF INDIAN BUSINESS WITH OTHER COUNTRIES

China's outstanding success in establishing itself as a reliable producer of manufactured consumer goods for mass markets in the industrialized countries. In 1990, India's total exports were $18.5 billion and China's total exports were $62 billion or a little over three times India's at present. India's exports are about $60 billion; whereas China's exports are $438 billion, or seven times as large as India's.

Keeping the total exports of India and China at $500 billion, if the two countries had retained the same relative shares as they had in 1990, India's exports would have been $120 billion and China's $380 billion. The extra $60 billion in exports for India translates into extra employment of about 5 to 6 million persons, which is more than 20 per cent of the total employment in the formal sector.

Export competitiveness also requires continued progress in restructuring trade policies away from the earlier approach followed in India and in other countries, which protected domestic producers behind tariff walls. While this helps the individual producer being protected, it has the inevitable result of raising the domestic cost structure of the economy making exports uncompetitive.

Trade liberalization is a process that has been underway in almost all developing countries. However, its pace has been much slower in India. Quantitative restrictions on imports were removed in stages beginning in 1992 and finally abolished only in 2001. Tariff levels for industrial goods have been reduced from an import weighted average of 80% in 1992 to around 20% in 2004-05, but these tariff levels are still among the highest in the world.

Policies towards foreign direct investment are extremely important in gaining competitiveness in a globalised world. China's example of the impact of foreign direct investment is relevant in this context since almost 50% of Chinese exports are associated with FDI. In our own case, the role of FDI in modernizing a sector can be seen from the experience of the automotive sector. It was the entry of Maruti Suzuki which initiated the modernization of the sector twenty five years ago. Subsequently foreign investment brought in other contemporary motor vehicles and the resulting upgradation of the auto components sector has generated strong export capability in this area. Most recently, the competitive environment has seen the entry of a purely Indian designed vehicle which is even being exported.

Once again, China's example indicates that we have not exploited the scope for FDI inflow fully. China attracts around $60 billion of FDI whereas FDI in India, on a comparable basis, is about $ 5 billion. The Chinese economy is three times the size of the Indian economy, which suggests that India should be able to absorb $20 billion. The Common Minimum Programme states that "India needs and has the ability to absorb two to three times the level of FDI than at present." This translates to a target of $15 billion per year, which is a very reasonable target given what China has achieved.

China and South East Asia know that India suffers from an enormous infrastructure deficit. It has already mentioned the need for massive investments in rural infrastructure, mainly irrigation, rural roads and watershed development. An effective effort is required to upgrade our industrial and urban infrastructure.

Urban infrastructure is another dimension of infrastructure development which is grossly neglected. Success in achieving our growth target of 7–8% growth per year will inevitably put a strain on our major cities, especially those located in areas most likely to lead the economic expansion. None of these cities is institutionally and organizationally equipped to cope with the demands that will be put on urban infrastructure including especially road transport, traffic management, urban water supply and sewage disposal. Part of the problem is that the management of our cities is not based on adequate empowerment of the cities and financial capacity based on a combination of property taxation and user charges.

Bangalore exemplifies the challenge posed by urban infrastructure. The city has benefited enormously from the software boom and has demonstrated the tremendous benefits that can be realized from globalization given an educated labour force an acceptable telecommunications infrastructure, and a base of technically competent private entrepreneurs. It has the promise of retaining its leadership role and emerging as one of Asia's premier cities. But it has yet to demonstrate that it can stay ahead of the curve in providing the infrastructure support needed to sustain its boom town image. Bangalore has the enormous advantage of being an early winner, but in this highly competitive world it is necessary to work hard to stay ahead.

2.6 COMMON PROBLEM OF INDIA IN ACHIEVING COMPETITIVE ADVANTAGES

The State government is aware of the problem and is taking steps to ensure that Bangalore retains its position as a beacon for private investment both domestic and foreign. This is not simply a matter of making investments in one or other facility to deal with bottlenecks as they arise. It is necessary to restructure the system of urban governance and empower cities to look after themselves.

Recognizing the importance of infrastructure in India's development, the Prime Minister has established a Cabinet Committee on Infrastructure under his Chairmanship to give high level attention to infrastructure related issues. The government hopes to use this forum to expedite decision making in this critical area.

The resources required to close India's infrastructure deficit are enormous. An estimate made some years ago was that it needs to invest approximately \$150 billion over a ten year period. Updated to today prices the amount would be closer to \$200 billion. Resources on this scale cannot be provided by the public sector alone and it is the need to encourage private public partnership to bring in private resources into infrastructure development to the maximum extent possible. However, one must be realistic about the scope for attracting private investment. It is relatively easy in telecoms, airports and ports. It will be possible in power, once the reforms of the State Electricity Boards are underway but meanwhile a large part of the services would have to come from the public sector. It is also possible in roads where traffic density is high enough but there may be need for some public sector support through viability gap funding. There are other types of infrastructure such as rural roads, irrigation, watershed development etc. where private investment is unlikely to come forth.

All this means that a very large part of infrastructure investment will have to come from the Public sector either in the form of direct public investment in areas where the private sector is unlikely to venture, or the public contribution to public private partnership. We are trying to ascertain how we can mobilize the resources needed to meet these needs. One possibility, is to find ways of increasing the fiscal deficit beyond the levels permissible under the FRBM Act, for the specific purpose of providing funds for critical infrastructure development projects, but linked to a process whereby the additional deficit would be neutralized by effective use of foreign exchange reserves.

2.7 MEASURES TO ACHIEVE THE COMPETITIVE ADVANTAGES BY INDIA

The policy responses specifically needed for exploiting the potential benefits of globalization. The most important advantage which globalization offers today lies in the opportunity for expanding exports of goods and services. India had done well in the area of information technology related services, as the prosperity of Bangalore testifies, but had not shown comparable dynamism in exporting manufactured products. And yet, growth of labour intensive manufactured exports provides an opportunity for expanding productive employment which is a critical objective at present.

What does it take to become a successful exporter and thereby benefit from globalization? In addition to providing quality infrastructure, we must ensure that our domestic production structures are adequate to ensure global competitiveness. Developments in retail markets abroad have created mass consumer markets where most simple consumer goods are sold through large departmental stores and discount chains. These retailers source consumer goods from all over the world, but they typically demand supplies in large quantities and conforming to strict quality specifications. Some of our policies, such as the reservation of certain areas for the small scale sector, have prevented us from exploiting world markets. These policies were expected to promote employment in the small scale sector, but over a longer period they have prevented us from penetrating export markets which could have generated a much larger volume of productive employment. Successive governments have, over the years, removed items with export potential from the reserved list. This process needs to continue and hopefully, this will help in future.

India tries to make the tariff levels down to East Asian levels. To do this, India would need to bring the average tariff level down to one third of the present level. It is appropriate to mention that in one area where the country has performed exceptionally well is in the software and IT sectors, where tariffs on inputs and capital goods were kept at low levels.

The Cabinet cleared the proposal to establish an Investment Commission in the Finance Ministry. The Commission has a broad mandate to explore the scope for encouraging private investment both domestic and foreign. One of its tasks will be to make recommendations which could lead to the realization of the foreign direct investment potential of the country.

The foreign investment means that successful exploitation of opportunities in global markets can only come from multi-nationals. Bangalore is surely the last city where one can make this statement since companies such as Infosys, WIPRO and BICON, all admired in their fields are Indian Firms. Similarly, in the pharmaceuticals sector, Ranbaxy, Dr. Reddy's laboratories, Cipla etc. are Indian firms. A competitive environment, including opening up to the sector to both trade and foreign investment, if we want to ensure that efficient firms thrive and grow properly done, it should lead to the emergence of Indian firms that define themselves as acting in the global arena. Firms that cannot compete with FDI in their own home market are unlikely to be able to do so in the global market place. Our companies in the software sectors, biotech and pharmaceuticals have demonstrated that we can compete and there is no reason why this should not be true in many other sectors.

Many cities of globalization point to the devastating effects of the East Asian Crisis as evidence of the dangers of the external liberalization. The fact is that the East Asian Crisis was not caused by either trade liberalization or liberalization of FDI. It was caused by premature liberalization of the capital account, especially short term capital, in the face of weaknesses in the banking system. India's liberalization has deliberately avoided these pitfalls. We have consciously limited short term debt and followed a reserve management policy that has been abundantly cautious. Our reserves today are for above the level needed to manage the external payments situation, including any possible threats from short term capital out flows. Indeed that is why we are considering ways of using the reserves to build much needed infrastructure.

Does market volatility in export markets pose a risk? This is indeed an important issue. Exporting for world markets in today's environment involves both market risk and technology risk. A change in technology, or in tastes, or the sudden emergence of a new low cost source of supply in some other emerging market country could lead to a sudden loss in export orders. However, this factor can also go in our favour. The extra-ordinary market share carved out by China in so many simple manufactured goods offers an opportunity for India to persuade international buyers to shift at least part of their demand to India, provided we can match China's quality and prices. What is a market opportunity for us is clearly a market risk for China.

The globalization of World trade provides large potential benefits but also some risks. It is for countries to decide when they want to be on the risk reward frontier. As business school students you know that it is difficult to imagine high rewards without some risks. An important implication is that firms need to be flexible and nimble to survive in this environment. It is for this reason that many analysts argue that flexibility in labour laws is important. The government recognizes this, but also recognizes that this is a difficult and sensitive subject. We hope to build a consensus on this issue through discussion with all concerned.

As students of management recognizes that what we are engaged in is a typical SWOT analysis. It will review the country's strength and weaknesses, our opportunities and our threats. Out of this should come a reshaping of our development strategy. We need to leverage our strengths, re-inforce ourselves in areas where we are weak, aggressively exploit our opportunities especially in areas where we have strengths, and finally take precautionary steps to deal with threats.

CHAPTER 3

Emerging Trends in Globalization

3.1 INTRODUCTION

The globalization process has been neatly described as "the expansion of free-market relations and economic liberalism". A. Financier George Soros has defined its essence as "the development of global financial markets, the growth of transnational corporations, and their increasing domination over national economies. A less restrictive definition by Peter Dicken sees globalization, or "the complex interaction between Trans-National Corporations and states set within the context of a volatile technological environment" as something much less fundamentally economic than the previous quotations suggest.

Seemingly determined to place globalization within a more inter-disciplinary conceptual framework, Britain's Department for International Development define the big G as "the growing interdependence and interconnectedness of the modern world through increased flows of goods, services, capital, people and information. The process is driven by technological advances and reductions in the costs of international transactions, which speed technology and ideas, raise the share of trade in world production and increase the mobility of capital". Or, in laymans terms, "how our lives are becoming increasingly intertwined with those of distant people and places around the world—economically, politically and culturally."

Thus, in many ways, globalization is many things to many people, the definitions each adopts largely conforming to his or her own particular worldview or set of social and economic circumstances, experiences or prejudices. Seeing globalization merely in terms of economic liberalism ignores the powerful effects of cultural exchange, both benign and destructive. Seeing globalization as some battle for hegemony between nation states and powerful non-state actors ignores the non-global actuality of most trans-national business. As human geographers point out, global processes are in fact complex strata of varied relationships and interactions connecting and influencing people in diverse places and organizations. World environments and histories are not shaped in some predetermined fashion from above. Rather, they're shaped by a multitude of forces, frequently change, and are experienced differently from place to place and person-to-person.

3.2 GLOBALISATION OF MARKETS

The new commercial reality is the emergence of global markets for standardized consumer products on a previously unimagined scale of magnitude. Technology, by bilateral communication, transport and travel drives the world toward a converging commonality. Well equipped companies had emphasis on customizing items to offering globally standardized products that are advanced, functional, reliable and low priced. They benefit from enormous economies of scale in production, distribution, marketing and management.

Globalisation is intrinsically connected to the market. Increasingly, markets become interdependent and transnational and the market is often understood as the driving force of the globalization processes. Often it is assumed that globalizing markets lead to uniformity of the way in which people conduct their economic activities.

The key questions that are dealt with: What insights does anthropology and development sociology offer when they study rapidly expanding markets? What are the consequences for societies when markets change, new markets develop, or when existing markets become marginalized? Who are the winners and losers of new economic opportunities? How is trust in markets generated and sometimes broken down again? What are people's concerns about wealth and profit? What is the imaginary realm of markets?

3.2.1 Globalised Market Contributes To

The worldwide success of a growing list of products that have become household names is evidence that consumers the world over, despite deep-rooted cultural differences, are becoming more and more alike—or, as the author puts it, "homogenized." In consequence, he contends, the traditional MNC's strategy of tailoring its products to the needs of multiple markets may put it at a severe disadvantage vis-a-vis competitors who apply marketing imagination to the task of developing advanced, functional, reliable standardized products, at the right price, on a global scale. A powerful force drives the world toward a converging commonality, and that force is technology. It has proletarianized communication, transport and travel. It has made isolated places and impoverished peoples eager for modernitys allurements. Almost everyone everywhere wants all the things they have heard about, seen, or experienced via the new technologies. The result is a new commercial reality—the emergence of global markets for standardized consumer products on a previously unimagined scale. Corporations geared to this new reality benefit from enormous economies of scale in production, distribution, marketing and management. By translating these benefits into reduced world prices, they can decimate competitors that still live in the disabling grip of old assumptions about how the world works.

The days are gone when accustomed differences in national or regional preference found and also the days are gone when a company could sell last year's models — or lesser versions of advanced products — in the less developed world.

The days are also gone when prices, margins and profits abroad were generally higher than at home. The globalization of markets is at hand. With that, the multinational commercial world nears its end, and so does the multinational corporation.

The multinational and the global corporation are not the same thing. The multinational corporation operates in a number of countries, and adjusts its products and practices in each —at high relative costs. The global corporation operates with resolute constancy — at low relative cost — as if the entire world were a single entity; it sells the same things in the same way everywhere.

3.3 GLOBAL VS. MULTINATIONAL

Which strategy is better is not a matter of opinion but of necessity. Worldwide communications carry everywhere the constant drumbeat of modern possibilities to lighten and enhance work, raise living standards, divert and entertain. The same countries that ask the world to recognize and respect the individuality of their cultures insist on the wholesale transfer to them of modern goods, services and technologies. Modernity is not just a wish but also a widespread practice among those who cling, with unyielding passion or religious fervor, to ancient attitudes and heritages.

(I) Is it who can forget the televised scenes during the 1979 Iranian uprisings of young men in fashionable French-cut trousers and silky hody shirts thirsting with raised modern weapons for blood in the name of Islamic fundamentalism?

(II) In Brazil, thousands swarm daily from preindustrial Bahian darkness into exploding coastal cities, there quickly to install television sets in crowded corrugated huts and, next to battered Volkswagens, make sacrificial offerings of fruit and fresh-killed chickens to Macumban spirits by candlelight. During Biafra's fratricidal war against the Ibos, daily televised reports showed soldiers carrying bloodstained swords and listening to transistor radios while drinking Coca-Cola. In the isolated Siberian city of Krasnoyarsk, with no paved streets and censored news, occasional western travelers are stealthily propositioned for cigarettes, digital watches and even the clothes off their backs.

The organized smuggling of electronic equipment, used automobiles, western clothing, cosmetics and pirated movies into primitive places exceeds even the thriving underground trade in modern weapons and their military mercenaries. A thousand suggestive ways attest to the ubiquity of the desire for the most advanced things that the world makes and sells — goods of the best quality and reliability at the lowest price. The world's needs and desires have been irrevocably homogenized. This makes the multinational corporation obsolete and the global corporation absolute.

Market forces are powerful and can be so for good. But, left unchecked, they can yield socially deleterious outcomes. Markets may be important and market incentives can indeed be powerful, but they are neither all-pervasive, nor do they solve all problems. In their proper context, with appropriate safeguards and institutions, markets and their incentives can do much good. It is also, of course, well-known that great harm can be done when governments try to replace or outdo markets in circumstances where they do not have the capacity effectively to do so. The trick for society, both at the national and at the global level, is to harness the power of markets in the social interest. That, and not the defence, or attempts at the "perfection", of markets, through thick and thin, have been the traditional role of the economist.

These and other limitations of the pure market model and market system are not disputed among professional economists, much less social scientists of broader competence. Whatever one may think of a market-driven economy, no one would want a completely market-driven society. Hence the universal agreement on the need for laws, rules, and institutions to "govern" the functioning of markets and of individual and corporate behaviour. What these look like is, of course, the very stuff of politics, as well as of moral philosophy.

Global financial integration has substantially increased in recent decades. Initially, it manifested itself in growing capital flows between developed countries. In response to the removal of capital controls, financial innovation and technological progress, financial integration has subsequently spread to emerging market countries. Gross and net capital flows between developed and emerging economies have increased. Financial integration has also been evident in frequently high correlations between asset yields or prices, particularly for certain asset classes such as high-yield corporate bonds and sovereign bonds and equities in developed and emerging markets.

A critical rethinking of finance has been prompted by the present crisis. It is also implicating the very notion of the market economy and the globalize form that it has taken in recent years. *Finance,* the *market* and *globalization* are at risk of being jointly demonized, including by normally moderate observers of economic affairs. Recollecting a few basic arguments in favour of the trio may not be useless at this juncture.

Lending is an ancient human activity. Embedded in it is the suspicion of immoral conduct on the part of the lender, seen as the one who, for personal profit, either encourages the borrower's spendthrift ways or exploits the borrower's genuine needs. Which is why in some human communities, at certain times in the past but also today charging interest on money loaned was/is forbidden by either law or religion.

The very concept of money was probably devised at the dawn of humanity along with that of credit, and perhaps even at its service, as a means of transferring spending power over time by detaching it from any specific physical good. Money flanked and possibly surpassed credit as a source of negative symbols in the popular imagination.

Yet money and credit are part of what has enabled human beings to free themselves from the barbarism of immanence, from the savagery of a life ruled by the consumption for survival, which is spent in an instant. They teach man to think about the unfolding of time and they do so by appealing to the most powerful of all psychological levers, that of desire and need. Learning how to project a desire into the future or to predict a need is a fundamental step in evolution. It pushes people to design a method for satisfying future desires or needs, and that method is saving. If everyone's savings is lent to someone else, both the personal (if the loan is interest-bearing) and the social utility are augmented, because two ends are simultaneously met: that of investors who have in mind their future consumption (needs-desires) and that of those who instead require additional immediate purchasing power, motivated by the mere urge to consume, but possibly – and this is the most socially interesting case – by the desire to increase their own productive capacity, and therefore by a plan that is equally far-sighted and future-oriented.

In a monetary economy, finance – consisting of markets and intermediaries whose job is to assure the optimal allocation of resources and risks – is what makes the saving-credit-investment gears turn. It is one of humanity's great intellectual achievements. Yet it does not enjoy the universal admiration accorded to such other intellectual watersheds as the wheel or the number zero. The problem is that everybody can use the wheel and the number zero profitably, easily and naturally while by definition finance creates a conflict of interest between two major, and equally deserving categories: lenders and borrowers. The first group will want to see high interest rates and broad guarantees, be they real collateral or based on reputation. The second group will want low interest rates and the possibility of providing the minimum possible guarantees.

The unalterable fact that the objectives of these two groups are, at least in part, conflicting leads to tensions being inevitably offloaded onto professional intermediaries. They always run the risk of being seen as parasites who are happy to sit back and let others toil – the people who produce tangible goods and save up to ensure that they can retire in peace – before fleecing them mercilessly. It must be acknowledged that the victims of this prejudice often do practically nothing to dispel it; indeed, at times their conduct seems designed to lend it credence. Evident examples of this are to be found in the current global financial crisis.

Yet, the pivotal role of finance in our lives has never been apparent as in the present turbulent days.

3.4 MARKET: DID IT FAIL?

In this crisis, who has failed State or Market? People argue that it is more a State failure, but by virtue of a paradox. One firmly established conclusion of centuries of economic science is that the market must be "regulated" or it is no market. If the government practices absolute laissez-faire, the free competitive market cannot last; it is strangled by the monopolistic spirit of operators. This is a law of nature, a sort of economic entropy. The pure competitive market is the optimal regime from the standpoint of "buyers," i.e., the community as a whole, but the worst possible for the "sellers," a powerful minority constantly trying hard to oppose it. Such a market is a limiting condition that the public authorities may seek to approximate only by virtue of unflagging effort. Clear, comprehensive, specific rules are essential; and farsighted, attentive regulators and supervisors who cannot be captured by the "sellers" are indispensable. They must obviously be efficient: the burden of the regulatory apparatus that inevitably weighs on private agents ought to be non-distorting, light and non-bureaucratic. But it cannot do without that.

This forms the essence of what to human mind is the most advanced contribution of liberalism to economic thought. Nobody should confuse the great principles of liberty with the arbitrariness of complete laissez-faire. Eighty years ago, an Italian champion of liberalism in politics and a neatly pro-free-market economist, Luigi Einaudi, wrote:

The maxim of economic liberalism (is) taking on a third – I would call it a religious – meaning. In this interpretation, "economic liberals" are those who accept the maxim of laissez-faire, laissez-passer almost as if it were a universal principle. (...) The whole subsequent history of the doctrine demonstrates that economic science (...) has nothing to do with the religious conception of economic liberalism.

The "religious" notion that Einaudi stigmatized so scathingly was resuscitated in the second half of last century, as the consequence of a debate on the foundations of public economy. The standard theory of regulation as fundamental to the public interest came under increasing criticism in the 60s, and gave way to an alternative view, according to which markets themselves, or at the most civil courts, can remedy virtually all market failures, whereby government is necessarily incompetent, possibly corrupt and "captured" by the very interests it is supposed to regulate, so it can only make things worse.

The schools of thought backing this view are unquestionably among the high points of twentieth-century economics. Unfortunately, in the last twenty years, especially in Britain and America, that view has been used to forge a properly religious dogma, as Einaudi understood it, and the policies today under indictment were born of that religion. The global financial crisis of these past two years turns the empirical evidence overwhelmingly against it. The fundamental problem underlying the crisis has been one of rules and their effective application. The laissez-faire fundamentalists may be seen paradoxically as State interventionists, in that they wanted the government, allying with vested interests, to purposely deprive the competitive market of the air it breathes, namely rules and supervision. If this view is correct, by a twist of language it can call it a State failure: a failure by inaction, not excessive action, due to the refusal to see, to counter or to correct an evident series of market failures.

3.5 GLOBALIZATION: THE ACCOMPLICE

In the frenzied hunt for a scapegoat during this delicate conjuncture, there has been no lack of anathemas proclaimed against globalization. In past years detractors and enthusiasts of globalization have squared off for some time, but the former are rapidly gaining ground since the outbreak of the financial crisis.

The problems are serious and concrete, but the target is too generic to be useful. Globalization involves various aspects: production, trade, finance, migrations, the diffusion of ideas and knowledge. These aspects all have one characteristic in common: the heightened mobility made possible by the ICT revolution. Technology, then, is the prime mover, even if the trade and financial liberalization policies adopted in many countries in the 1990s assisted the process.

In effect, globalization and innovative finance are two sides of the same coin minted by technological innovation. Because of that deep nature, they are neither good nor bad, they just represent an opportunity for individuals, for societies, for economies; they must be understood and governed, and cannot be stopped, except at the cost of accepting backwardness and marginality.

3.6 TRENDS IN GLOBALIZATION

Globalization is in the tip of every tongue in the world today. Most of those who talk about globalization are not aware of its fundamentals. Nevertheless there is a red hot debate about this much circulated concept in academic corridors, board meetings and bed rooms. In India, there is a wide confusion about the effects and affects of globalization. Widely people think that because of the surrender of the nation state to globalization all the perils are hunting and hurting.

There is no one single effect of globalization. It is a multiple effect phenomenon impacting differently the various sectors. Those countries who master the art of combating adversities and succeeding in the battle can be called the good boys and those who fail in this fight are bad boys of globalization. India is neither totally good nor totally bad. There is a mixture of benefits and problems affecting the long standing Indian society. People swing sweeping remarks in this or that way. Very few have understood the differential consequences of globalization in India.

Generally globalization can be understood as a process which compresses the world into a small space where business and technology play a predominant role in ushering new social relations. Although globalization has started with relaxation of economic rules to accommodate free market principles and foreign players, now it has grown beyond the comprehension of economists. Today it is a massive social process demanding an all together different method to understand the developments in culture, society, religion, polity and personal relations. These factors and characteristics of society needs separate analysis to know the globalization fully well.

Although some aspects of globalization were tried by governments, time and again, it was the P.V. Narasimha Rao led minority government in 1991 introduced the full fledged new liberal economic reforms. The import duties were reduced, export relaxation was given, license raj in the industrial development was lowered, red tape was cut, and more importantly a red carpet was rolled out for the foreign investors. A large scale disinvestment was carried out to take the government hands off from the loss making public sector enterprises. The state protection given to the sick enterprises were withdrawn. The step motherly treatment given to the private sector was withdrawn and they were encouraged to enter the holy fields of telecommunications, aviation, power, ports, energy and other crucial infrastructural building projects. So much so a world impressive communications revolution was triggered by the neo liberal reforms.

3.7 IMPACT OF GLOBALIZATION ON INDIAN SOCIETY

Positive	Negative	No Improvement
Technology	Agriculture	Governance
Gender	Urban infrastructure	
Economy	Rural economy	
Civil society	Corruption	
Local languages		
Media		

To respond to the reforms, there was a massive acknowledgement from the global capitalists. They started honoring the Indian government invitations and come with billion dollars to kick start production units across the country. Coupled with the inflow of foreign investments, the demand for Indian software talents throughout the world increased the nation's clout. A huge army of software talents migrated to the Western world and facilitated an enormous amount of foreign exchange to India. This solved two major crises haunting the Indian economy. One, the foreign exchange problem started diminishing. Two, the increasing foreign investment pushed the infrastructural growth around the nation. Once primary infrastructure started growing the investor confidence kept increasing. Within fifteen years of the neo liberal economic reforms a fissionary nation was created. The divide was clear between India and Bharath. Suffering India and shining Bharath. The rich and poor, rural and urban, service class and agriculturalists, men and women, the bi polar opposites started troubling the social development. Is the globalization process a villain behind this divided society?

3.8 EFFECTS OF GLOBALIZATION

Effects of Globalization on Indian Industry started when the government opened the country's markets to foreign investments in the early 1990s. Globalization of the Indian Industry took place in its various sectors such as steel, pharmaceutical, petroleum, chemical, textile, cement, retail and BPO.

Globalization means the dismantling of trade barriers between nations and the integration of the nations economies through financial flow, trade in goods and services, and corporate investments between nations. Globalization has increased across the world in recent years due to the fast progress that has been made in the field of technology especially in communications and transport. The government of India made changes in its economic policy in 1991 by which it allowed direct foreign investments in the country. As a result of this, globalization of the Indian Industry took place on a major scale.

The various beneficial effects of globalization in Indian Industry are that it brought in huge amounts of foreign investments into the industry especially in the BPO, pharmaceutical, petroleum, and manufacturing industries. As huge amounts of foreign direct investments were coming to the Indian Industry, they boosted the Indian economy quite significantly. The benefits of the effects of globalization in the Indian Industry are that many foreign companies set up industries in India, especially in the pharmaceutical, BPO, petroleum, manufacturing and chemical sectors and this helped to provide employment to many people in the country. This helped reduce the level of unemployment and poverty in the country. Also the benefit of the Effects of Globalization on Indian Industry are that the foreign companies brought in highly advanced technology with them and this helped to make the Indian Industry more technologically advanced.

The various negative Effects of Globalization on Indian Industry are that it increases competition in the Indian market between the foreign companies and domestic companies. With the foreign goods being better than the Indian goods, the consumer preferred to buy the foreign goods. This reduced the amount of profit of the Indian Industry companies. This happened mainly in the pharmaceutical, manufacturing, chemical, and steel industries. The negative Effects of Globalization on Indian Industry are that with the coming of technology the number of labour required decreased and this resulted in many people being removed from their jobs. This happened mainly in the pharmaceutical, chemical, manufacturing, and cement industries.

The effects of globalization on Indian Industry have proved to be positive as well as negative. The government of India must try to make such economic policies with regard to Indian Industry's Globalization that are beneficial and not harmful.

3.9 GLOBALIZATION AND STRUCTURAL CHANGES IN THE INDIAN INDUSTRIAL SECTOR

Globalization and Structural Changes in the Indian Industrial Sector took place in the early 1990s when the government decided to open the markets to foreign investments by forming new economic polices.

Structural Changes in the Indian Industrial Sector and Globalization were initiated because the government wanted to encourage growth by doing away with supply bottlenecks that stopped efficiency and competitiveness.

Globalization implies the dismantling of trade barriers between nations and the integration of the economies of the nations through financial flow; trade in services and goods, and corporate investments between nations. Globalization has increased in the recent years due to the rapid progress that has been made in the area of technology especially in communications and transport. The Indian policies with regard to the industrial sector before globalization had imposed many restrictions on the sector with regard to the use and procurement of capital and raw material, type and nature of industry where the entry of private sector was allowed, the operation scale, and the various markets where they could supply. The Indian industrial policies favoured firms of small size that were labour intensive.

The Structural Changes in the Indian Industrial Sector was brought about by the New Economic Policy of 1991 which did away with many of the regulations and restrictions. The various advantages of Globalization and Structural Changes in the Indian Industrial Sector are that it brought in huge amounts of foreign investments and this gave a major boost to this sector. Many foreign companies entered the Indian market and they brought in highly technologically advanced machines into the country as a result of which the Indian Industrial Sector became technologically advanced. With new companies being set up in the Indian Industrial Sector it provided employment opportunities for many people in the country which in its turn helped to reduce the level of poverty in the country. The number of factories in India in 1990-1991 stood at 110,179 and in 2003-2004, the figure increased to 129,074.

The various disadvantages of Globalization and Structural Changes in the Indian Industrial Sector are that with many foreign companies entering the sector increased the competition for the domestic companies. With foreign goods being better than the Indian products, the consumer in the country preferred to buy the foreign goods. This reduced the profit levels of the Indian companies and they had to resort to lowering the prices of their products which in turn further lowered their levels of profit. With highly advanced technology entering the Indian Industrial Sector, the number of labour required in the sector reduced. The number of labour in the Indian Industrial Sector in 1990-1991 was 81,62,504 and in 2003-2004, the figure has decreased to 78,70,081. Thus, Globalization and Structural Changes in the Indian Industrial Sector poses advantages and disadvantages for the country. So the government of India must take steps in order to ensure that the changes in the structure of the Indian Industrial Sector are such that it facilitates globalization in a manner that is gainful and constructive for a country like India.

3.9.1 Globalization of Indian Pharmaceutical Industry

Globalization of Indian Pharmaceutical Industry started in the early 1990s when the government opened its markets to foreign investments. Indian Pharmaceutical Industry's Globalization took place with the coming of the foreign companies in the sector.

Globalization means the dismantling of the trade barriers and the integration of the economies of the nations through trade in goods and services, corporate investments, and financial flow between nations. Globalization has increased the world over in recent years due to the rapid progress that has been made in the field of technology especially in communications and transport. The government of India opened its economy to foreign companies through changes in its economic policy in 1991 and this led to the Globalization of Indian Pharmaceutical Industry.

The various advantages of Globalization of Indian Pharmaceutical Industry are that it brought in huge amounts of foreign currency into the industry which in its turn helped to boost the Indian economy. With many foreign pharmaceutical companies entering the Indian Pharmaceutical Industry it increased the number of jobs that were available to the people of the country. The benefits of Globalization of Indian Pharmaceutical Industry are that the foreign pharmaceutical companies also brought in highly advanced technology into the industry and this improved the quality of medicines that were available to the people. Many Indian pharmaceutical companies took over international pharmaceutical companies such as Ranbaxy merged with Croslands, Wockhardt with Merind and Nicholas Piramal with Sumitra Pharma. This helped the Indian pharmaceutical companies to grow and make even more profits.

The various disadvantages of Globalization of Indian Pharmaceutical Industry are that the competition increased in the Indian market between the foreign pharmaceutical companies and domestic companies. This reduced the profit levels of the Indian pharmaceutical companies as a result of which many had to close down such as Hindustan Ciba Geigy, Park Davis, Boehringer Mannheim, and Abbot. This has resulted in many people losing their jobs and in Mumbai's Thane region which is in Maharashtra more than 30,000 people lost their jobs between 1997-1999. Further the disadvantages of Globalization of Indian Pharmaceutical Industry are that many foreign pharmaceutical companies are taking over the Indian pharmaceutical companies such as SKB merged with Sterling, Ciba Geigy merged with Sandoz, and Rhone Poulenc merged with Fashions. This has led to the fear that foreign pharmaceutical companies will take over the Indian Pharmaceutical Industry.

Globalization of Indian Pharmaceutical Industry has had some positive as well as some negative effects. The government of India must make sure that the Indian Pharmaceutical Industry's globalization proves beneficial for the country.

3.9.2 Globalization of Indian Textile Industry

The initiation and development of globalization and Indian textile industry took place simultaneously in the 1990s. The Indian textile industry, until the economic liberalization of Indian economy was predominantly an unorganized industry. The economic liberalization of Indian economy in the early 1990s led to stupendous growth of this Indian industry. The Indian textile industry is one of the largest textile industries in the world and India earns around 27% of the foreign exchange from exports of textiles and its related products. Further, globalization of India textile Industry has seen a paradigm increase in the 'total industrial production' factor of this Industry, which presently stands at 14%. Furthermore, the contribution of the Indian textile Industry towards the gross domestic product (GDP) of India is around 3% and the numbers are steadily increasing. The process of globalization and Indian textile industry development was the effect of rapid acceptance of 'open market' policy by the developing countries, much in the lines of the developed countries of the world.

The initiation and its subsequent development of globalization and Indian textile industry respectively, were effected by the Ministry of Textiles under the Government of India. The aggressive policy that was undertaken for the rapid development of globalization and Indian textile industry were really praiseworthy. The most significant step amongst them was introduction of "The National Textile Policy 2000". This policy envisaged to address the following issues:

- Increased global competition in the post 2005 trade regime under WTO
- Huge import volume of cheap textiles from other Asian neighbours
- High production cost with respect to other Asian competitors
- Use of outdated manufacturing technology
- Poor supply chain management and huge transit cost
- Huge unorganized and decentralized sector.

Further, this policy also aims at increasing the foreign exchange earnings to the tune of US $ 50 billion by the end of the year 2010. It includes rational projections for the overall development and promotion of all the sectors involved directly or indirectly with the Indian textile industry. Furthermore, this policy also envisages the inclusion of the huge unorganized and decentralized Indian textile sector under the organized textile industry. This is because the unorganized textile manufacturing sector in India accounts for 76% of the total textile production.

The globalization of the Indian textile sector was the cumulative effect of the following factors:

- Huge textile production capacity
- Efficient multi-fiber raw material manufacturing capacity
- Large pool of skilled and cheap work force
- Entrepreneurial skills
- Huge export potential
- Large domestic market
- Very low import content
- Flexible textile manufacturing systems.

The Indian textile industry consist of the following sectors:

- Man-made Fiber
- Filament Yarn Industry
- Cotton Textile Industry
- Jute Industry
- Silk and Silk Textile Industry
- Wool & Woolen Industry
- Power Loom Sector.

An approximate number of textile manufacturing companies operating in India are given below:

- Badges, emblems ribbons and allied products - 175
- Bed covers, curtains, cushions and other draperies - 2471

- Carpets and rugs - 270
- Embroidery and embroidered garments, made ups and furnishing - 848
- Fabrics and textiles - 3013
- Yarns and threads - 1201
- Jute products - 337
- Kids apparel and garments - 1052
- Ladies apparel and garments - 2932
- Men's' apparel and garments - 2936
- Miscellaneous garments, textile and leather accessories - 1658
- Yarns and threads - 1201
- Wool, woolen garments, blankets and accessories - 468
- Textile chemicals, dyeing and finishing chemicals - 239.

The overall growth of the Indian textile industry can be attributed to the globalization. Today, the Indian textile industry employs around 35 million personnel directly and it accounts for 21% of the total employment generated in the economy. Globalization of the Indian textile industry has also facilitated introduction of modern and efficient manufacturing machineries and techniques in the Indian textile sector. Thus, much of India's economic growth is largely dependent on textile manufacturing and exports.

Globalization and the Indian Petroleum Industry go hand in hand since Globalization of the Indian Petroleum Industry started soon after the independence of the country.

The Indian Petroleum Industry was dependent from the very beginning on foreign capital, expert personnel, and technology, which led to the industry's globalization. Globalization entails the integration of the nations' economies through corporate investments, financial flow and trade in goods and services between nations. Globalization also means the dismantling of trade barriers between nations and it has increased in the last few years due to the massive progress that has been made in the area of technology, especially in transport and communications. The Indian Petroleum Industry's Globalization took place since foreign involvement in the various important stages such as production, refining, exploration, and transportation increased over the years. In order to further encourage the Globalization of the Indian Petroleum Industry, the government of India took certain measures in the early 1990s when the country opened its markets to foreign investments.

The various measures taken by the government to encourage Globalization and the Indian Petroleum Industry are converting the legal status of the Oil and Natural Gas Commission to a corporation. In order to encourage the involvement of the private sector in production and exploration, the government set up the Directorate General of Hydrocarbon. The government in an effort to encourage Indian Petroleum Industry's Globalization has offered the contract of discovered fields to foreign and private companies. The various companies that have helped in the Globalization of the Indian Petroleum Industry are Enron Oil and Gas Company, Videocon Petroleum Ltd, Reliance Industries Ltd., Ravva Oil Ltd., and Command Petroleum.

The Indian government in an attempt to further boost the Globalization of the Indian Petroleum Industry formed the Exploration Licensing Policy by which it tried to attract the foreign and Indian companies to production and exploration. The incentives that were declared by the government to encourage Globalization and the Indian Petroleum Industry are that on imports that were required for petroleum operations custom duty would not have to be paid, state participation is not compulsory, no tax on the production of crude oil, provisions for liberal depreciation, tax holidays for 7 years from the day that production starts and the freedom to sell natural gas and crude oil in the domestic market at prices that are related to the market.

Globalization and the Indian Petroleum Industry has been going together as has been seen for the past many years. The government of India has taken several measures in order to ensure that the Globalization of the Indian Petroleum Industry is successful for the industry. In the future, the government is likely to ensure that Indian Petroleum Industry's Globalization is beneficial for the industry and not harmful.

3.9.3 Globalization of Indian Chemical Industry

The process of globalization of Indian chemical industry was initiated in the early 1990s. The erstwhile Indian chemical industry suffered due to the absolute monopoly of the Government of India enterprises.

But with the opening of the Indian markets to Foreign Institutional Investors (FII) and Foreign Direct Investments (FDI) the monopoly of these Government institutions were curtailed substantially. This gave rise to the opening up of the Indian chemical industry to host of untapped opportunities. With the introduction of the open-market economic policy by the Government of India the process of globalization of Indian chemical industry took a steady rise. The Department of Chemicals & Petrochemicals under Government of India is the concerned highest authority that regulates the Indian chemical industry and the allied areas of environmental concern. The chemical Industry of India is at par with world standard and it shares a good portion of chemical business in world market. Asian countries, African countries and even Arab world buys Indian chemical products. The demand for Indian chemical products is high across the world. The reason for this popularity is its high quality and competitive pricing. India's low cost and high end chemical products manufacturing expertise coupled with world class manufacturing infrastructure is the main leveraging factor for the rise of this industry. India offers high class chemical products at a substantial discount than its western counterparts while delivering the same grade of output.

The globalization of Indian chemical industry was initiated by the following bombastic chemicals:

Basic chemicals are:

- Ethylene
- Propylene
- Butadiene
- Styrene

- Benzene
- Toluene
- Orthoxylene
- Paraxylene
- Mixed xylenes
- Ethylene oxide

Chemical intermediates are:

- Monoethylene glycol
- Phthalic anhydride
- DMT
- Vinyl Chloride
- Caprolactin
- Acrylonitrile
- Linear Alkyl Benzene

Synthetic fibers are:

- Acrylic fiber
- Nylon filament yarn
- DMT
- Polyester staple fiber
- Polyester filaments yarn

Polymers are:

- LDPE / LLDPE
- HDPE
- PVC
- Polystyrene
- Poly propylene

3.9.4 Globalization of the Indian Manufacturing Sector

The initiation and development of globalization of the Indian manufacturing sector took place simultaneously in the 1990s. The widespread acceptance and development of globalization of the Indian manufacturing sector effected astronomical growth of this industry.

The introduction and the subsequent development of globalization of the Indian manufacturing sector respectively helped India to shed its age old tag of being 'an agriculture based country'. The main growth driver of the Indian manufacturing sector are Information Technology and hardware, telecommunication hardware, automobile, pharmaceutical, biotechnology, infrastructure, electronic, electrical, textiles, etc. The effect of globalization of Indian manufacturing industry is reflected in the GDP's share of Indian manufacturing sector which has grown considerably over the years.

The share of Indian manufacturing industry towards India GDP has grown from 25.38% in 1991 to 27% in 2004. Further, the contribution of the Indian manufacturing sector to the Indian export sector has increased from 52% in 1970 to 59% in 1980 and 71% in 1990 and 77% in 2000-01. Furthermore, the Indian manufacturing exports accounted for a little over 5% (in 1990) of the value of output of the Indian manufacturing sector but today it is close to 10%.

India exports manufactured products worth about US$ 50 billion and a recent study on Indian manufacturing industry has forecast an annual growth of 17% by the end of the year 2015. In other words at this rate of increase the quantum of India's manufacturing exports will cross the US$ 300 billion mark by the end of the financial year 2015. Most of this business would be in the domain of auto components, pharmaceutical, apparel, specialty chemicals and electrical and electronic equipment sectors. The Indian sectors which grew tremendously as a result of globalization of the Indian manufacturing sector are as follows:

- Capital goods
- Chemicals
- Chemicals and fertilizers
- Consumer non-durables
- IT Hardware and peripherals
- Leather and leather products
- Steel and non-ferrous metals
- Water equipment.
- Engineering goods
- Petroleum
- Packaging
- Electronics
- Gems and jewelry
- Mining
- Textiles and apparels

The positive effect of the globalization of the Indian manufacturing sector can be corroborated from the following facts:

- The Indian industrial growth exceeded 10%
- Manufacturing growth rate exceeded 12%
- Manufacturing of consumer durables and non-durables have also recorded upswings
- Telecommunication sector with inflows of US$ 405 million has registered the maximum growth of 950%
- Merchandise exports recorded strong growth
- The automotive industry achieved a growth rate of over 20% in 2006-07
- The biotechnology industry witnessed another good year in 2006-07 and registering more than 40% of growth
- The US$ 47 billion Indian textile industry is expected to grow to US$ 115 billion by the year 2012
- The US$ 6.4 billion Indian retail industry is expected to grow over 20% annually to US$ 23 billion by 2010
- The robust pharmaceutical market in India ranks 4th worldwide and is expected to cross business worth Rs. 1,00,000 crore in formulations and bulk drug production by 2010.

Although, the process of globalization of the Indian manufacturing sector have contributed immensely for the overall development of the Indian economy but it still suffers from some bottlenecks, like the following:

- Use of primitive technology or under utilization of technology
- Poor infrastructure
- Over staffed operations
- Expensive financing and bureaucracy.

India is slowly shedding its image from being an agriculture based country to a manufacturing based country and thus the above-mentioned bottlenecks should be immediately arrested and eradicated to ensure further growth of this industry. To ensure elimination of the above-mentioned aberrations form the

Indian manufacturing sector the government of India must focus on areas like improving the urban infrastructure, ensuring fair competition and access to markets, reduction of import duties, quality improvements in vocational and higher education, increased investment in R&D and support of SMEs.

The manufacturing industry is the backbone of any economy since it helps in the overall growth of productivity, employment, and it also strengthens agriculture and service sectors. The astronomical growth in worldwide distribution systems and Information Technology, coupled with opening of trade barriers, has led to stupendous growth of global manufacturing networks, designed to take advantage of low-waged yet efficient Indian work force. The globalization of the Indian manufacturing sector has brought down the percentage of Indians living below poverty line from 40% to 25%. The Indian manufacturing sector is successfully competing in the global marketplace and registering high growth on year-on-year basis since the 1990s.

3.9.5 Globalization on Indian Steel Industry

The effects of Globalization on Indian steel industry have been felt more profoundly in the past few years. The India steel industry is one of the major industries in India.

The effects of Globalization on Indian steel industry are not same throughout the country. The effects depend on the different regions, the type of raw materials used, the condition of the markets, technological advancements, the policies of the governmental authorities pertaining to the trade and business activities of the Indian steel industry, etc. In this age of the globalization, as the other industries of the developing countries, the Indian steel manufacturing sector needs to restructure itself, in order to have a sustainable growth. This will be very helpful for providing the correct strategies for the steel industry in India. The restructuring should depend on the different requirements of the steel industry.

The government played a very important role in the development of the steel industry in India. The India steel industry is experiencing a slow but steady growth. The steel industry in India has huge scopes in the future with massive scale of infrastructural development happening all across the country. The steel industry in India caters to many other industrial sectors such as construction industry, mining industry, transportation industry, automobile industry, engineering industry, chemical industry, etc. The steel segment includes the manufacturing of three different kinds of steel such as carbon steel, ferro-chrome steel and stainless steel.

The steel industry in India has further plans of development. Plans are being chalked out on setting up of three pig iron manufacturing units of the combined capacity of 6 lakh tons per year and a steel manufacturing unit of the capacity of producing one million ton yearly in West Bengal, with the technical and financial support of China. With all these developments steel industry in India is all set to become one of the most reputed industries not only in India but also in the international market as suggested by experts.

In order to survive the immense competition under the globalization, the Indian steel industry plans a reversal of the production of steel industry. The main objectives of the strategy is the derivation of the benefit from the optimum utilization of the plant capacity, the nullification of any form of drawbacks, to track the opportunities in order to get the maximum from it and to tackle the possible threats.

The strategy suggested for the reversal of the steel industry in India is double layered in nature, effecting the reversal and at the same time sustaining the reversal. The strategy has to be growth and survival oriented. The survival part would assure the survival of the industry in the fierce competitive atmosphere and the growth part would boost the sustainable growth of the industry. The two different parts of the strategy has to be integrated into one to have the expected results.

The reduction of the cost is another major factor in the survival of the Indian steel industry in the age of globalization. The cost reduction would be the main aspect of the improvement pertaining to the competitiveness of the industry. The manufacturers under the steel industry in India have to focus their attention in the areas such as:

- The reduction in the cost of operations
- The reduction in the costs pertaining to the working capital
- The reduction in the costs pertaining to the production inventory or stock that is not sold
- The improvement in the economics operating in the technological aspects of production
- The transposition of basic materials of production
- The sources of the procurement should be different.

3.10 BENEFITS OF GLOBALIZATION

Benefits of Globalization keep varying with respect to the changing trends in the different aspects of the world, be it economic, cultural, ecological, technological, social, or political.

The most significant changes brought about by the process of globalization are the increasing interdependence and integration at a worldwide scale. Globalization has brought about great revolutionary changes worldwide. Some of the significant advantages of globalization are the speedy and easy transportation of goods and services, reduction in the chances of war amongst the developed countries, increase in the free international trade between countries, growing connectivity with the development of global mass media, diminishing the cultural barriers, propagating democratic idealism, increasing interdependence between the nation-states, growing liquidity of capital, rising possibilities of investment of the developed countries in the developing ones, easy and flexible operations of corporations across borders, increase in the connectivity between the individuals and corporations all over the world, and policies undertaken in the developed countries for growing environmental protection.

Within the developing world, it has been assessed that globalization will increase the economic welfare and opportunity. Along with these the civil liberties will be enhanced and resources more efficiently used. As a result, all the nations participating in the free trade enjoys a profitable status. This in turn inculcates low prices, increase in employment and a better living standard in these developing countries of the world. Regarding the benefits of Globalization, one is that, there is always a positive chance for the new advanced skills and technologies aiding to increase the standard of life throughout the world. According to the liberals, globalization is an effective tool for eliminating pauperization and for permitting the poor people to get hold of a steady grip of the global economy. For instance, as per World Bank reports, within the two decades from 1980s to 2001, those people living on $1 or less per day, reduced from 1.5 billion to 1.1 billion. Alongside there is a rise in the total population of the world. So, it is an obvious conclusion that in the developing countries the percentage of those people got reduced from 40% to 20%.

Benefits of Globalization in the developing nations can also be observed in the improvement of the socio-economic status of women there. This is because in the competitive world of today the role of women has become more significant and more valuable, hence nations like Saudi Arabia cannot develop themselves with their this existing culture that exclude women from participating in the state affairs. The developed nations on the other hand, encourage education for women and this thereby improves the economic prospects of their respective states dramatically.

Among other globalization benefits, mention should be made of advancement in medicine new and amended public health policies, and increase in food supplies. All these have diminished the infant mortality rate and increased the expectancy of life. Again benefits of globalization are obvious with the increase in the income level of the country. This in turn declines the use of child labour. It should be noted that though there is still inequality within and between nations, but as a benefit of globalization, there have emerged a global middle class from the 1980 onwards. One can observe the growing process of integration of rich and poor nations with advancement in the medical facilities, technology, democratization of politics and finance. In the twenty-first century, globalization is considered as an outstandingly progressive, positive, and liberating force.

Regarding the benefits of Globalization on different aspects of the world, it can be stated that the regressive taboos are eradicated in the globalized nations and discrimination against people regarding gender, class, race, colour, and religious beliefs are diminished to a great extent. It is a remedy to the intolerant and fanatic fundamentalism oppressing millions even today. The best possible benefit globalization offers is the ray of hope among the still to develop nations of the world, which after observing the positive impact of globalization in the west, can demand for a better future and Western liberal traditions.

CHAPTER 4

International Trade and Theories

4.1 INTRODUCTION

Today most countries are still depending to each other. This dependency degree between the countries varies one nation to another. Most nations after the first and second World War tries to make protection policy and closed their borders for not having trade between the nations or they imposed a very high rate of tariff for the world. But, the result was against their policy and they realize the importance of International Trade and one by one country of the world adopted the liberalisation and free trade policy and tries to remove their deficit in the balance of payments. Now, the general question arises that why do the nations trade? Nations trade with each other because of unlimited wants of the nations, no nations are self-sufficient who can produce all the goods and services required inside the country, the factors of production differs among them, the geographical and demographical, climatic, mineral resources and mines, labour-capital resources, technological advancement, managerial and entrepreneurial skills differs from one nations to another. All these differences among the nations differs the production possibilities situation among them. This production possibilities differences show that a nation may be efficient in producing one particular goods in comparison to other and may have inefficiency in producing another product in comparison to other. For example, Korea and Japan can produce electronics and automobiles goods more efficiently than any other country in the world. India can produce cotton and jute more efficiently than other countries. Korea, Japan and India can therefore, export these goods to other countries at relatively lower prices. USA and UK, can import these products at lower price from Korea, Japan and India, and in return of it they can import USA machines and UK aircrafts at a lower price, because the cost of production of USA and UK in machines and aircraft respectively may be at lower price as comparison to Korea, Japan and India. In other words the nations trade not in a barter system but through the market mechanism by using money as a medium of exchange. By this means the nations found gains from the trade. In this way the gains were generate in the International Trade. For attaining more profit and gains from trade the nation specialize in the production and exports of those goods and services in which it has an absolute or a comparative advantage and in modern time having competitive advantage; and it purchases or imports those goods and services in which it has absolute or comparative disadvantage over other nations of the world. So, the basis of the International Trade between the nations is the gains or profits to get from the exchange of goods and services. If there are no gains or profits in exchange of goods and services then there would be not International Trade among the nations.

4.2 NATIONS TRADE PRACTICES

The International Trade depends on the product price of the product which differs from one nation to the other. This difference in the product price is found due to the difference in the production possibility of the product or differences in the product demands or may be both. Differences in the supply position (production possibility) may appear due to availability of natural resources, the degree of efficiency of factors of production, the technological advancement etc. So, it is assumed that the nation having excess in labour oriented product must export labour oriented product and the nation having excess of capital oriented product must export capital oriented product.

Now, we can illustrate why the nations trade with the help of chart.

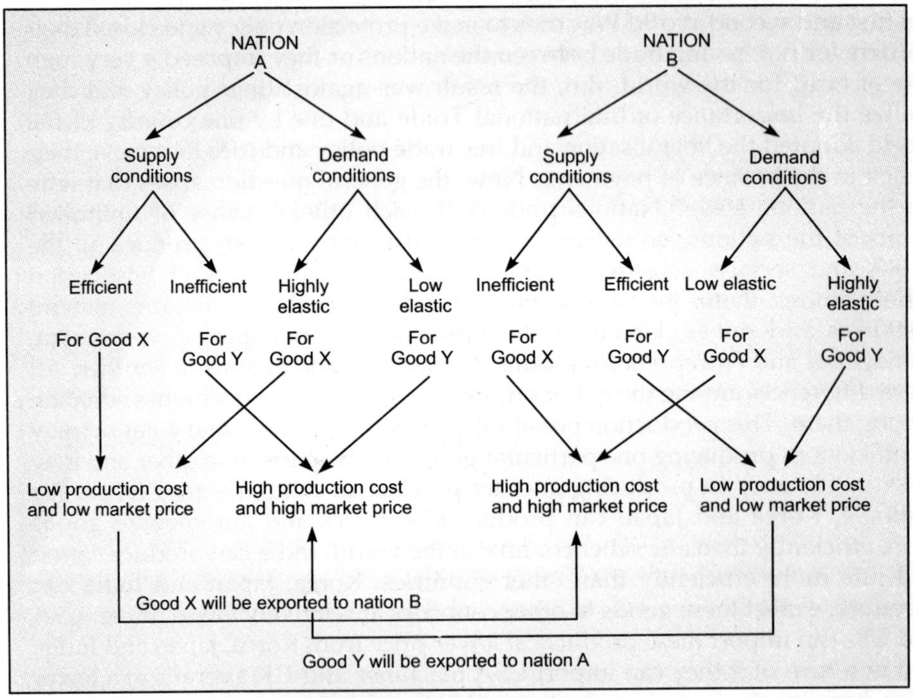

Fig. 4.1: Nations trade chart

From the above chart, it is quite clear that the Nation A had comparative advantage in production of Good X while the Nation B had comparative advantage in production of Good Y. With the exchange of goods between them, both the nations had gains from the trade therefore, the International

Trade will exist. Nation A had good supply condition in Good X and also having high elasticity for it but, inefficient in supply and demand of Good Y. So, it is better to import from Nation B instead of producing within the country and also increase the production of Good X so that more export occurs for Nation B and vice-versa.

From the above example it is clear that no nations are self-sufficient within self. There is always a degree of dependency found among the nations, therefore to fulfill their needs nations must go for the International Trade.

4.3 ABSOLUTE ADVANTAGE THEORY OF INTERNATIONAL TRADE

Adam Smith the Scottish Economist in his famous book "Wealth of Nation" propounded the Absolute Advantage theory of International trade in the year 1776. He argued against the mercantile type of International Trade and advocated free trade as the best policy for the nations of the world. Smith also argued that free trade for each country could specialize in the production of those commodities in which it had an absolute advantage and import those products having absolute disadvantage. This International specialization of factors in production would result in an increase in world output, which would be shared by the trading nation. Thus, a nation need not gain at the expense of other nations all nations could gain simultaneously.

The absolute advantage theory refers to theory posited by **Adam Smith** in the 18th century that asserts that a nation would benefit from manufacturing more output than others manufacture since it is in the possession of a particular resource or commodity. This particular resource can also be a certain method or knowledge that increases the production efficiency, and thus reduces the relative need to resources.

4.3.1 Assumptions of the Theory

1. Two countries and two commodities
2. Free trade policy
3. Factor of production is only labour
4. No transportation charges is added with the trade
5. No mobility of factor of product between the country but mobile within the country

For example, suppose there are two countries namely India & USA and two goods namely sugar & machine. As Adam Smith had argued that labour is the only production factor. Suppose India can produce one unit of sugar with the help of 10 unit of labours whereas it produces one unit of machine with 20 unit of labours. USA involved 20 units of labour to produce one unit of sugar whereas it take only 10 units of labour to produce one unit of machine. Therefore, India had absolute advantage in producing sugar where it has disadvantage in producing machine while USA had absolute advantage in producing machine and having disadvantage in producing sugar.

Particulars/Labour Production	10 Units of Labour	20 Units of Labour
India	1S*	1M*
USA	1M*	1S*

1S* One unit of Sugar
1M* One unit of Machine

If the two countries were to exchange the two goods at a ratio of one to one, i.e one unit of sugar for one unit of machine, India could get a unit of machine by using 10 units of labour to produce one unit of sugar and trading that with USA for one unit of machine, whereas if it produced machine itself then it would have to give up 20 units of labour. The 10 units of labour 'saved' can be used to produce another unit of sugar for home consumption.

The symmetry of the example makes it obvious that USA may make a similar gain by producing two units of machine, using 20 labour units and exporting one unit in exchange for one unit of sugar, rather than using the 20 units of labour to produce one unit of sugar itself. The implication is clearly that both countries could have more of both goods with a given effort, by trading.

This is a simple and very powerful illustration of the benefits of the International Trade and on it Adam Smith rested his view for non interference of International Trade and advocated for free trade as the best policy of developing a nation.

4.4 COMPARATIVE COST ADVANTAGE THEORY OF INTERNATIONAL TRADE

Comparative advantage was first described by Robert Torrens in 1815 in an essay on the Corn Laws. He concluded it was to England's advantage to trade with Portugal in return for grain, even though it might be possible to produce that grain more cheaply in England than Portugal.

However the term is usually attributed to David Ricardo who explained it in his 1817 book *On the Principles of Political Economy and Taxation* in an example involving England and Portugal. In Portugal it is possible to produce both wine and cloth with less labour than it would take to produce the same quantities in England. However the *relative costs* of producing those two goods are different in the two countries. In England it is very hard to produce wine, and only moderately difficult to produce cloth. In Portugal both are easy to produce. Therefore while it is cheaper to produce cloth in Portugal than England, it is cheaper still for Portugal to produce excess wine, and trade that for English cloth. Conversely England benefits from this trade because its cost for producing cloth has not changed but it can now get wine at a lower price, closer to the cost of cloth. The conclusion drawn is that each country can gain by specializing in the good that it has comparative advantage in and trading that good for the other.

In economics, **comparative advantage** refers to the ability of a person or a country to produce a particular good or service at a lower marginal cost and opportunity cost than another person or country. It is the ability to produce a product most efficiently given all the other products that could be produced. It can be contrasted with absolute advantage which refers to the ability of a person or a country to produce a particular good at a lower absolute cost than another.

Comparative advantage explains how trade can create value for both parties even when one can produce all goods with fewer resources than the other. The net benefits of such an outcome are called gains from trade.

Adam Smith developed the principle of absolute advantage. The economist Paul Craig Roberts notes that the comparative advantage principles developed by David Ricardo do not hold where the factors of production are internationally mobile. Limitations to the theory may exist if there are single kind of utility. The very fact that people want food and shelter already indicates that multiple utilities are present in human desire. The moment the model expands from one good to multiple goods, the absolute may turn to a comparative advantage. However, global labour arbitrage, where one country exploits the cheap labour of another, would be a case of absolute advantage that is not mutually beneficial.

The theory explains that a country tends to specialize in the production of that commodity in which it has a comparative cost advantage by virtue of its natural resources, climatic conditions, human resources, demographical, infrastructure, financial status and capital equipments.

The term Comparative Advantage means the special ability of a country to provide a particular commodity or services relatively at a lower cost than other commodities or services. A country will according to the theory, concentrate on the production of such goods and services in which it has comparative cost advantage and export them in exchange for other commodities in which has a positive cost disadvantage. The commodity in which is most suited to it, will be produced at a large scale. The production of other commodities in which it has little cost advantage will not be carried on any longer. The country will specialize in the production of the relatively most cost advantageous commodity that it will export and the lesser cost advantageous commodity will be import from other countries. It is thus, the comparative cost advantage in the production of goods and services, which gives rise to International Trade, according to the Comparative Cost Theory of International Trade.

4.4.1 Assumption of the Theory

- **Two countries and two goods:** Only two countries and two commodities are to be considered at a time.
- **Full employment:** if one or other of the economies has less than full employment of factors of production, then this excess capacity must usually be used up before the comparative advantage reasoning can be applied.
- **Only labour is the factor of production:** Labour is the only factor of production. The cost of production is expressed only in terms of so many units of labour. The labour productivity is homogeneous.

- **Perfect mobility of factors of production within countries:** The factors of production are perfectly mobile within the country but totally immobile between the countries.
- **Negligible transport cost:** It is assumed that there is no transportation cost would be incurred in International Trade.
- **Assume that half the resources are used to produce each good in each country:** It is also assumed that both the countries are producing both the goods but with different cost of production.
- **Perfect competition:** Another assumption is that the domestic and International markets is done under perfect competition which make efficient allocation of productive resources in an idealized free market.
- **Constant return to scale:** The law of constant returns to scale applies to both the countries.

In his example, Ricardo imagined two countries, England and Portugal, producing two goods, cloth and wine, using labour as the sole input in production. He assumed that the productivity of labour (i.e., the quantity of output produced per worker) varied between industries and across countries. However, instead of assuming, as Adam Smith did, that England is more productive in producing one good and Portugal is more productive in the other; Ricardo assumed that Portugal was more productive in both goods. Based on Smith's intuition, then, it would seem that trade could not be advantageous, at least for England.

However, Ricardo demonstrated numerically that if England specialized in producing one of the two goods and if Portugal produced the other, then total world output of both goods could rise! If an appropriate terms of trade (i.e., amount of one good traded for another) were then chosen, both countries could end up with more of both goods after specialization and free trade then they each had before trade. This means that England may nevertheless benefit from free trade even though it is assumed technologically inferior to Portugal in the production of everything.

As it turned out, specialization in *any* good would not suffice to guarantee the improvement in world output. Only one of the goods would work. Ricardo showed that the specialization good in each country should be that good in which the country had a comparative advantage in production. To identify a country's comparative advantage well requires a comparison of production costs across countries. However, one does not compare the monetary costs of production or even the resource costs (labour needed per unit of output) of production. Instead, one must compare the *opportunity* costs of producing goods across countries.

A country is said to have a comparative advantage in the production of a good (say cloth) if it can produce cloth at a lower opportunity cost than another country. The opportunity cost of cloth production is defined as the amount of wine that must be given up in order to produce one more unit of cloth. Thus England would have the comparative advantage in cloth production relative to Portugal if it must give up less wine to produce another unit of cloth than the amount of wine that Portugal would have to give up to produce another unit of cloth.

Overall, this condition is rather confusing. Suffice it to say, that it is quite possible, indeed likely, that although England may be less productive in producing both goods relative to Portugal, it will nonetheless have a comparative advantage in the production of one of the two goods. Indeed, there is only one circumstance in which England would not have a comparative advantage in either good, and in this case Portugal also would not have a comparative advantage in either good. In other words, either each country has the comparative advantage in one of the two goods or neither country has a comparative advantage in anything.

Another way to define comparative advantage is by comparing productivities across industries and countries. Thus, suppose, as before, that Portugal is more productive than England in the production of both cloth and wine. If Portugal is twice as productive in cloth production relative to England but three times as productive in wine, then Portugal's comparative advantage is in wine, the good in which its productivity advantage is greatest. Similarly, England's comparative advantage good is cloth, the good in which its productivity disadvantage is least. This implies that **to benefit from specialization and free trade, Portugal should specialize and trade the good in which it is "best" at producing, while England should specialize and trade the good in which it is "least worse" at producing.**

Note that trade based on comparative advantage does not contradict Adam Smith's notion of advantageous trade based on absolute advantage. If as in Smith's example, England were more productive in cloth production and Portugal were more productive in wine, then we would say that England has an absolute advantage in cloth production while Portugal has an absolute advantage in wine. If we calculated comparative advantages, then England would also have the comparative advantage in cloth and Portugal would have the comparative advantage in wine. In this case, gains from trade should be realized if both countries specialized in their comparative, and absolute, advantage goods. Advantageous trade based on comparative advantage, then, covers a larger set of circumstances while still including the case of absolute advantage and hence is a more general theory.

4.4.2 Cost Differences

Recardo had defined three costs differences on which the International Trade may hold. These costs are:

1. Absolute Cost Difference
2. Equal Cost Difference
3. Comparative Cost Difference

1. *Absolute Cost Difference*

Absolute differences in cost refer to the differences in the cost of production of certain commodities in the large proportion in one country than in the other country. Sometimes, absolute differences in production costs between two countries develop. In such case, International Trade between them is inevitable. We can explain it with the help of an illustration.

One Labour Unit Production

	Jute	Cotton
INDIA	02	01
EGYPT	0.5	01

Suppose India can produce with one unit of labour either two units of jute or one unit of cotton. Egypt, on the other hand produces with one unit of labour either one unit of cotton or half unit of jute. It is evident here that India has natural advantage in the production of jute while Egypt enjoys natural advantage in production of cotton. Hence, India will specialize in the production of jute and Egypt in cotton. India will export jute to Egypt in exchange for cotton. The exchange rate between the two countries is based on labour costs.

The International Trade between India and Egypt will continue so long as India is able to get more than one unit of cotton so long as India is able to get more than one unit of cotton in exchange for two units of jute. If India gets only one unit of cotton for two units of jute, International trade will not be possible because there is no gain in this trade to India. Similarly, Egypt and India will continue trade so long as Egypt gets more than half units of jute from India in exchange for one unit of export of cotton. If Egypt gets less than or equal to half unit of jute against one unit of cotton, no trade is possible between India and Egypt. Thus, International Trade between two countries is possible if both the countries are in advantage.

2. *Equal Cost Difference*

If there are equal differences in production costs, there is hardly any possibility of International Trade between the two countries, as there is no gain to either country.

One Labour Unit Production

	Jute	Cotton
INDIA	02	02
EGYPT	01	01

In the above example, the costs of production of jute and cotton in both the countries are in the ratio of 1:1. In India, one unit of jute = one unit of cotton holds good for Egypt. Now, if India produces jute only and imports cotton, it cannot get more than one unit of cotton in place of one unit of jute. Similarly, if Egypt specializes in the production of cotton, it cannot get more than one unit of jute in place of one unit of cotton. No country will be in advantage in exchanging the goods because the ratio of costs is the same in the two countries. Thus, there is no possibility of trade between these two countries equal there are equal differences in costs.

3. *Comparative Cost Difference*

If the production cost in the two countries are comparative between two countries, international trade will inevitably take place between them because the International Trade will benefit both. This can be illustrated with the following example:

One Labour Unit Production

	Jute	Cotton
INDIA	02	01
EGYPT	02	02

Suppose either India can produce with one unit of labour two units of jute or one unit of cotton or Egypt can produce with one unit of labour two units of jute or two units of cotton. Here India had comparative advantage in producing Jute as compare to cotton while Egypt has equal advantage in producing jute and cotton. At first sight, it seems that there would be no chance of having International Trade between them. But, when India transfer its resources from cotton to jute for increasing the opportunity for creating more trade Egypt also found the opportunity to gains from the trade.

One Labour Unit Production

	Jute	Cotton
INDIA	02/01 = 02	01/02 = 0.5
EGYPT	02/02 = 01	02 /02 = 01

Now, India will produce Jute only and imports Cotton from Egypt similarly Egypt producs Cotton to imports Jute from India. This exchange certainly benefited both the countries. India will receive half unit of cotton as a trade gain while Egypt will receive one unit of Jute as a trade gains. So, in this way through comparative advantage both the countries having International Trade gains. It is quite clear that with the domestic trade both the countries are not having trade gains but when these two countries involve in bilateral trade both the countries having trade gains. Generally, these types of International Trade we see in the real world. Recardo argued for this trade only as the best International Trade.

4.4.3 Criticism of the Theory

1. The theory assumed labour as the only production factor. According to all factors are equally important and resources have opportunity cost.
2. Two by two, model is rigid. It fails to explain multi-commodity and multi-lateral trade.

3. By considering barter system the theory neglected important international issues like currencies, conversion, international payments and liquidity.
4. Barter system and free trade did not exist in modern trade.
5. Transport cost is significant part of international trade, which is not explained.
6. Trade between countries of unequal development tend to benefit advanced countries.

4.5 MODERN THEORY OF INTERNATIONAL TRADE

Modern economists were critical of the classical theory of International Trade on various grounds. Although they accepted that comparative cost differences are the basis of trade that was considered not adequate, as they have not explained why comparative cost differences take place. The real basis of trade is something what modern economists have explained. In particular, Hechscher and Ohlin have applied the general equilibrium tools to the analysis of International Trade. According to them, International Trade is but a special case of Inter-local or Inter-regional trade. E.F.Heckscher first wrote his book "The effects of Foreign Trade on the Distribution of Income" in 1919. Bertil Gotthard Ohlin (23 April 1899 – 3 August 1979) was a Swedish economist and politician. He was a professor of economics at the Stockholm School of Economics from 1929 to 1965. He was also leader of the People's Party, a social-liberal party which at the time was the largest party in opposition to the governing Social Democratic Party, from 1944 to 1967. He served briefly as Minister for Trade from 1944 to 1945 in the Swedish coalition government during World War II.

Ohlin's name lives on in one of the standard mathematical model of international free trade, the Heckscher-Ohlin model, which he developed together with Eli Heckscher. He was jointly awarded the Nobel Memorial Prize in Economic Sciences in 1977 together with the British economist James Meade "for their pathbreaking contribution to the theory of international trade and international capital movements".

In 1933 Ohlin published a work that made him world renowned, *Interregional and International Trade*. In this Ohlin built an economic theory of international trade from earlier work by Heckscher and his own doctoral thesis. It is now known as the Heckscher-Ohlin model, one of the standard model economists use to debate trade theory.

The model was a break-through because it showed how comparative advantage might relate to general features of a country's capital and labour, and how these features might change through time. The model provided a basis for later work on the effects of protection on real wages, and has been fruitful in producing predictions and analysis; Ohlin himself used the model to derive the Heckscher-Ohlin theorem, that nations would specialize in industries most able to utilize their mix of national resources efficiently. Today, the theory has been largely disproved, yet it is still a useful framework by which to understand international trade.

The Heckscher-Ohlin Theorem, which is concluded from the Heckscher-Ohlin model of international trade, states: trade between countries is in proportion to their relative amounts of capital and labour. In countries with an abundance of capital, wage rates tend to be high; therefore, labour-intensive products, e.g. textiles, simple electronics, etc., are more costly to produce internally. In contrast, capital-intensive products, e.g. automobiles, chemicals, etc., are relatively less costly to produce internally. Countries with large amounts of capital will export capital-intensive products and import labour-intensive products with the proceeds. Countries with high amounts of labour will do the reverse.

The following conditions must be true:

- The major factors of production, namely labour and capital, are not available in the same proportion in both countries.
- The two goods produced either require relatively more capital or relatively more labour.
- Labour and capital do not move between the two countries.
- There are no costs associated with transporting the goods between countries.
- The citizens of the two trading countries have the same needs.

The theory does not depend on total amounts of capital or labour, but on the amounts per worker. This allows small countries to trade with large countries by specializing in production of products that use the factors which are more available than its trading partner. The key assumption is that capital and labour are not available in the same proportions in the two countries. That leads to specialization, which in turn benefits the country's economic welfare. The greater the difference between the two countries, the greater the gain from specialization.

Wassily Leontief made a study of the theory that seemed to invalidate it. He noted that the United States had a lot of capital; therefore, it should export capital-intensive products and import labour-intensive products. Instead, he found that it exported products that used more labour than the products it imported. This finding is known as the Leontief paradox.

Ohlin started with the comparative cost theory of the classical writers but built into it the general theory of value and the mutual interdependence in price theory between commodity prices and factor prices and analysed the demand and supply factors to arrive at the fundamental equilibrium, under the general theory of value. While the classical theory is a single market theory based only on time dimension, Ohlin's theory is a multi-market theory based on time and space dimensions to explain the phenomenon of International Trade.

4.5.1 Elements of the Theory

This model is also a two factors and two commodities and two-country model as that of classical writers but the latter had based only on one factor. The basis of trade is the relative cost differentials of commodities as between countries. These cost differences are the same thing as price differences in the classical theory, as price is equal to the marginal cost of the commodity.

Ohlin explains these price differences by differences in factor prices resulting from differences in factor endowments in the different countries. Thus, in the final analysis, differences in factor endowments explain International Trade.

That is why this theory also called as factor proportions analysis. Some countries have abundance of labour, they are labour rich, and others have abundance of capital, they are capital rich. The labour rich countries have lower wages rates as specialize in the production of labour intensive goods, which will necessarily be produce at lower costs and lower prices; while the capital rich countries specialize in the production of capital-intensive goods, which will be produced at relatively lower costs and prices.

4.5.2 Assumptions of the Theory

The modern theory of International Trade assumes the following points:

1. There is perfect competition in commodity and factor markets such that the price of a commodity is equal to its marginal cost and the price of a factor is equal to its marginal product.
2. It is a two-factor (labour and capital) two-commodity (X and Y) and two-country model. One country is labour abundant and the other one is capital abundant. Good X is capital-intensive and good Y is labour intensive.
3. Demand conditions are identical in both countries.
4. Production functions are homogeneous of the first degree, which results in constant costs of production.
5. There are no restrictions on trade and no transport costs.

From the above assumptions, it is quite clear that International Trade takes place based on differences in factor endowments.

According to this theory there are two countries USA and India and having bilateral trade between them. It is also assumed that USA is a capital abundant country while India is labour abundant country, USA specialize in producing machine tools while India in agricultural products and primary products. This is because the capital abundant country specializes in capital-intensive goods and a labour abundant country specializes in labour-intensive goods.

This type of specialization leads to lower costs and lower commodity prices of the respective commodities. Differences in factor prices and in factor intensities used in the production of goods lead to different costs of production and prices. These differences in prices would cause the international trade to take place. Thus, the capital abundant country exports capital-intensive goods which are relatively cheap and in which it specializes and labour-intensive goods are imported as labour is more expensive, relatively in that country. The reverse is true in the case of a labour abundant country.

4.5.3 Price Criterion

This theory can be represented with the help of the price ratios.

$(P_o K_U/P_o L_U)$ USA. < $(P_o K_I/P_o L_I)$ India

Here P_o is the price of factors, K_U and L_U stand for capital and labour of USA, whereas K_I and L_I stand for capital and labour of India. Let us assume that there are two commodities like machine tools (capital intensive) and tea (labour-intensive) produced by both the countries. If machine tools is cheaper in USA, it is due to the use of cheaper factor of capital more in USA, in the case of tea it is cheaper in India due to large use of labour which is relatively cheaper in India. Thus, the capital are uses more in the capital abundant country because it is a cheaper resource in the country while the labour are uses more in the labour abundant country because it is found in excess. That is why, the machine tools has less cost of production in USA as compare to machine tools cost of production in India. Similarly the production cost of tea in India is very less as compare to USA with the price differences in their products both the countries get gains from the trade because they specialise their production where less factor or resources required.

4.5.4 Factor Proportion Theory

Let assumes again, India is labour-abundant country where the labours wage rate are very low therefore the agricultural products like tea can produce cheaply by using the larger quantity of labour relative to capital. On the other hand, in USA capital is found excess as compare to labour and its interest cost is very low, so it can produce the machine tools very cheaply as compare to agricultural products like tea. The trade takes place when USA exports machine tools and imports tea and India exports tea and imports machine tools. Now, it can be demonstrated with the help of a diagram.

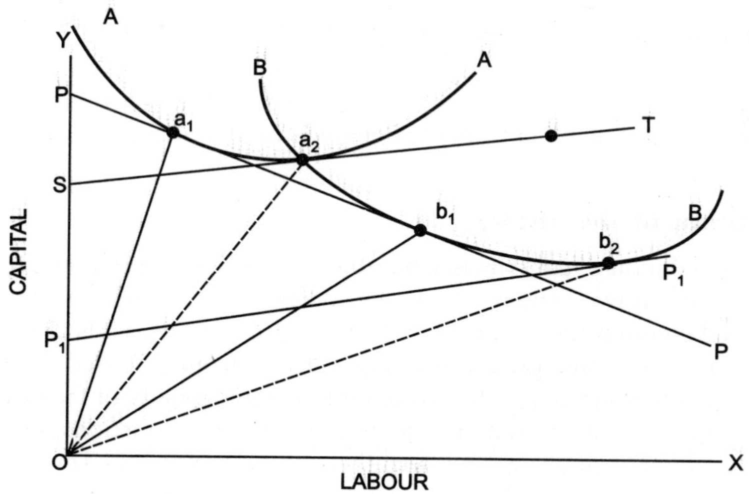

Fig. 4.2: Explanation of international trade of modern theory

From the above analysis, it is clear that commodity A is relatively cheaper in USA (PP) and expensive in India (P_1P_1). Commodity A is a capital-intensive good, while commodity B is a labour-intensive good. Thus, the capital abundant country like USA has a comparative cost advantage in the production of capital-intensive goods. The capital-abundant country *i.e.,* USA can export its cheaper capital-intensive goods to India, while India being labour abundant country can export its labour-intensive good. Trade can thus take place between India and USA in the commodities A and B.

In the figure 4.2 AA and BB are equal product curves, reflecting the factor proportion. The equal product curve AA is capital-intensive as it is nearer to the vertical axis Y representing capital. In the same context equal product curve BB is labour-intenisve as labour falls on the horizontal axis 'X'.

Now, suppose that both commodity can be produced in USA and India. The price line PP has a slope reflecting the factors of productions (labour and capital), in USA. The tangent point to the equal product curves AA and BB is at a_1b_1, indicating the equilibrium conditions for factor proportions. The price ratio, (PP) Oa_1 and (PP) Ob_1, represent equilibrium factors intensities for A and B commodities in USA. On the same lines, P_1P_1 represents the slope of the factor price ratio in India and ST is parallel to that reflecting the same slope while P_1P_1 is tangent to BB equal product curve at b_2, its parallel ST representing the same factor price ratio as P_1P_1, is tangent to AA equal product curve at a_2. Thus, the equilibrium factor proportions are Oa_2 for commodity A and Ob_2 for commodity B in India.

In USA the cost of using capital for both the commodity A and B, is the amount of OP, which is the point at which PP cuts the capital axis Y. In India, the costs of producing A and Y goods are OS and OP_1. It means that in India, production of good A is more costlier in terms of capital input as OS (for good A) is higher than OP_1 (for good B).

It is assumed from the above propositions that the demand conditions and factor endowments are fixed. The factor price ratios data which is used in the diagram 3 are achieved from the interaction of demand and supply of factors. The supply relates to the factor abandonment and endowments and the demand for factors is derived demand from the demands for the final products, like A and B goods.

4.5.5 Criticism of the Theory

Many of the economist had criticises the theory that there were nothing new in the theory and it was centered to the Ricardiam theory. They also changes that Ohlin's theorem is the supplements of Recardo's theory as it is also based on comparative cost and price advantages. This theory is based on some unrealistic assumptions like perfect competition, homogeneity of factor units, absence of product differentiation, identical production functions, etc. The main points of criticism against modern theory of International Trade are as follows:

1. **Supplements of Recardo's theory:** Prof Viner has claimed that Heckscher-Ohlin theorem is not new, it is just the supplement of the Recardo's theory of comparative cost advantage theory. There were no innovative ideas behind the theory.

2. **Unrealistic idea of Identical factors in both the countries:** The factors of production in both the countries are supposed to be identical which is not realistic. In the real world the factors of production cannot be identical. There were always a variety of production capacity found in the factors so, it cannot be identical.
3. **Importance of factor's demand was ignored:** The modern theory only emphasises on the relative supply of factors of production and does not give importance to demand.
4. **The assumption of constant returns to scale is unrealistic:** In the real world no constant returns to scale exist only increasing or diminishing returns to scale exist. So, the assumption of constant returns to scale in the theory is unrealistic. The prices of the factors also changes with the change in the economic conditions therefore, the constant returns to scale cannot exist.
5. **Production functions are homogeneous in both the country:** The production function in both the countries are supposed to be homogeneous and linear. It ignores the technological changes and changes in factor prices. So, it is not possible that the technology of the country sustain. Therefore, the assumption of homoginity in production functions is unrealistic.
6. **No transportation costs assumption is unrealistic:** In today's business scenario transportation play a vital role in determining the trade between domestic border and International, we cannot ignore the transportation cost. It may be happen that the transportation cost per unit is more than the cost of production per unit. As well as the transportation cost may be higher within the domestic region and low internationally. For example, if sugar is exporting to Nepal and sold to Tamil Nadu from U.P. then the transportation cost will be lower in exporting Nepal while higher to Tamil Nadu.
7. **Capital-rich country export capital intensive product and Labour-rich country export labour intensive product is not always true:** The Heckscher-Ohlin argument that capital rich country export capital oriented product and labour rich country export labour oriented product. Leontief studied American exports and imports and concluded that though USA was capital-rich, her exports were mainly labour intensive and her imports were capital-intensive. Today also USA is the largest producer of crude oil but it imports crude-oil from Arabian countries of central Asia.

   Heckscher-Ohlin theorem is more important than the classical theory in that it includes almost all the aspects of International Trade. They had considered all the factors of production, demand and supply of the factor, the prices of it and finally the resources availability of a country. These all things makes a country to dominate the another. With this advantages one country can increase its trade gains in the International Trade.

4.5.6 Comparison between Classical Theory of International Trade vs. Modern Theory of International Trade

Classical Theory	Modern Theory
1. Classical theory emphasises only on the both demand and supply of the product and factor.	1. Modern theory considerd both demand and supply of the product and factors.
2. Labour is the only factor of production.	2. Labour and capital both are the factor of production.
3. The main constraint of the theory is the comparative cost advantage of one country to another.	3. It depicts the basis of International trade as differences in factor endowments.
4. It is based on the constant returns to scale on factor side.	4. It considers all types of returns to scale—increasing, constant and dminishing.
5. The production function of a commodity will be differ from one country to another.	5. The uniform production function for the same commodity is between the trading countries.
6. It provokes that international trade theory is differ from domestic trade theory.	6. It provokes that international trade theory is an extension of domestic or inter-regional trade theory
7. It only emphasises on the cost of production as the basis of trade.	7. It considered the relative prices of the factors of production as the basis of trade.
8. It emphasises on the mobility of factor of production within country but immobility in international.	8. It is based on the available quantity of the factors domestically and mobility is less material to the theory.
9. The classical theory is nothing else it is an improvement of the Absolute cost Advantage theory of Adam Smith.	9. The modern theory is not a new theory, it is the supplements of the Recardo's comparative costs advantage theory.

4.6 VERNON'S INTERNATIONAL PRODUCT LIFE CYCLE

Reymand Vernon propounded this theory. According to him all the product which is internationally marketed has to go the process of product life cycle. The developed countries where in the introduction stage during the industrial revolution. Then when the industrial grew at rapid rate, they moved to other parts of the country to trade and formed colonies. The International Product Life Cycle had four stage i.e., Introduction, Growth, Maturity and Decline which determine the Production Location, Market, Competitive Factors and Production Technology.

Particulars	Introductory	Growth/Development	Maturity/Boom	Saturation/ Decline
LOCATION FOR PRODUCTION	Domestic industrial, small scale industry, cottage, retail industry etc	Innovating, Research & Development and other Industrial Countries	Multiple/ multi-lateral Countries and their trading partners	Mainly in up growing, Less Developed Country
MARKET PLACE	Innovating Country with some exports	Basically deals in Industrial Countries for exports market as foreign production replaces export in some countries	Growth and Development in Less Develop Countries with diminishing in Industrial Countries	Basically for Less Develop Countries and Export Oriented Countries
COMPETITIVE FACTORS	Tendency of Monopolistic behaviour in sales and specific pricing for product differentiation	Increased trends of demand, high competitor, cartel in pricing with product quality for survival in the market	Stationary state of demand, Competitors decrease, Importance of pricing strategy	Continuous diminishing in demand, Importance of pricing strategy, Competition decreases due to exit of production houses
PRODUCTION METHODOLOGY	Short-run production, production increases with the increase in demand as well as factors of production also imitate the same	More technology used and incensement in capital investment making more qualitative and competitive product in the market	Long-run production is preferred with huge capital investment required skilled labour only & reduction in the labour involvement in production	Decrease in the capital investment, Long-run production continues, unskilled labours are more employed in the production

CHAPTER 5

Instrument of Trade Policy

5.1 INTRODUCTION

A general phenomenon of a country is to maintain its trade balance properly. The world is dominated by developing and less developing countries who always suffer with deficit balance of payments. This is because, the need requirement of these countries is very high and their resources are very less in number therefore, they imports more and due to lack of capital and capital equipments they are not able to increase their exports. Hence, they faced the deficit in their balance of payments.

India has also facing the same problem as the other developing nations are facing. The share of India to the World Trade was 2.5% during Fifties but it reduces to only 0.5% in nineties. After adaptation of LPG (Liberalisation, Privatisation and Globalisation) it is almost 1.0% but still a very large deficit is lying with our balance of payments. Indian government had adopted the trade policy as export promotion and import substitution.

Today, every government of the nations imposing so many trade instruments to reduce the import and to reduce the deficit in the balance of payment. Some of the important instruments of trade are as follows:

- Tariff
- Import Quotas
- Voluntary Export Restraints
- Anti-Dumping Policies
- Administrative Policies

5.2 TARIFFS

Tariffs can be expressed in absolute or in relative terms, they may be discriminatory, they can be imposed on imports or on exports, and they may be prompted by considerations of revenue or protection to domestic industries.

5.2.1 Types of Tariffs

1. **Specific Tariffs:** Specific tariffs are those which are assessed on the basis of the physical weight of the product which is imported or exported. They are expressed in absolute terms of dollars and cents per unit e.g. per tonne, or per pound of weight of the imported (or exported) quantity. Specific duties can be levied on goods like wheat or rice or sugar, but they can not be adopted for all goods and services especially in the case of valuable goods. For instance specific tariffs cannot be levied in the case of say, diamonds, modern art paintings, transistors, television sets etc.
2. **Advalorem Tariffs:** In this tariff it is levied on the basis of the value of the product measured by their money price, it is called as advalorem tariff. This tariff is a percentage tax.
3. **Compound Tariff:** It combines with advalorem duty with specific duty. The distinction between the two types of tariffs is of some significance. As the prices of imported goods rise, the advalorem tariff based on a given fixed percentage brings greater revenue to the tariff imposing country, whereas specific tariffs lack such revenue elasticity with respect to import price changes.
4. **A Discriminatory Tariff or Non-Discriminatory Tariff:** It calls for different rates of duties or non-discriminatory tariff depending on the country of origin or the destination of the product for example, a country from, say, Australia and lower rates of duty on goods coming from Thailand. A non-discriminatory tariff, on the other hand, imposes a uniform rate of duty regardless of their source of origin.
5. **Revenue Tariff:** Revenue tariffs are those which are imposed primarily to produce revenue for the government. With the introduction and expansion of income taxes and other direct taxes, the importance of tariff as a source of revenue has considerably gone down, especially in developed countries. The less developed countries, however, still rely on tariffs as a substantial source of government revenues. In Malaysia, for example, the import and export duties together amount for well over 40% of the total government revenues.
6. **Protective Tariffs:** When the tariffs are imposed primarily to protect the domstic industries from foreign competition, the country is said to have protective tariffs. The motive, here is not revenue but protection of the domestic economy from foreign competition.
7. **Retaliatory and Countervailing Tariffs:** When country A imposes duties against the products from country B, it is possible the country B will retaliate and levy duties on goods imported from country A. Country B's tariffs are then described as retaliatory tariffs. A countervailing tariffs is subsidy in the country of origin.

5.3 IMPORT QUOTAS

The tariff is measured by price, the volume of imports are restricted by increasing the domestic price, so discouraging consumption and encouraging domestic production. Different countries had a devised for whole range of import-restricting policies that do not operate directly thorough the price mechanism, which is known as the non-tariff barriers to trade. One of the important of such policy instrument is called as quota. Quota limits the volume of imports to some specified quantity in a specified time period, that volume being less than the usual volume of trade. In other words a quota is a direct limitation of the physical quantity of exports and imports permitted in the country. The effect of the quota is of course to raise the domestic price of the product which restricts the supply to the domestic market, and in different ways the effects of a quota are identical to those of a tariff.

5.3.1 Types of Import Quotas

There are two types of import quotas:

1. **Bilateral Quotas:** A bilateral quotas imply the mutual agreement between countries through their negotiation. The benefit of these quotas is that they do not revealed retaliation. This type of quota is to generate benefit between the two countries having mutual understanding in their import and export.
2. **Unilateral Quotas:** In the case of unilateral quotas, quota is fixed in global terms and any country can supply the fixed amount by quota at it minimum price. The quota imposing nation gets the price benefit. This type of allocation of the quota however, involve allocating and distributing the quota among different nations on the perdetermined criteria basis. The unilateral quotas are discriminatory, it means the quotas are fixed differently to different countries. Sometimes in unilateral quotas the imposing nation doesn't benefited from it.

We can explain the import quotas with the help of a figure.

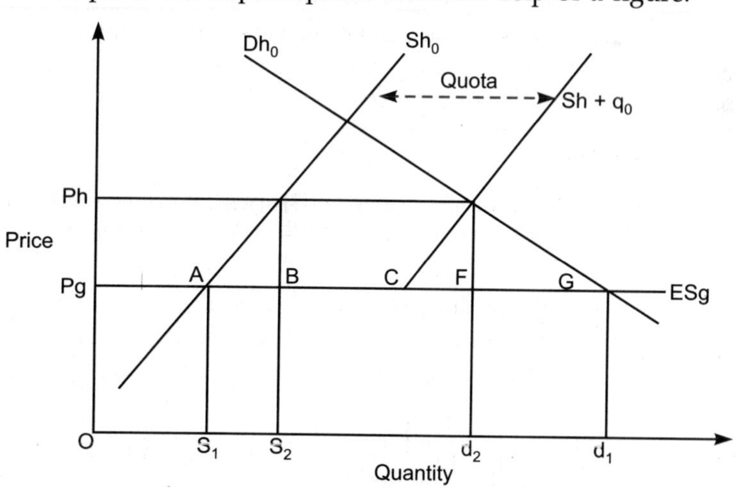

Fig. 5.1: Exporting country imposing an import quota

From the above figure the imports of the domestic country under free trade is $d_1 - s_1$, shows the difference between the domestic consumption and production. As from the figure it is clear that the Ph is the domestic price and Pg is the global price for the product. The other countries are not interested to export goods in the domestic country if its price is less than the global price but when they found the domestic price is more than global price they keenly interested in supplying the product in domestic country. Now, due to high price government of domestic country introduces a quota on imports equal to $d_2 - s_2$. The aggregate supply curve facing the domestic consumes will thus follow the domestic supply curve (Sh) for prices below Pg, and will follow the global excess supply curve (ESg) at price Pg until the quota limit is reached, it then follows the line Sh + q which is parallel to Sh for prices above Pg.

The market in the importing country will then clear at price Ph, and imports will be $d_2 - s_2$, which is equal to the quota. As with the tariff, it will be a loss to the consumer surplus, shown in the areas A, B, C, F and G, and a gain in producer surplus will be A. Due to imposition of quota by government the per unit profit to the volume of the quota will be Ph-Pq. This is due to price of the domestic product as Ph and the imports brought at price Pg.

The government will issue the licences for the import of various propositions of the quota. If the licences are issued free to change then the holders of those licences will gain all the rent shown by the area C + F, and if it is the domestic agents then this area will be an internal transfer from consumers to other in the economy. If the government sells the licences then part of the rent will accrue to the government; if the licences are sold for the maximum amount possible to the area C + F, then the revenue from these sales will equal the revenue from the equivalent to tariff.

5.4 DIFFERENCE BETWEEN QUOTAS AND TARIFFS

The important differences between quotas and tariffs are as follows:

1. Tariffs are the revenues to the government whereas quotas do not have the same. Under tariffs, a part of consumer's loss goes to the government whereas in quotas system the extent of consumer's loss will be more or less the same, but to whom that surplus goes is ambiguous.
2. Distribution of import licences which is associated with quotas may give rise to corruption and bribery on the past of government officials whereas import tariffs don't create such evils of government corruption etc.
3. In case of the inelastic domestic demand and supply curves for the import goods quotas are more effective than the import tariff. In other words it has less impact regarding the demand and supply of domestic products.
4. The terms of trade, with the tariff effect can be predictable but effect from the quotas are unpredictable.
5. Quotas are easy to impose, remove, change and administer but this could not work with tariff.
6. In quotas it is more permissive in international attitude whereas the tariffs are not so permissive in international attitude.

7. A rate of tariff may resque the country for short period but it may be very harmful to the public image of the protected industry in the long run.
8. As the total demand for the product grows, a given quota fixed in absolute terms would be more protective to the domestic producers. A tariff, on the other hand, would not prevent foreign imports gaining their share of the expanded market in the protected sector of the economy.
9. Quotas allow atleast some imports into the country while tariff make stricktly prohibited imports in the country.
10. Quotas provide more possibilities of profit by imposing it while tariff has loss possibilities of earning profit.

5.5 VOLUNTARY EXPORT RESTRAINTS

The voluntary export restriction (VER) is a relatively new but popular way of restricting the imports of a country. Under voluntary export restraints an importing country negotiates with the foreign suppliers quantitative restrictions on the amount of exports they will supply to the domestic market. These negotiations may be between the governments, associations of manufacturers acting with government approval. In some respect voluntary exports restraints (VER) has similar effects like quota, if the VER is applied instead of quota in the quota imposing figure 5.1 then the impact on the price, production, consumption and imports would be the same. The effects of the VER on consumer and producer surplus would also be rigid.

The difference between VER and Quota lies in the destination of the rents arising from the quantitative restriction on the imports. The supplier who are holding a part of the overall VER quantity will be able to sell that quantity in the importing country at the domestic price Ph, and this way it secure the rent, which was going in the favour of domestic importing company. If all the rents from the VER goes to foreign companies then the net loss to the importing country to VER will be the sum of areas, B, C, F and G in the above mentioned table.

Since VER is usually specified in quantity terms, foreign suppliers may be able to increase their rents by supplying higher cost items for example *n* expensive or luxury cars for standard cars. Those foreign supplier who didnot join in the VER scheme may find it difficult to enter the scheme at a later date, so that those who join early are themselves given a protected position as suppliers to the importing country's market. It might be happen that foreign supplier had the fear to lose their competitive edge in the future, in other hand the foreign suppliers will contitune to supply the importer's market.

VER is an 'implicit stick' taken by the government of the importing country. If the country presume of failure to agree to participate in a voluntary scheme to restrict the trade which might lead the government for imposing other forms of trade restriction, like tariff, which definitely decrease the imports to the same level as the VER, but will not allow the foreign suppliers to gain the rents from the restriction.

5.6 IMPORT SUBSIDY

The government of the importing country decides to increase imports by subsidising them, it is made with the intention that the price paid by the customer will be driven below the world market price. The operation of this type of policy can be explained with the help of the diagram.

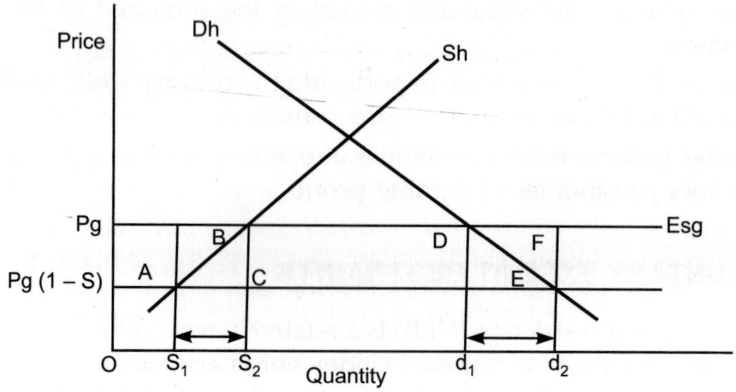

Fig. 5.2: An Importing country imposing a subsidy

Suppose the subsidy is paid at an advalorem rate of S on the global price then the domestic price will be Pg(1 – S) where Pg is the global price. The domestic production will reduce and fall down to S_2, while its impact to the demand will be positive, so the consumption increases to d_1. The domestic country's import expand from $s_1 - d_1$ to $d_2 - s_2$. Due to this the maximum benefit will goes to consumers, the consumer surplus can be measured by the sum of areas A, B, C, D and E. The producer must face the loss, the reduction of the producer surplus will the areas A and B. The cost of the subsidy to taxpayers will be SPg per unit over the new volume of imports which is the sum of areas B, C, D, E and F. The benefits of the consumer will be less than the losses of the producer surplus and the taxpayers, and the net loss to the economy is area B + F.

Import expansion by the use of a subsidy with therefore reduce the welfare of a country. The best policy on imports for a country is the free trade.

5.7 EXPORT SUBSIDY

The export subsidy as provided by the government tends to increase the production of the domestic country. This will encourage the other enterprise to do so. The increase in the production will result in fall of consumption and the export of that product will increase. This can also explain with the help of the diagram.

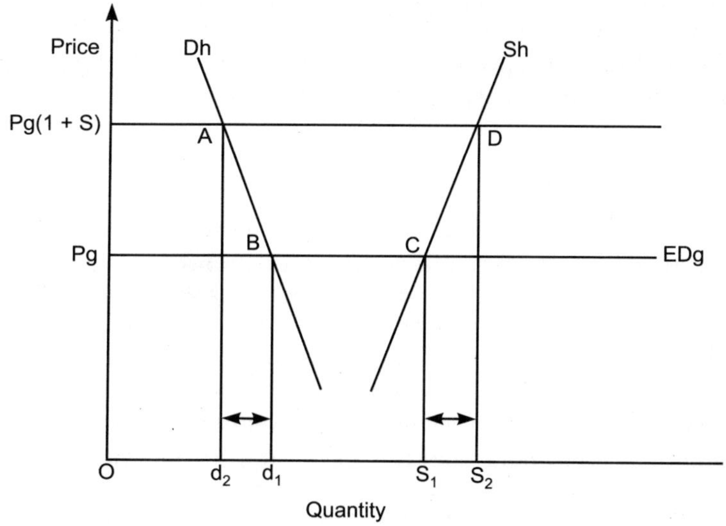

Fig. 5.3: An exporting country imposing a subsidy

Under free trade the price prevailing in the domestic country will be the global price Pg. S_1 level of quantity will be produced with this price and d_1 demand will be occur with this price. The amount of demand d_1 will be consumed in the domestic country and rest of product will be exported.

If an export subsidy is paid at an advalorem rate of S on the global price Pg, then the country's domestic price for the product will be Pg(l + S), since domestic producers will be receiving that price inclusive of the subsidy for exports. The demand for the product will fall from d_1 to d_2, while the supply and production increase to S_2 and therefore, the export will expand from $s_1 - d_1$ to $s_2 - d_2$.

In this case, the consumer have to face the loss, the total loss of the consumer will be the area A and B, the benefit to the producer can be defined with the area A, B and C, so that gains to producers exceed losses to consumers. However, this subsidy will cost taxpayers an amount equal to the sum of the areas B, C and D, so that overall there will be a loss to the area B that is equal to consumption loss and with the area of D *i.e.*, the production loss. After analysing all these, we can conclude that the certain trade policy is still inferior to free trade.

5.8 ANTI-DUMPING

The concept of dumping refers to a particular situation where a foreign supplier sells goods in another country below his cost of production or below the price prevailing in his own domestic market. Haberler defined dumping as, "the sale of goods abroad at a price which is lower than the selling price of the same goods at the same time in the same circumstances at home, taking account of differences in transport costs. To find out whether dumping is being practised, comparison is to be made between the transaction price of exports and the price charged in the domestic market".

Mostly the nations restrict import of dumped good or subject them to the imposition of anti-dumping duties to rectify the trade distortive effects of dumping. These duties are additional duties levied if there is dumping and a casual level is established between dumping and injury to the domestic industries.

5.8.1 Types of Dumping

There are three types of dumping. These are as follows:

1. **Intermittent Dumping:** When the production of a product is more than its demand in the domestic market, the producer sells the surplus of its product in other nations of the world at a lower price without deducting the price in the domestic market.
2. **Persistent Dumping:** Under this type of dumping the producer sells his excess production in other nations continuously at a lower price.
3. **Predatory Dumping:** Under this the producers intentions is to charge a low price initially to foreign market with a view to drive away the competitors and increase the price after the competitors leave the field.

5.8.2 Effects of Dumping

The effects of dumping on importing and exporting countries can be defined as

- Domestic industry might be affected adversely by a decline in sales and profits. For examples Indian product market had faced the effects from the Chinese product.
- The survival of the domestic industry will be threatened if the dumping continued for a longer period.
- Dumping may affect the balance of payment directly or indirectly.
- In case of the exporting country it will find market for its surplus production.
- For exporting country it will be able to strengthen its balance of payments position.
- The importing country's consumers benefited with low price of the product whereas for exporting country's consumer have to pay higher prices for their purchase of the commodity dumped.

It cannot be called that any product which is imported in India and sell into a lower price, lower than the domestic price may not be called as dumping. It is a known fact that producers sell their goods at different prices in different markets to suit the competitive situation prevailing in the markets concerned. Indian exporter also doing the same as they match their prices to the current prices in the International markets for products concerned. It is only when the practice of selling below domestic prices causes injury to the domestic industry in the importing country, dumping attracts attention and is liable for action.

5.8.3 Anti-Dumping Duties Imposed by India

The recent anti-dumping duties imposed by India are:

1. Provisional anti-dumping duty was imposed on the import of petroleum based chemical chlorine chloride in April, 2001.

2. Recently the central government initiated anti-dumping investigations on the imports goods from China.
3. The government propose to impose anti-dumping duty on black and white photo paper imported from the UK, France and Hungary.
4. The government also impose the anti-dumping duties against the Korean optic fibre on the ground that it has been exported to India at a low price normal value and thus caused material injury to the domestic industry.
5. The anti-dumping duty was also proposed on seamless tubes imported from Austria, Czech Republic, Russia and Romania.

5.9 ADMINISTRATIVE POLICY

Every government of the country looks after its administrative policy regarding maintaining its trade balance. To regulate properly the foreign trade and maintaining the trade document the government administer some policy. In India, this practice is also adopted for maintaining the deficit balance of payment. As India, having high import as compare to export the government impose some measures to reduce the deficit in the balance of the payments. This is the common practice adopted by government. Some of the Indian administrative policies are as follow:

5.9.1 Exports and Imports Free Unless Regulated

Exports and Imports shall be free, except in cases where they are regulated by the provisions of this Policy or any other law for the time being in force. The item wise export and import policy shall be, as specified in ITC (HS) published and notified by Director General of Foreign Trade, as amended from time to time.

5.9.2 Compliance with Laws

Every exporter or importer shall comply with the provisions of the Foreign Trade (Development and Regulation) Act, 1992, the Rules and Orders made there under, the provisions of this Policy and the terms and conditions of any licence/certificate/permission granted to him, as well as provisions of any other law for the time being in force. All imported goods shall also be subject to domestic Laws, Rules, Orders, Regulations, technical specifications, environmental and safety norms as applicable to domestically produced goods. No import or export of rough diamonds shall be permitted unless the shipment parcels are accompanied by Kimberley Process (KP) Certificate required under the procedure specified by the Gem and Jewellery Export Promotion Council (GJEPC).

5.9.3 Interpretation of Policy

If any question or doubt arises in respect of the interpretation of any provision contained in this Policy, or regarding the classification of any item in the ITC (HS) or Schedule of DEPB Rate the said question or doubt shall be refer to the

Director General of Foreign Trade whose decision thereon shall be final and binding as well as if any question or doubt arises whether a licence/certificate permission has been issue in accordance with this Policy or if any question or doubt arises touching upon the scope and content of such documents, the same shall be refer to the Director General of Foreign Trade whose decision thereon shall be final and binding.

5.9.4 Procedure

The Director General of Foreign Trade may, in any case or class of cases, specify the procedure to be followed by an exporter or importer or by an licensing or any other competent authority for implementing the provisions of the Act, the Rules and the Orders made thereunder and this Policy. Such procedures shall be included in the Handbook (Vol.1), Handbook (Vol.2), Schedule of DEPB Rate and in ITC (HS) and published by means of a Public Notice. Such procedures may be amending from time to time.

The Handbook (Vol.1) is a supplement to the Foreign Trade Policy and contains relevant procedures and other details. The procedure of availing benefits under various schemes of the Policy are given in the Handbook (Vol.1).

5.9.5 Exemption from Policy/Procedure

Any request for relaxation of the provisions of this Policy or of any procedure, on the ground that there is genuine hardship to the applicant or that a strict application of the Policy or the procedure is likely to have an adverse impact on trade, may be made to the Director General of Foreign Trade for such relief as may be necessary. The Director General of Foreign Trade may pass such orders or grant such relaxation or relief, as he may deem fit and proper.

The Director General of Foreign Trade may, in public interest, exempt any person or class or category of persons from any provision of this Policy or any procedure and may, while granting such exemption, impose such conditions as he may deem fit. Such request may be considered only after consulting Advance Licensing Committee (ALC) if the request is in respect of a provision of Chapter-4 (excluding any provision relating to Gem and jewellery sector) of the Policy/Procedure. However, any such request in respect of a provision other than Chapter-4 and Gem and Jewellery sector as given above may be considered only after consulting Policy Relaxation Committee.

5.9.6 Principles of Restriction

DGFT may, through a notification, adopt and enforce any measure necessary for:

(*i*) Protection of public morals.

(*ii*) Protection of human, animal or plant life or health.

(*iii*) Protection of patents, trademarks and copyrights and the prevention of deceptive practices.

(*iv*) Prevention of use of prison labour.

(*v*) Protection of national treasures of artistic, historic or archaeological value.

(*vi*) Conservation of exhaustible natural resources.

(*vii*) Protection of trade of fissionable material or material from which they are derived; and

(*viii*) Prevention of traffic in arms, ammunition and implements of war.

5.9.7 Restricted Goods

Any goods, the export or import of which is restricted under ITC (HS) may be exported or imported only in accordance with a licence/certificate/permission or a public notice issued in this behalf.

5.9.8 Terms and Conditions of Licence/Certificate/Permission

Every licence/certificate/permission shall be valid for the period of validity specified in the licence/certificate/permission and shall contain such terms and conditions as may be specified by the licensing authority, which may include:

- The quantity, description and value of the goods;
- Actual user condition;
- Exprot obligation
- The value addition to be achieved; and

5.9.9 Licence/Certificate/Permission Not a Right

No person may claim a licence/certificate/permission as a right and the Director General of Foreign Trade or the licensing authority shall have the power to refuse to grant or renew licence/certificate/permission in accordance with the provisions of the Act and the Rules made there under.

5.9.10 Penalty

If a licence/certificate/permission holder violates any condition of the licence/certificate/permission or fails to fulfil the export obligation, he shall be liable for action in accordance with the Act, the Rules and Orders made there under, the Policy and any other law for the time being in force.

5.9.11 State Trading

Any goods, the import or export of which is governed through exclusive or special privileges granted to State Trading Enterprise (s), may be imported or exported by the State Trading Enterprise (s) as specified in the ITC (HS) Book subject to the conditions specified therein. The Director General of Foreign Trade may, grant a licence/certificate/permission to any other person to import or export any of these goods. In respect of goods the import or export of which is governed through exclusive or special privileges granted to State Trading Enterprise (s), the State Trading Enterprise (s) shall make any such purchases or sales involving imports or exports solely in accordance with commercial considerations, including price, quality, availability, marketability, transportation and other conditions of purchase or sale. These enterprises shall act in a non-discriminatory manner and shall afford the enterprises of other countries adequate opportunity, in accordance with customary business practices, to compete for participation in such purchases or sales.

5.9.12 Exemption from Bank Guarantee

All the exporters who have an export turnover of at least Rupees 5 crore in the current or preceding licencing year and have a good record or accomplishment of three years of exports will be exempt from furnishing a BG for any of the schemes under this Policy and may furnish a LUT in lieu of BG.

5.9.13 Private/Public Bonded Warehouses for Imports

Private/Public bonded warehouses may be set up in the Domestic Tariff Area as per the terms and conditions of notification issued by Department of Revenue. Any person may import goods except prohibited items, arms and ammunition, hazardous waste and chemicals and warehouse them in such private/public bonded warehouses. Such goods may be clear for home consumption in accordance with the provisions of this Policy and against licence/certificate/permission, wherever required. Customs duty as applicable is paid at the time of clearance of such goods. If such goods are not clear for home consumption within a period of one year or such extended period as the custom authorities may permit, the importer of such goods shall re-export the goods.

5.9.14 Free Exports

All goods may be export without any restriction except to the extent ITC (HS) or any other provision of this Policy or any other law regulates such exports for the time being in force. The Director General of Foreign Trade may, specify through a public notice such terms and conditions according to which any goods, not included in the ITC (HS), may be export without a licence/certificate/permission.

5.9.15 Export of Spares

Warranty spares, whether indigenous or imported, of plant, equipment, machinery, automobiles or any other goods, except those restricted under ITC (HS), may be exported along with the main equipment or subsequently but within the contracted warranty period of such goods subject to approval of RBI.

5.9.16 Export of Imported Goods

Goods imported, in accordance with this Policy, may be export in the same or substantially the same form without licence/certificate/permission if the item to be imported or export is not mention as restricted for import or export in the ITC (HS). Exports of such goods imported against payment in freely convertible currency would be permit against payment in freely convertible currency. Goods, including those mentioned as restricted item for import (except prohibited items) may be imported under Customs Bond for export in freely convertible currency without a licence/certificate/permission provided that the item is freely exportable without any conditionality/ requirement of licence/ permission as may be required under ITC (HS) Schedule II.

5.9.17 Export of Replacement Goods

Goods or parts thereof on being exported and found defective/damaged or otherwise unfit for use may be replaced free of charge by the exporter and such goods shall be allowed clearance by the customs authorities provided that the replacement goods are not mentioned as restricted items for exports in ITC (HS).

5.9.18 Export of Repaired Goods

Goods or parts, except restricted ITC (HS), thereof on being exported and found defective, damaged or otherwise unfit for use may be imported for repair and subsequent re-export. Such goods shall be allowed clearance without a licence/ certificate/permission and in accordance with customs notification issued in this behalf.

5.9.19 Private Bonded Warehouses for Exports

Private bonded warehouses exclusively for exports may be set up in DTA as per the terms and conditions of the notifications issued by Department of Revenue. Such warehouses shall be entitled to procure the goods from domestic manufacturers without payment of duty. The supplies made by a domestic supplier to the notified warehouses shall be treated as physical exports provided the payments for the same are made in free foreign exchange.

5.9.20 Denomination of Export Contracts

All export contracts and invoices shall be denominated either in freely convertible currency or Indian rupees but the export proceeds shall be realised in freely convertible currency. However, export proceeds against specific exports may also be realized in rupees provided it is through a freely convertible Vostro account of a non-resident bank situated in any country other than a member country of ACU or Nepal or Bhutan. Additionally, the rupee payment through the Vostro account must be against payment in free foreign currency by the buyer in his non-resident bank account. The free foreign exchange remitted by the buyer to his non-resident bank (after deducting the bank service charges) because of this transaction can be taken as the export realization under the export promotion schemes of this Policy. Contracts for which payments are received through the Asian Clearing Union (ACU) shall be denominated in ACU Dollar. The Central Government may relax the provisions of this paragraph in appropriate cases. Export contracts and Invoices can be denominated in Indian rupees against EXIM Bank/Government of India line of credit.

5.9.21 Export Promotion Councils

The basic objective of Export Promotion Councils is to promote and develop the exports of the country. Each council is responsible for the promotion of a particular group of products, projects and services. The list of the councils and their main functions are given in Handbook (Vol.1).

5.9.22 Registration-cum-Membership Certificate

Any person, applying for (*i*) a licence/certificate/permission to import/export, [except items listed as restricted items in ITC (HS)] or (*ii*) any other benefit or concession under this policy shall be required to furnish Registration-cum-Membership Certificate (RCMC) granted by the competent authority in accordance with the procedure specified in the Handbook (Vol.1) unless specifically exempted under the Policy.

5.9.23 Regularization of EO Default and Settlement of Customs Duty and Interest through Settlement Commission

With a view to providing assistance to firms who have defaulted under the Foreign Trade Policy for reasons beyond their control as also facilitating the merger, acquisition and rehabilitation of sick units, it has been decided to empower the Settlement Commission in the Central Board of Excise and Customs to decide such cases also with effect from 01.04.2005.

5.9.24 Easing of Documentation Requirements

Pending the finalization of Single Common Document (SCD) for international trade, the government departments dealing with exports and imports will honour the permission/licence/certificate issued by the other government departments based on the verification of the export documents like shipping bill, bank realization certificate, packing list, bill of lading etc. and will not insist upon fresh submission of these documents.

CHAPTER 6

Foreign Exchange Market

6.1 INTRODUCTION

The foreign exchange market is the market where the currency of one country is exchanged for that of another country and where the rate of exchange is determined. The genesis of Foreign Exchange (FE) market can be traced to the need for foreign currencies arising from:

- International Trade
- Foreign Investment
- Lending to and borrowing from foreigners.

In order to maintain an equilibrium in the FE Market, demand for foreign currency (or the supply of home currency) should equal supply of foreign currency (or the demand for home currency). In operational terms, the demand for and supply of home currency should be equal. In the event of a disequilibrium situation, the monetary authority of the concerned country normally intervenes/steps in to bring out the desired balance by:

- variation in the exchange rate: or
- changes in official reserves: or
- both.

6.2 PARTICIPANTS IN THE FOREIGN EXCHANGE MARKET

Major Participants in the FE market are:

1. Large commercial banks (through their dealers) operating either at retail level for individual exporters and corporations, or at wholesale level in the interbank market.
2. Central banks of various countries that intervene in order to maintain or to influence the exchange rate of their currencies within a certain range. As also to execute the order of government.

3. Individual brokers or corporations. Bank dealers often use brokers to stay anonymous since the identify of banks can influence short-term quotes.

6.3 FOREIGN EXCHANGE RATE DETERMINATION

The foreign exchange is determined by the demand for and supply of foreign exchange. As per the commodities relative demand and the supply arrangement according to it mainly determined the foreign exchange rate. Gustav Cassel determined the foreign exchange rate on the basis of purchasing power parity theory as the foreign exchange rate is determined by the relative purchasing powers of the two currencies depicting a parity between them.

The demand for foreign exchange depicit the requirement of foreign currency to purchase good and services from foreign country as well as in addition of capital exports. In other words, the demand for foreign exchange arises out of debt transactions in the balance of payment's current and capital accounts. The foreign exchange may be required for; to buy foreign goods and services, to make unilateral transfer payments; to hold deposits in overseas banks, to make long and short term lending to foreign residents, business firms or governments etc.

The supply of foreign exchange means that a country earns foreign currency by exporting various goods and services, receiving unilateral transfer payments & long-term and short-term capital imports. The supply of foreign exchange is derived from the credit transactions in the balance of payment's current and capital amounts of the home country.

In short we can say that all the spending and lending of foreign exchange is considered as demand foreign exchange while the foreign receipts and borrowings is considered as supply of foreign exchange. The foreign exchange is determined where demand for foreign exchange and supply of foreign exchange is intersecting each other the foreign exchange rate is determined.

From the figure 6.1 it is clear that the demand and supply curves intersect at point E the OQ_0 quantity of foreign exchange supply which exactly matches the demand for foreign exchange. This point will be considered as the equilibrium point where foreign exchange demands and supply are equal, and therefore, the balance of payment will also be balanced, RoE line show the equilibrium line of balance of payment is in balance. This is nothing else but, the equilibrium exchange rate. It prevail under the existing demand and supply conditions of foreign exchange. But, the exchange rate does not sustain at equilibrium rate it could fluctuate up and down, around the equilibrium rate in the foreign exchange market. (In the figure 6.1 it is shown by R_1 and R_2 as Rs 50 = $1 and Rs 40 = $1). If suppose the demand for dollar increase (as it shift to R point in the figure 6.1) the exchange rate will also change accordance of it, say Rs 50 = $1 at R_1 point then in the foreign exchange market the supply also respond in the same way and slowly the new foreign exchange rate Rs 50/$1 again return back to Rs 45/$1. Similarly, if the demand for dollar reduces and the new exchange rate becomes Rs 40/$1 then also supply for dollar respond in the same way and the change exchange rate again come to its original exchange rate.

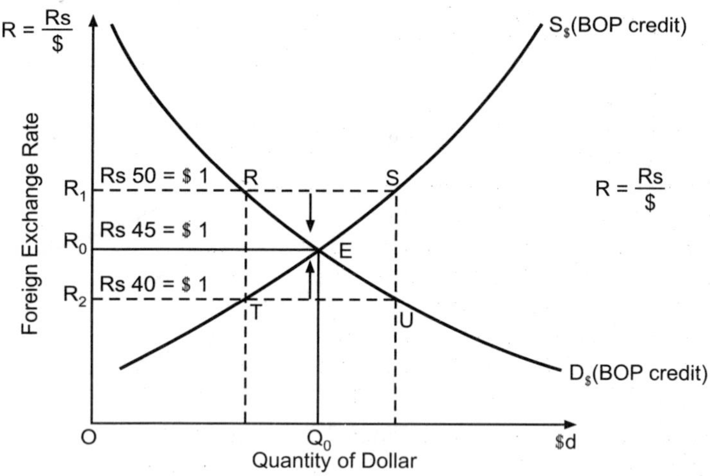

Fig. 6.1: Foreign exchaing rate

In the figure 6.2, the exchange rate is determined at the point E, where the demand for dollar d. $ curve and supply of dollar S$ curve cuts each other. The equilibrium foreign exchange price is suppose Rs 45/$1. Let us assume that the Indian foreign export increases, so the demand for rupee in the foreign market appreciated. This also impact to the dollar-rupee conversions and exchange rate. Therefore, it also effect to the domestic market and demand curve will shift from D_0\$ to D_1\$. Let, the rupee appreciated and became Rs 40/$1 then Indian Balance of Payment is in surplus. Now, the new equilibrium point suppose E_2. This will decrease the value and exchange price of dollar. Due to low rate of exchange of dollar to rupee the domestic speculators start, purchasing dollar from the exchange market in expectation of selling in high exchange price in future. This tendency of speculator leads the foreign exchange market favourable for the dollars and so only the demand for dollar increase which tends fill the foreign exchange for dollar to rupee to its original exchange rate, i.e. Rs 45/$1. Similarly, suppose the Indian foreign imports increases, so the demand for dollar in domestic market will increase. The demand curve will shift to D$ to D_2\$ and the new exchange rate become Rs 50/$1 then Indian Balance of Payment is in deficit. Now, the new equilibrium point become E_1. This will increase the value and exchange price of dollar. Due to high exchange price of dollar to rupee the domestic speculators starts selling the dollar in the exchange market for getting more profit, and this will increase the supply of dollar in the domestic exchange market which naturally leads the foreign exchange market to its original exchange rate equilibrium. i.e. again Rs 45/$1. This fluctuation of foreign exchange in domestic market also find in the other foreign exchange market and vice-versa.

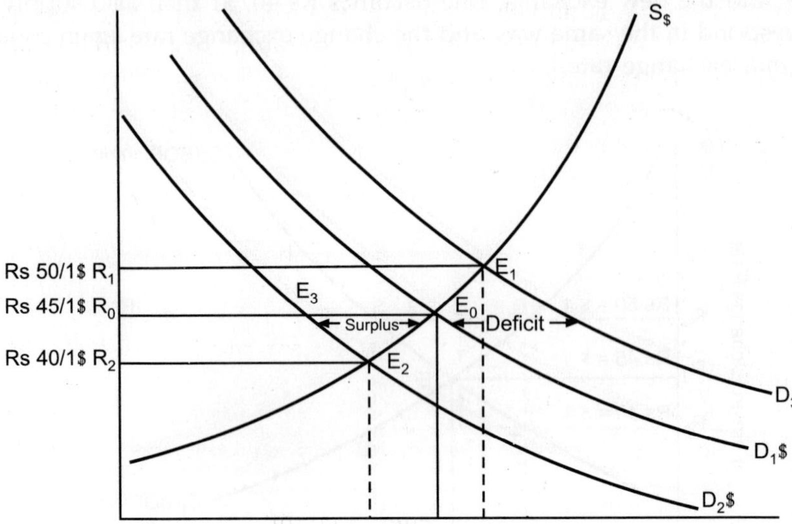

Fig. 6.2

6.4 CAUSES OF FLUCTUATION IN EXCHANGE RATE

The market rate of exchange rate, is subject to fluctuations in response to the supply of and demand for international money transfers. Factually, there are numerious factors which affect the demand for and supply of foreign currency which are ultimately responsible for the short-term fluctuations in the exchange are, some of the causes are as following:

1. **Trade Movement:** The change in the export or import certainly cause a change in the rate of foreign exchange. If the exports exceed the import the demand for foreign currency will down, hence the exchange rate move in favour to the country, if the import having over than exports. The demand for foreign currency will rise, thus, the rate of exchange moves against to the country.
2. **Capital Movement:** The movement of capital internationally from one nation to another would be for short periods to avail of the high rate of interest prevailing abroad or for long periods. For the purpose of making long-term investment abroad. Any trade of capital from one nation to another will bring about a change in the rate of exchange. If suppose a large amount of capital is shifted from USA to India, the demand for Indian rupees (or the supply of US dollar) in the exchange market increases so that the exchange value of the rupee in terms of US dollar increases. The Indian rupee will appreciate in terms of US $. The reverse will be found with Indian rupee where US $ will appreciate in terms of Indian rupee.
3. **Stock Exchange Operations:** It includes granting of loans, payment of interest on foreign debt, repatriation of foreign capital, purchase and sale of foreign securities etc. which definitely impact to the demand

for foreign funds and through it to the foreign exchange rate. For example, when a debt is given by the domestic country to a foreign country, the demand for foreign money increases and the rate of exchange tends to more unfavourably for the domestic country. In case of foreigners repay their loan, the demand for domestic currency exceeds its supply and the rate of exchange becomes favourable.

4. **Speculative Transactions:** It include transactions ranging from anticipation of seasonal movements in the exchange rate for the maximum extent, means, the outgoing of the capital. In the time of political instability, there is large speculation take place in terms of foreign currency. There is a scramble for purchasing particular currencies and few currencies are unloaded. These speculative activities bring about wide range of fluctuations in the foreign exchange rate.
5. **Banking Operation:** Banks are the major player and dealer of foreign exchange. They on the behalf of the International traders sell the drafts, transfer funds, issue of letter of credit, accept the foreign bills of exchange, take-up arbitrage operations etc. These operations impact the demand for and supply of foreign exchange and particularly effecting the foreign exchange rates. Bank rate also exerts a tremendous impact on the foreign exchange rate. An increase in the bank rate attracts the foreign funds, which tends the demand for domestic currency increase and the foreign exchange rate will rise upward. The reverse caused when the bank rate is lowered.
6. **Monetary Policy:** A growth oriented monetary policy has generally an inflationary impact, while a contractionist monetary policy reflects the deflationary impact. This show itself in a similar change in the external value of currency. Inflation means a rise in the domestic price level, a fall in the domestic purchasing power of money of the people and therefore a decline in the exchange rate. On the other hand in a deflationary leads to decline in the domestic price level, increase in the purchasing power of the people and tends to rise in the exchange rate.
7. **Political Conditions:** A proper maintenance or stability in the foreign exchange rate needs a stable political system in the country. The political stability of the government may leads the foreigners to invest in the country which make movement of foreign currency in the country. Due to supply of the foreign currency the domestic currency in respect to the foreign currency will appreciate. But, if the instability of political system found in the country make foreigners to withdraw their investment from the domestic market which may negative impact to the valuation of the domestic currency. So, its value depreciated. Thus, political condition also influence the foreign exchange of any country.

6.5 FIXED AND FLEXIBLE EXCHANGE RATES

Under the inconvertible paper money standard, there are of two types of exchange rates—Fixed and Flexible.

According to the International Monetary Fund (IMF) monetary system the fixed or stable exchange rates are known as pegged exchange rates or par values. The main objective of establishing IMF was to establishing the rates of exchange, with proper safe guards for adjustments whenever necessary. On the other hand, flexible exchange rates are left freely by the monetary authorities to be determined by the conditions of demand for and supply of foreign exchange and are perfectly free to fluctuate according to the changes in the demand and supply of the foreign exchange. If no restrictions on buying and selling in the foreign exchange market. The floating rate is based on the speculation in the foreign exchange market. Here, the Govt. does not interrupted the functioning or floating of exchange.

6.5.1 Advantage of Fixed Exchange Rate

The following are the advantages of fixed exchange rate:

1. Fixed exchange rates ensure certainly and confidence and also promote the International Trade. The foreign traders can easily know how much they have to pay and how much they receive in terms of their home currency. Flexible exchange rates constitutes an additional risk in International Trade which hampers its growth.
2. A system of fixed exchange rates will facilitate long-term International Investments. With an instable exchange rate, the lenders and investors will not be prepared to land for long-term investments. Thus, the fixed exchange rate system is essential for the orderly growth of international investment markets.
3. A fixed rate of exchange is more suited to a world of currency areas, such as the sterling area.
4. Fixed exchange rates will remove the dangerous possibilities of speculation. In a system of stable exchange rate there will be no panic flight of capital from one nation to another.
5. A fixed exchange rate will assist in domestic economic stabilisation. Whenever the chances of changes in the exchange rate appears the Govt interfere and established the exchange rate, which helps the economy to grow stable and smoothly.
6. Small countries like Sri Lanka and Singapore whose economy the foreign trade plays a critical role, stabilization of the exchange rate is the only right policy. For if the country does not stabilize her exchange rate, fluctuations in the rate of exchange will disturb her foreign trade and with it the prosperity and growth of the country.

6.5.2 Disadvantages of Fixed Exchange Rate

The fixed exchange rates system have following draw backs:

1. The fixed exchange rate may cause a large-scale of destabilizing speculation in the foreign exchange markets. Speculation causes the movement of funds from weak to strong currencies, so that a more drastic devaluation may force a country to resort to rigorous exchange controls.

2. Fixed exchange rates is not an absolute condition for long-term capital investment internationally. Over a very long-period a lender cannot expect the exchange rate to be stable. It means the expectation of getting more in the future is not found in the case of fixed exchange rate.
3. Stable exchange rates are not inevitable in a system of currency area like the sterling area. Typical economic, political and social forces have induced various countries to constitute the sterling block and these forces would not be enfeebled if the sterling is allowed to have flexible exchange rates.
4. The system of fixed exchange rates has many inherent weaknesses. Given with severe exchange control, it props up currency speculation and endangers the stability in the external value of the domestic currency ultimately leading to devaluation of the currency.
5. Another major weakness of fixed exchange is that it does not reflect the existing and true cost-price relationship between two currencies. When the nations follow different economic rules and regulation, cost-price relations after frequently and the economic stability will be hampered.

6.5.3 Advantage of Flexible Exchange Rate

The following are the advantage of flexible exchange rate:

1. In the flexible exchange rate system, the exchange rate moves in a free market to equate supply and demand, so that the market is cleared off and the problem of scarcity or surplus of any one currency is automatically solved. Therefore, under this exchange rate system, the countries do not have to make extra efforts including changes in prices and incomes in order to maintain equilibrium in the balance of payments.
2. This system of exchange rate facilitates continuous adjustments, so that the adverse effect of prolonged period of disequilibrium is avoided.
3. It permits the continued existence of free trade and convertible currencies. This system does not require the use of exchange controls, which is generally associated with the system of fixed rate.
4. The flexible exchange rate system also prefer more independence on the countries in the domestic policies. It is facilitating because flexible rates minimise the transformation of economic effects through monetary channels than otherwise might interfere with the pursuit of internal policies aimed at achieving or maintaining growth and full employment.
5. Sohmen* as a reference (* Sohmen E ∴ Flexible Exchange Rates Theory and Controversy. PP. 83-90) argues that flexible rates system tends to reinforce the effectiveness of monetary policy. For example, when a country seeks to expand output, it may lower interest rates. But, the lowering the interst rate, under the flexible exchange rate systems, will cause an outflow of capital, a rise in the spot rate, and a rise in exports

relative to imports. The trade balance, as such will move favourable which will reinforce the expansionary effect of lower interest rate on domestic spending, thus making the monetary policy more effective.

6.5.4 Disadvantage of Flexible Exchange Rate

The following are the disadvantage of flexible exchange rate:

1. The elasticities for demand and supply of foreign currencies in international markets are too low for exchange rate variations to operate successfully in bringing about automatic adjustment in the equilibrium. When the elasticities for demand & supply of currency is too low, the exchange market becomes unstable, hence the depreciation of the weak currency would tend to worsen the deficit payment further.
2. The instability and uncertainty of the exchange rate is found under the flexible exchange rate system. This instability and uncertainty of foreign exchange rate may leads to the reduction of the volume of international trade. This exchange rate system undoubtly increase the exchange rate run in the international and domestic exchange market.
3. This type of exchange rate are determined on the basis of speculation in the exchange rate market. In short run it would effect highly to the export and import of the country. This uncertainty will discourage the stable equilibrium conditions in the exchange market.
4. Flexible exchange rate system involves greater possibility of inflationary effect of exchange depreciation on the domestic price level of a country, causing a further depreciation. The pegged exchange rate system, on the other hand, imposes a strong discipline on the domestic policies to prevent inflation in order to maintain the external value of the currency.
5. The immobility of factor's of production deprives the flexible rates system of its advantage in free monetary and other policies used for maintaining internal stability. But, it does not work for high changes in the factors of production and it forcefully make impact to the movability of the factors of production.
6. The flexible exchange rate system does not work effectively in case of critical position of economy or in the case of emergency like war, with other country and civil war it is totally failure.

6.6 QUOTING IN THE FOREIGN EXCHANGE MARKET

Foreign exchange rates are quoted either for immediate delivery (spot rate) or for delivery on a future date (forward rate). In practice delivery in spot market is made two days later.

A FE quotation is the price of a currency expressed in the units of another currency. The quotation can be either direct or indirect. It is direct when quoted as "so many units of local currency per unit of foreign currency." For example, Rs 45 = US $1, is a direct quotation for US $ in India. Similarly, a quotation in the USA will be \$0.22 = FFr1. Whereas in France, it would be FFr 3.3 = DM1, etc.

On the other hand, an indirect quotation is the one where exchange rate is given in terms of variable units of foreign currency as equivalent to a fixed number of units of home currency. For example, in India US\$ 2.22 = Rs 100 is an indirect quotation.

6.7 SPOT RATE OF EXCHANGE

When the exchange of one currency to another currency on the second working day after the date of the agreement, it is called as spot rate of exchange. The time period is allowed to banks to process the necessary paper work and transfer the funds. Such, transfers to the bank and from banks will be effected when their overseas currency accounts are either credited or debited, depending on whether the bank is buying or selling. If the agreement is made on telephone is called as contract date or the value date. The value is the one when the deposit is credited or debited. Normally, a deal is done on Tuesday will be settled on Thursday while a deal done on Friday will be settled on the following Tuesday. A business day is defined as one in which both banks are open for business in both settlement countries. Mostly, the exchange rate are dealed in spot.

For instance, a deal done by an Indian trader with American trader in terms of Rs/\$ and the spot day decided as Tuesday. So the settlement is normally expected on Thursday. But, a holiday in USA announced for Wednesday than this settlement changed to Friday. Similarly, any holiday occur in India is between the settlement time than the settlement with extended to next day. In case, this deal of Rs/\$ done in London, the occurrence of bank holiday in the UK during the spot period is entirely irrelevant. This is because all bank account transfers are made in the settlement country rather than the dealing centre.

Settlement of both sides of a foreign exchange deal should be mode on the same business day. So, the settlement of the deal of the exchange rate depends upon the holiday to the centre for exchange in different countries. Sometimes, the countries far to each other found this type of problems like India and USA but for the USA & Canadian currencies US \$/can\$ transactions, a spot transaction can be done in one day only. This is only be done on the convention and agreement among the market participants.

6.8 FORWARD RATE OF EXCHANGE

If the exchange of currencies takes place after more than two working days, it is called the forward rate of exchange. In the forward rate of exchange the contract between a customer and a dealer for the purchase or sale of a specific quantum of a certain foreign currency for executing by delivery and payment at a future time agreed upon when making the contract. It is expressed on the basis of premium/discount on the spot rate for the forward period premium on one country's currency implies discount on another country's currency. For example, if the US $ is at a premium vis-a-vis Indian Rupee, it obviously implies that the Rs is at a discount vis-a-vis to the US $.

This rate of exchange is not found in a specific location and place. The deals in the forward is made on the basis of telephonic talk, telex etc. The major player of the forward markets are the banks who actually cover the orders for their clients. The forward rate are quoted by a dealer for any future date except then the spot date. Normally this is quoted for one, two, three or six months.

Quotation for the forward rates are mode on the basis of two ways.

(*i*) They can be made in terms of the exact amount of domestic currency at which the trader quoting the rates will buy and sell a unit in foreign currency. This quotation of the forward rate is called as the 'outright rate'.

(*ii*) Another method is to quote in terms of points of the discount or in other term discount on the spot rate used in inter banking quotation.

The forward rate of exchange is determined on the basis of a mechanism. Under it, if the first forward quote is smaller than the second forward quote, then there is a premium. So, under this circumstances the points are added to the spot rate. In the reverse case if the first quote is greater than the second, then it is considered as discount instead of premium. If however, both the figures of the quote is the same, then the trade has to specify the forward rate is at premium or discount. This mechanism ensures that the purchase price is lesser than the selling price, and the trader points from the spread between the two prices:

For Example:

	Spot	**1 month**	**3 months**	**6 months**
Rs/$	45/1	46/1	47/1	46.5/1

or in the dealing terms it can be defined as:

$/Rs	45.2321/2340	25/20	40/32	20/26

In the outright terms, these quotes would be expressed as

Maturity	Bid/Buy	Sell/offer/Ask	Spread
Spot	Rs 45.2321 per US $	Rs 45.2340 per US $	0.0019
1 month	Rs 45.2296 per US $	Rs 45.2320 per US $	0.0024
3 months	Rs 45.2281 per US $	Rs 45.2308 per US $	0.0027
6 months	Rs 45.2341 per US $	Rs 45.2366 per US $	0.0025

6.9 AN ARBITRAGE BETWEEN TWO CURRENCIES

Suppose two Traders A and B are quoting the following rates:

Trader A (India)	Trader B (USA)
Mumbai	New York
Rs 45/1$	1$/0.022 Rs

Fig. 6.3

We assume that buying & selling rates for these traders. We find out the reciprocal rate of the quote given by the trader B which is Rs 47/1$ (=1/0.022). A combeste buys, say $ 10,000 from the trader A by paying Rs 45 per $. Then he sells these US $ to the trader B and receive Rs 4,70,000. In the process, he gains Rs 20,000 (= 4,70,000 – 4,50,000).

Since, in practice, buying & selling rates are likely to be different, so the quotation is likely to be as follows.

Trader A	Trader B
Rs 43/1$—Rs 45/1$	$0.021—$0.022
	$0.023—$0.023

Fig. 6.4

Ask price and bid price

Spread

$$\text{Per cent spread} = \frac{\text{Ask price} - \text{Bid Price}}{\text{Ask price.}} \times 100$$

Arbitrage can be defined as an operation that consists in deriving a profit without risk from a differential existing between different quoted rates.

6.10 PURCHASING POWER PARITY (PPP) THEORY

The theory was enunciated by Gustav Cassel a Swedish economist in 1920. Purchasing power of a currency is determined by the amount of goods and services that can be purchased with one unit of that currency. If there is more than one currency, it is fair and equitable that the exchange rate between there currencies provides the same purchasing power for each currency. This is reffered to as **purchasing power parity.**

The rate of exchange tends to rest at the point which expresses equality between the respective purchasing powers of the two currencies. This point is called the purchasing power parity.

Suppose USA and India were both on paper currency inconvertible into metal. Then how many Rupees would have to paid to get a $? Obviously as many as would have the same purchasing power in India as one $ has in USA.

Let us suppose that in USA $1 purchases X commodities and in India, X commodities costRs 45. Then the rate of exchange will obviously tend to be

$$\$1 = \text{Rs } 45$$

Now suppose the price levels in the two countries remain the same but some how the exchange rate moves to

$$\$1 = \text{Rs } 50$$

This means that the purchasing power of $ 1 in India is more than Rs 45. It will pay people to convert $ dollar into Rupees at this rate, purchase X commodities in India for Rs 45 and sell them in USA for $1 again, making a profit of Rs 5 per dollar worth of transaction. This will create a large demand for Rs in USA, while supply there of will be less because very few people would export commodities from USA to India. The value of the Rs in terms of the \$ dollar will, therefore, move up until it reaches \$1 = Rs 45. At that point imports from India will not give abnormal profits \$1 = Rs 45 is called the purchasing power parity between the two countries.

Let us consider two countries, A and B. The rate of inflation in the country A is higher than that in the country B. As a result, imports of the country A increase since the prices of foreign goods tend to be lower. Similarly, exports from the country A decrease since the prices of its goods appear to be higher to foreigners (residents of country B- included). This situation cannot persist for long. In consequence, the currency of the country A will depreciate with respect to that of the country B.

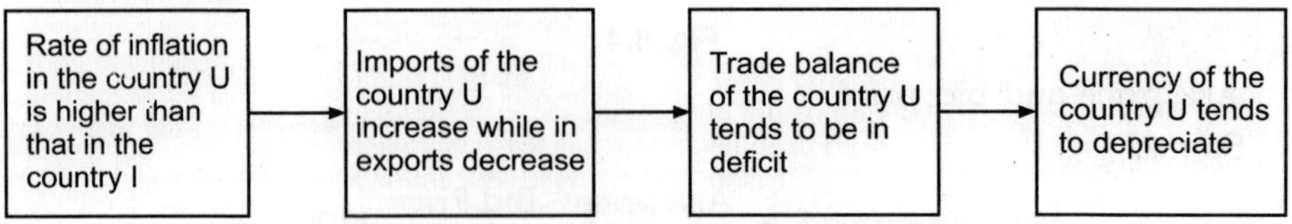

Fig. 6.5: Fluctuation in exchange rates

Suppose at a particular time period, the price index in the country U is P_{1U} while that in the country I is P_{1I} and the exchange rate is $S_{1A/B}$, the relation between price indices and exchange rate is expressed as equation 1.

$$P_{1U} = S_{1U/I} \times P_{1I} \qquad ...(1)$$

Now, suppose at the period second-

$$P_{2U} = P_{1U}\,(1 + r_U)$$

and
$$P_{2I} = P_{1I}\,(1 + r_I)$$

where r_U and r_I are the rates of inflation in the two countries respectively.

Thus, at the period second, the exchange rate will be

$$P_{2U} = S_{2U/I} \times P_{2I}$$

or
$$P_{1U}\,(1 + r_U) = S_{2U/I} \times P_{1I}\,(1 + r_I)$$

Putting the value of P_{2U} and P_{2I} in the second period then we get

$$P_{1U}/P_{1I} = S_{2U/I} \times [(1 + r_I) / (1 + r_U)]$$

or
$$S_{1U/I} = S_{2U/I} \times [(1 + r_I)/(1 + r_U)]$$

or
$$S_{2U/I} = S_{1U/I} \times [(1 + r_U)/(1 + r_I)] \qquad ...(2)$$

So, the above description of the equation 2 for the period second shows that in country I the inflation rate is high as compare to country U. Due to high inflation rate in country I, it value in domestic currency will depreciated and the purchasing power of the people of country I become lower which definately leads the currency of country U to appreciate. Thus, we can that due to the change in the purchasing power of the currency leads to effects the exchange rate without interfering the exchange rate system mechanism. This can be well explained with the help of a example.

Suppose at a particular period a consumer spend \$ 10 to buy a certain quantity of goods. Alternatively, the same quantity can be bought for Rs 450. So, the parity holds such that

$$\$\ 10 = S_1\ \$/Rs \times Rs\ 450$$

or S_1 \$/Rs = \$ 10/Rs 450 or \$ 0.022/Rs 1

Let, to buy same quantity of goods at the second period. Suppose, we spend either \$ 11 or Rs 540. So, the resultant relationship will be

\$ 11 = S_2 \$/Rs × Rs 540

or S_2 \$/Rs = \$ 11/Rs 540

or \$ 0.020/Rs 1

It can clearly see that during period 1 and period 2 the US \$ had appreciated as compare to Indian Rupee. This appreciation is found due to the different rate of inflation between the two countries.

6.10.1 Criticism of the Theory

The purchasing power parity theory has criticises on many grounds like

1. This theory helps only in determining the change in the exchange rate, not the absolute exchange rate. Therefore PPP theory cannot be applied to the absolute levels of prices.
2. In case of the wholesale price index number on which purchasing power parity theory based does not give an accurate measure of a change in purchasing power.
3. The purchasing power of currency in terms of only internationally funded goods & services is relevant for its external value, the wholesale price index number includes prices of all the commodities.
4. Apart from the goods, many other items of services like banking, insurance, consultancy, telephones inter the foreign transactions and a huge capital transfers take place between the nations which do not enter the wholesale price index number.
5. The imposition of embargo, tariffs and provisions of subsidy for exports very often causes deviations in the purchasing power which are not accounted for by the purchasing power parity theory.
6. The change in exchange rate depends on the elasticities of the reciprocal demand whereas purchasing power parity theory recognises the changes in the exchange rate due to only changes in relative prices.
7. This theory assumes that the relative commodity prices are the sole determinants of international transactions and the change in the relative prices is the sole determinant in exchange rate, which is not true. Changes in the exchange rate also take place to disequilibrium caused by capital transfers, service payments and change in real income.

Despite these shortcomings, the PPP theory is very much useful in determining the first approximation to an equilibrium rate of periods of serious and frequent price changes. For more accurate measure of the exchange rate, other factors like flows and changes in faster, techniques and real incomes would have to be taken into account.

6.11 THEORY OF INTEREST RATE PARITY

The interest rate parity theory describe the change of any currency's premium and discount due to the differencial of interest rate between the two currencies.

In case of perfect market condition and no interference or restriction on the money flow. One should be in a position to gain the similar real value on one's monetary assets irrespective of the country where they are held. For instance

$$r\uparrow \rightarrow S\uparrow \rightarrow I\downarrow \rightarrow X\downarrow \rightarrow M\uparrow$$

It means that when rate of interest is high ($r\uparrow$) then the saving are also high ($s\uparrow$), which adversely effect to the investment ($I\downarrow$), due to low investment the export ($X\downarrow$) will also be decrease whereas the Import will increase ($M\uparrow$). When import is greater than export, then the quantity demanded for foreign currency will high, which means the domestic currency will be depreciated. This decrease in the value of domestic currency is due to increase in the interest rate.

$$r\downarrow \rightarrow s\downarrow \rightarrow I\uparrow \rightarrow X\uparrow \rightarrow M\downarrow$$

Similary, in the reverse of the above example, if the interest rate is low ($r\downarrow$) the savings ($s\downarrow$) of the people will also be low, people prefer investing their money instead of saving it. Thus the Investment ($I\downarrow$) will increase. This helps in increasing the export ($X\uparrow$) and discourage the Import ($M\downarrow$). Due to high increase in export tends to a high quantity demanded of the domestic currency which means, the value of domestic currency will appreciate in terms of foreign currency. This appreciations in the domestic currency will be due to change in interest rate, mean low interest rate. Therefore, we can say that if the interest rate is low in the domestic country than the value of the domestic currency will appreciated and foreign currency depreciated and when the interest rate become high then the value of domestic currency will depreciated and foreign currency appreciated.

For example: An investor has a sum of \$1 today. The exchange rate is say, \$1Sr/.Rs 45, means, he can convert his \$1 to get Rs 45. (Here Sr means the spot rate of exchange). Further, the net interest per rupee in i_{Rs} while per dollar it is $i_{\$}$. The investor has two choices before him

(*i*) He places his money in \$ to receive $1\times (1 + i_{\$})$ after a period T;

(*ii*) He converts his money into rupee and places it in rupee market to receive $Sr \times (1 + i_{Rs})$

In order that he be indifferent in placing his money either in \$ or in Rs, the two sums, at the end of the period T, should be equal as:

$$Sr\ (1 + i_{Rs}) = 1(1 + i_{\$}) \qquad ...(1)$$

$$\text{or} \quad \$1 = Rs\ Sr\ [(1 + i_{Rs}) \ / \ (1 + i_{\$})]$$

where, i_{Rs} interest rate per rupee

$i_{\$}$ interest rate per dollar.

So, the rate of exchange after the period T is Rs Fr/\$ (Here Fr means the forward rate of exchange). So, in general we can determined it as

$$Fr = Sr\ \frac{1+i_D}{1+i_F}$$

where,
Fr = Forward Rate
Sr = Spot Rate
i_D = Domestic rate of interest
i_F = Foreign country's rate of interest

This equation can be rearranged such as.

$$\frac{Fr - Sr}{Sr} = \frac{i_D - i_F}{1 + i_F}$$

If i_F is considered small compared to 1, then

$$\frac{Fr - Sr}{Sr} = i_D - i_F \qquad ...(2)$$

Thus, premium or discount should be almost equal to the difference between the rates of interest rate of the two currencies.

Illustration: If the current exchange rate between the US $ and Indian Rs is Rs 45/$1 and interest rate for the period for the one year are 7.5% (US $) and 9.0% (Rs) respectively, determine the expected exchange rate after one year.

Solution.

Here, Sr = Rs 45/US $1

T = 1 year

Investor will get after one year Rs 49.05 = (Rs 45 × 1.09)

Investor will get after one year US $ 1.075 = (US $ 1 × 1.075)

Therefore

Fr = 45 × [(1 + 0.090)/(1 + 0.75)] = 45.627

6.12 EXCHANGE RATE RISK OF AN ENTERPRISE

Multinational enterprises are subject to the following three types of risk exposures:

- Transaction Exposure
- Consolidation Exposure (Translation)
- Economic Exposure

6.12.1 Transaction Exposure

Whenever there is a commitment to pay foreign currency or possibility to receive foreign currency at a future date, any movement in the exchange rate will affect the domestic value of the transaction. The following situations give rise to transaction exposure.

- Trade transactions with foreign countries when billing is done in foreign currencies like exports or imports.
- Banking and Financial transactions done in foreign currencies like lending and borrowing or equity participation, etc.

Suppose an enterprise is unquely in the export business. Its exposure will be calculated from its position in terms of amount receivables from debtor companies in different currencies and amount payable to creditor companies. Let us assume that an Indian business firm has its position of receivable in Indian rupees.

Table 6.1

Currency	Indian Rupees	US dollars in Rs	Pound Sterlings in Rs	Japanese Yen in Rs	Total Exchange Exposure
Receivables	200,000	100,000	50,000	70,000	+ 220,000

The exchange exposure position of the enterprise is equal to Rs 220,000 (= 100,000 + 50,000 + 70,000). This results from credits given in US dollars, Pound sterlings and Japanese yens. Since the amount is receivable it is shown by a positive (+) sign and is technically referred to as long position.

Now, suppose the enterprise is uniquely of importing type. Its exchange exposure is calculated from the sum payable to creditors.

Table 6.2

Currency	Indian Rupees	US dollar in Rs	Pound Sterlings in Rs	Deutsch marks in Rs	French Franks in Rs	Total Exchange Exposure
Supplies	– 125,000	– 50,000	– 60,000	– 100,000	– 30,000	– 240,000

The exchange exposure position of the enterprise is equal to Rs 240,000. This is a debt on the company and as such, is represented by a negative (–) sign.

A transaction gain or loss occurs because the exchange rate has varied between the date of contract involving foreign currency and the completion of the contract. For every period, exposure position is calculated in each currency. If for a particular currency, the balance is zero, we say the exchange position is closed.

6.12.2 Translation Exposure

This position is reflected in the balance sheet (B/S) of an enterprise. Different methods of translation of balance sheet are in use. We will apply them to the one balance sheet of a company ABC, presented in Table. Let us assume the company ABC, is a subsidiary of an American company.

Table 6.3: Balance Sheet of the Company ABC

In Indian Rupee

Assets		Liabilities	
Fixed assets	200,000	Owner's equity	140,000
Stocks	50,000	Long-term debt	80,000
Receivables	30,000	Short-term debt	70,000
Cash	10,000		
Total	290,000		290,000

The same balance sheet is presented in Table in terms of US dollars, using a conversion rate of Rs 45 = US $1

Table 6.4: Balance Sheet of the Company ABC

(In US Dollars)

Assets		Liabilities	
Fixed assets	200,000/45 = 4444.44	Owner's equity	140,000/45 = 3111.11
Stocks	50,000/45 = 1111.11	Long-term debt	80,000/45 = 1777.77
Receivables	30,000/45 = 666.66	Short-term debt	70,000/45 = 1555.55
Cash	10,000/45 = 222.22		
Total	$ 6444.43		$ 6444.43

All assets and liabilities, except the owner's equity, are converted on the basis of the exchange rate prevailing at the closing day of the accounting year. Say, this rate is Rs 46/US$1. Then, the BS will appear as

Table 6.5: Balance Sheet of the Company ABC

(In US Dollars)

Assets		Liabilities	
Fixed assets	200,000/46 = 4347.82	Owner's equity	140,000/45 = 3111.11
Stocks	50,000/46 = 1086.95	Long-term debt	80,000/46 = 1739.13
Receivables	30,000/46 = 652.17	Short-term debt	70,000/46 = 1521.73
Cash	10,000/46 = 217.39		
Total	$ 6304.33		$ 6371.97

It may be noted that all items, save equity in the balance sheet have been converted, using the closing exchange rate of dollar. A general reason for excluding equity (for conversion at the closing rate) is that loss/profits an account of foreign exchange changes exclusively are to be borne/accused to the owner. For the same reason, equity is excluded in other (second & third) methods. There is a loss due to consolidation of US $ 67.64 (= $ 6371.97 – $ 6304.33).

6.12.3 Economic Exposure

The impact of appreciation or depreciation of local currency on the cash inflows and outflows. If the local currency appreciates, it is very likely that exports will be reduced as they become less competitive; the extent of reduction depends on the degree of competitively of the products exported. Similarly, sales of local products on local market may decline if there exists competition on the local market. Interest received on the money placed in foreign countries, and converted in local currency, will diminish as well.

If, on the other hand, the local currency depreciates, cash flows are affected exactly in the opposite way. Exports should increase as manufactured products are more competitive. But if the company imports a significant part of its inputs, its expenses will increase and thus its cost of production will go up. If the company has borrowed abroad, its financial charges will also increase.

6.13 INTEREST RATE RISK

All banks & firms, domestic or multinational are sensitive to interest rate movements. The interest rate risk results from a mismatch of maturity of assets and liabilities. For example, a bank faces interest rate risk if the sources of funds have a shorter term to maturity than that of its advances. A multinational runs an interest rate risk arising from mismatched timing in repricing those assets and liabilities that are sensitive to interest rate.

6.13.1 Importance of Interest Rate Risk

It concerns with

- Present credits and debts,
- Future credits and debts; and
- Conditional credits and debts.

An interest rate position either on the asset side or on the liability side is subjected to fluctuations of rates. When an enterprise is faced with a situation of interest rate risk, it can

- either decide to do nothing and keep into position uncovered.
- or cover itself by taking recourse to organised market of interest rate options and futures,
- or cover itself on over-the-counter (OTC) markets, future rate agreements, forward-forward agreements interest rate option, caps, floor, swaps etc.

6.13.2 Interest Rate Risk Manifestation

There is a close nexus between IRR and prices of financial securities. Therefore, it would be useful to know, how the prices of financial securities vary. The price of a financial security is equal to the present value of cash inflows (F_t) that it generates during its life. In general, the price of a fixed rate financial security P, refundable at the end of the borrowing period, depends upon:

- **The Coupon amount;** Coupon (C) is equal to the product of nominal value of a bond and interest rate.
- **The mode of capital refund;** Normally, refund (R) is done in one lot at the end of the life of a bond, but it can be done in installments over a period of a number of years.
- Market interest rate (r).
- Maturity period (N) of the borrowing.

$$P = \sum_{t=1}^{n} \frac{F_t}{(1+r)^t} = \frac{C}{(1+r)} + \frac{C_2}{(1+r)^2} + \ldots + \frac{C_n + R}{(1+r)^n}$$

where F_t represents the cash flows generated by the fixed–income security.

When market interest rate increases, the price of the fixed income security decreases and conversely when market interest rate decreases, the price of the fixed-income security increases.

Example: In 1970, a company bought bonds whose nominal value was Rs 1 million. Coupon is 5% or Rs 50,000 per year and the maturity period is 25 years. So, the value of the bond is

$$P_{(70)} = \sum_{t=1}^{25} \frac{\text{Rs}\,50{,}000}{(1.05)^t} + \frac{\text{Rs}\,1{,}000{,}000}{(1.05)^{25}} = \text{Rs}\,1{,}000{,}000$$

But, in 1980, the market rate become 12% making the value of the bond to be

$$P_{(80)} = \sum_{t=1}^{15} \frac{\text{Rs}\,50{,}000}{(1.12)^t} + \frac{\text{Rs}\,1{,}000{,}000}{(1.12)^{15}} = 523{,}000$$

It can be seen that the capital loss is very large (to the tune of 48%). On the other hand, a decrease in market yield induces a price increase that results into capital gain if the investor liquidates his bonds. However, if the bond is held till its maturity, there is no risk resulting from market variations.

6.14 MEASUREMENT OF INTEREST RATE RISK

Interest rate risk is measured by sensitivity and duration.

6.14.1 Sensitivity

Sensitivity (S) in the price of a fixed-income financial security indicates the percentage change in the price for each 1 per cent change in the market interest rate (r)

$$S = \frac{\Delta P / P}{\Delta r} \qquad \text{...(1)}$$

$$= -\frac{1}{P}\sum_{t=1}^{N} \frac{t F_t}{(1+r)^{t+1}} \qquad \text{...(2)}$$

The value of sensitivity depends upon several factors.

- life of the security
- interest rate on the security
- market interest rate

If for example, S = 3, it means that a 1% change in the interest rate causes a 3% change in the price of the security (in the negative direction).

Example: A 3 year bond, with nominal value of Rs 100, carries an interest rate of 6% and is refundable at the end of its life. Sensitivity calculations are

$$S = \frac{1}{100}\left[\frac{6}{(1+0.06)^2} + 2\times\frac{6}{(1+0.06)^3} + \frac{3\times 100+6}{(1+0.06)^3}\right] = 2.673$$

This means that a 1% change (increase from 6 to 7%) in the market interest rate would result into 2.67% loss of capital. Conversely, a 1% decrease in interest rate from 6 to 5 will yield capital appreciation of 2.67%.

6.14.2 Duration

Duration is an index of time during which an investor recovers his funds initially invested. Duration is calculated by finding the ratio of (*i*) sum of the product of period and the corresponding present value of cash flows generated by the security, and (*ii*) present value of the security. It is expressed in terms of years. It enables to compare bonds issued with different conditions. Duration (D) is computed using the formula

$$D = \frac{1}{P}\sum_{t=1}^{N} t \times \frac{F_t}{(1+r)^t} \qquad \text{...(1)}$$

duration is also equal to the product of sensitivity and the factor (1 + r).

Example: With the same example (Previous one).

$$D = \frac{1}{100}\left[1\times\frac{6}{1+0.06} + 2\times\frac{6}{(1+0.06)^2} + 3\times\frac{6}{(1+0.06)^3}\right]$$

$$= 2.83 \text{ years.}$$

But, if after one month, the rate rises to 7% the duration will change to

$$D = \frac{1}{100}\left[\frac{11}{12}\times\frac{6}{(1.07)^{11/12}} + \frac{23}{12}\times\frac{6}{(1.07)^{23/12}} + \frac{35}{12}\times\frac{6}{(1.07)^{35/12}}\right]$$

$$= 2.68 \text{ years.}$$

The securities with longer duration have greater volatility than those of shorter duration. Thus, the higher duration greater risk. If the duration of the asset is higher than that of liability, the financial firm is holding a long position and then the risk comes from the increase in rates, as decrease in the value of assets held will be higher than the advantage accruing from a decrease in sum payable. On the other hand, if the establishment holds a short position i.e. the duration of the asset is smaller than that of liability, the risk emanates from a decrease in rates.

6.15 TECHNIQUES OF HEDGING

There are several techniques which can be used in this category to reduce the exchange rate risk:

- Choosing a particular currency for invoice
- Leads and lags.
- Indexation clauses in contracts
- Netting
- Swaps

6.15.1 Choosing a Particular Currency for Invoice

In order to avoid the exchange rate risk, many companies try to invoice their exports in the national currency and try to pay their suppliers in the national currency as well. This way an exporter knows exactly how much he is going to receive and how much he is to pay, as an importer.

This method is a noble one. However, an enterprise suffers under this method if the national currency appreciates; this is likely to result into a loss of market for the products of the company if there are other competitors.

6.15.2 Leads and Lags

This technique consists of accelerating or delaying receipt or payment in foreign exchange as warranted by the position expected position of the exchange rate. The principle involved is rather simple.

If depreciation of national currency is apprehended, importing enterprises like to clear their dues expeditiously in foreign currencies; exporting enterprises prefer to delay the receipt from their debtors abroad. These actions, however if generalised all over the country, may weaken the national currency.

The converse will hold true if an appreciation of national currency is anticipated, importing enterprises delay their payments to foreigners while the exporting ones will attempt to get paid at the earliest. These actions may have a snowballing effect on national currency appreciating further.

6.15.3 Indexation Clauses in Contracts

Several clauses of Indexation are used by international trader for protecting against the exchange rate risk. Under it, a contract which contains a clause defining the price adjustment in such a manner that the fluctuations of exchange rate are absorbed. Suppose, the exporting country's currency appreciates, the price of exports will increased to the same proportion and if the exporting country's currency depreciate, the price of the export reduce in the same proportion. Due to the change in the price of export and change in the exchange rate the exchange rate risk is borne by the exporter country. To remove this exchange rate risk a variety of third currency or a basket of currencies is used. This clause has the repercussion for both the parties to the contract.

There is another option is that the contracting parties may decide to share the risk. They may stipulate that part of exchange rate variation, intervening between the date of contract and payment and can be shared by both the parties as equally, one-third, two-third, one-fourth etc.

6.15.4 Netting

Netting is the process by which a trader minimise the exchange rate risk by making and receiving payments in the same currency. The overall exchange rate risk exposure depends on the net balance. Under it, the trader tries to reduce the number of currencies invoices. One single currency choice is not sufficient as well as the dates of settlement must be similar during the netting.

Types of Netting: There are two types of netting.

(*i*) Bilateral (*ii*) Multilateral.

6.15.4.1 Bilateral netting

Bilateral netting means two trader of two different countries having trade relations and having exporting and importing their goods reciprocally. This is generally found that a company having subsidiary company in another country. The Parent company may sell their semi–finished product to their foreign subsidiary and the repurchase the final product from the latter. For examples Coca-Cola a parent company of USA and Coca-Cola India Ltd is a subsidiary of it, they had a trade and the following transaction take Place:

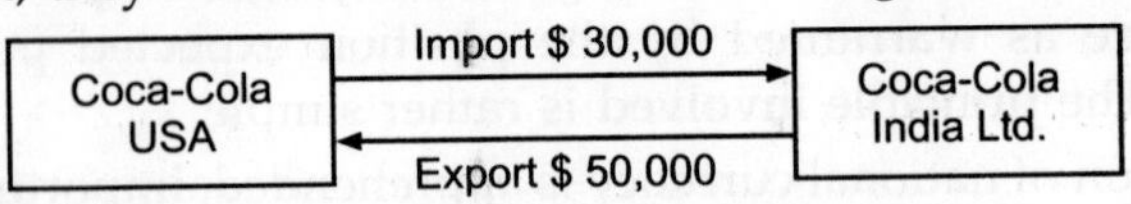

the above situation is found without netting between them. Now, when both the companies recourse to netting then the actual movement of the fund will be

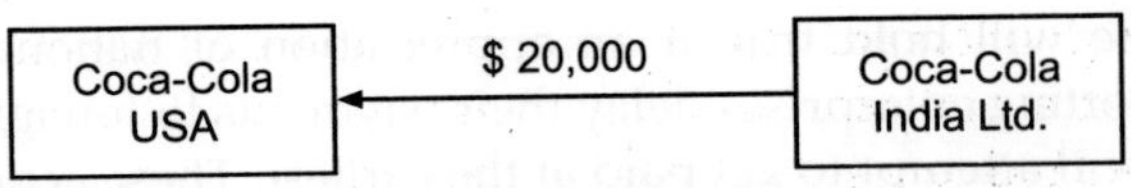

So, In this way with involving the netting the exchange rate risk of $ 80,000 reduces to only 20,000. So, with the help of netting both the countries are able to reduce the exchange rate risk exposure.

6.15.4.2 Multilateral netting

The netting can also be done on multilateral trading system. This is done when many subsidiary company trading with its parent company as well as with subsidiary companies. The group of subsidiary and parents company get together and for a netting to reduce the transaction among themselves and reduce the exchange rate risk exposure we can explain it with the help of a example.

Suppose, the Coca-Cola of USA having three different subsidiary companies all over the world. They may have the transaction as

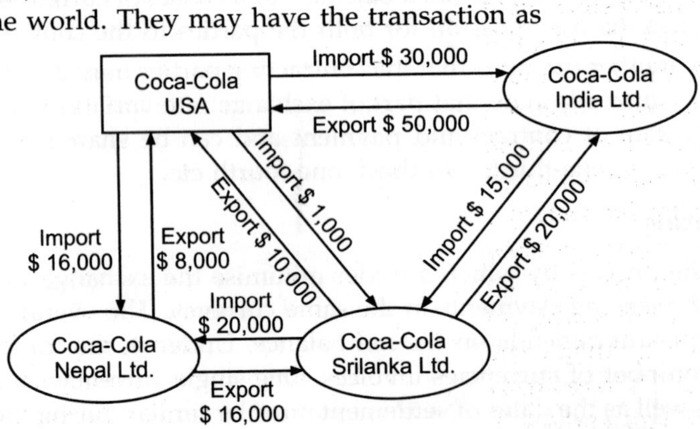

This situation found before the netting. After, involving of the netting, the total exchange rate risk exposure will reduce as

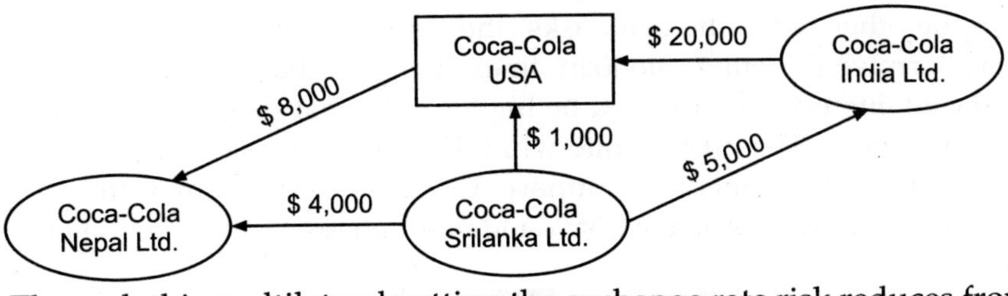

Through this multilateral netting the exchange rate risk reduces from $ 1,94,000 to only $ 38,000.

6.15.5 Swaps

A swap in the exchange rate market is an agreement between two or more traders. To transact the liabilities arising from two or more debt instruments. The swap involves two simultaneous operations; one spot and another in forward.

Types of Swap: I. Interest Rate Swap II. Currency Swap.

6.15.5.1 Interest rate swap

It involves the exchange of the interest payments. When a firm needs fixed rate funds but, actually receive the floating rate funds. Similarly any another firm who wants floating rate funds but able to get the fixed rate funds. This problem of both the firm is remove by a third party, the swap dealer, usually the bank act this role. The basic condition for the interest rate swap is that the loan amount must be identical and the periodic interest payment takes place in one currency. At the same the, one firm gets cheaper fixed rate funds and other gets cheaper floating rate funds. This can be determined with the help of a example

Example: Suppose Firm X needs fixed rate funds which is available to it at 7.5% to be computed half yearly but it has access to cheaper floating-rate funds available to it at LIBOR + 0.3%. Firm Y needs floating rate funds available to it at 6 month. LIBOR flat, but has access to cheaper fixed rate funds available to it at 7.0% to be computed half yearly.

The interest rate swap will take place in the following stages.

Stage I: If firm X has deal to floating-rate loan market, it will borrow from floating rate market. Similary firm Y will access to fixed rate loan market to borrow fixed rate loan.

Stage II: As both the firm not borrowed according to their requirement, both firms will approach to a swap dealer. Since firm X required fixed rate loan, the bank who may be the swap dealer ask it to pay fixed-rate interest to the bank, as it has borrowed fixed rate loan. This fixed rate loan interest payable by the bank which would be higher than what firm Y has to pay to the lender in the fixed-rate loan market but lower that what firm X has to pay to the lender if it had borrowed the fixed rate loan from the fixed rate loan market. Suppose it is 7.25%. In exchange, the swap dealer pays firm X the interest at 6 month LIBOR. Firm X pays LIBOR + 0.3% to the lender on its floating-rate debt.

On the other hand, the bank asks the firm Y to pay 6 month LIBOR as if it has borrowed floating rate loan. In exchange of that, the bank pays firm Y fixed rate interest which would be higher that what firm Y would have to pay to the lender. The interest rate what the bank has received from firm X minus (–) its own commission. Suppose it is 7.15% At this point, firm Y gets interest from the swap dealer at 7.15% and pays interest to the fixed rate lender at 7.0%.

Firm X will be attracted for the swap deal because the fixed rate of interest payable by it is lower than what it had to pay for borrowing from the fixed-rate loan market. Firm Y attracted for the swap deal because it gets from the bank an interest rate which is higher than what it has to pay to the ultimate lender. The bank is attracted to the swap deal because it earns from such a deal.

Stage III: At the maturity, both the firms repay the debt. Firm X repays the floating-rate loan and firm Y repay's fixed-rate loan.

6.15.5.2 Currency swap

The currency swap deals the exchange of principal and fixed rate interest payments on approximately equivalent loan in another currency. As compared to Interest rate swaps currency swaps involved larger volatile exposure since an exchange of principal is involved. This swaps are also arranged by banks. Under it bank enters into off setting swap arrangement with two parties at the same time. This can also be define with the help of a example.

Example: Suppose, Firm X can borrow Indian Rupee. At a fixed rate of 8.0% or it can borrow US dollar at a floating rate of one-year LIBOR. Firm Y can borrow Indian Rupee at a fixed rate of 9.2% and can borrow US dollar at one-year LIBOR. If firm Y needs fixed-rate Indian Rupee, it will approach to a bank provided firm X needs floating-rate US dollar. The swap deal will be conducted in different stages as follows:

Stage I: Firm X borrows Indian Rupee at 8% interest rate whereas firm Y borrows US dollar at LIBOR.

Stage II: Both the firms exchange the borrowed currencies with the help of the bank. After the exchange, Firm X will possess US dollar. Firm Y possess Indian Rupee.

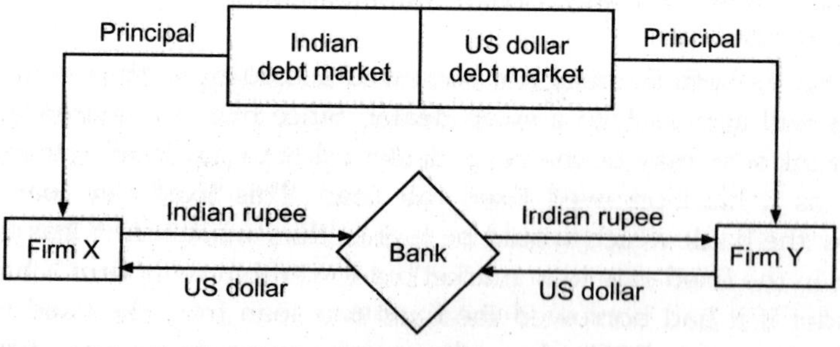

Stage I & II

Stage III: Now, the interest rate will be involved, the payment of interest rate will flow, firm X will pay LIBOR on US dollar that will reach the US dollar market through, firstly the bank and then through to Firm Y. Similarly, Firm Y will pay fixed rate interest that will flow to the fixed rate Indian Rupee market through the bank and through Firm X. Firm Y will pay fixed rate of interest to the bank that will be more than 8.0% but less than 9.2%. Suppose it is 8.6%. The bank will take its own commission and shall pay to Firm X in this case only, suppose at 8.4%.

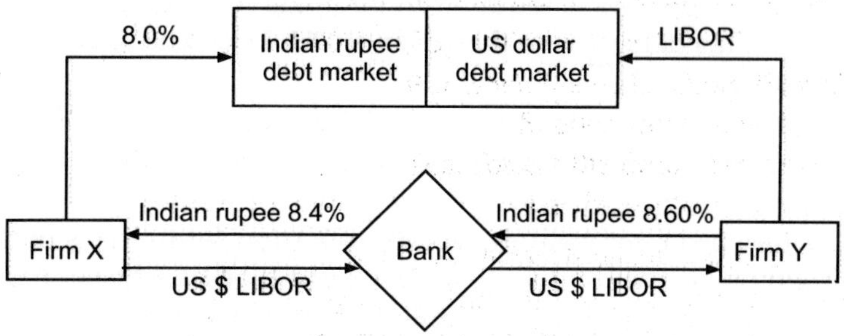

Stage III

Stage IV: In this stage, the two principals are again exchanged between the two firm *i.e.* Firm X and Y. Firm X gets back Indian Rupee and repays it to the lender. Firm Y gets back US dollar and repays it to the lender.

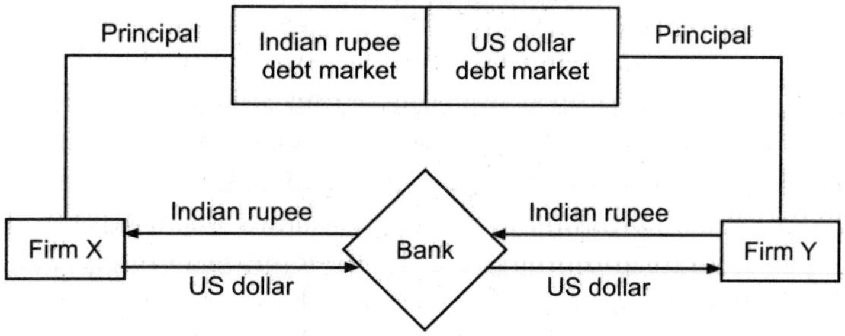

Stage IV

Due to the this swaps both the firms benefited. As Firm X gets the currency of it own choice while Firm Y also gets the currency of its own choice. The cost of borrowing gets reduced, which brings in gains to firm X as well as to Firm Y.

6.16 HEDGING TECHNIQUES IN DERIVATIVE MARKET

6.16.1 Covering in Foreign Exchange Futures Contract Market

A currency futures contract is a commitment to buy or to sell a specified quantity of a currency on a future date, at the predetermined/decided price existing on the date of the contract. These contracts have the following characteristics:

- Transactions are traded in standard lots.
- Quotations are made in terms of US$ per unit of another currency.

- Fluctuations differ according to currencies. The smallest variation (also called 'tick') is 0.01%. So if the contract is of the value FFr. 125,000, the value of minimal fluctuation is $125{,}000 \times \frac{0.01}{100}$ = FFr. 12.50
- Maturity periods are also standardised, say March, June, September and December.
- A guarantee deposit is required to be made for selling or buying of a contract. This deposit is of the order of US$ 1,000 and is made with the clearing House.

Futures rates differ from spot rates for the same reasons as forward rates. They are very close to forward rates of the same currency for the same maturity date.

In fact, if forward rates were much different from future rates of the same maturity, it would be easy to buy in the forward market if the currency was cheaper and sell futures contracts in the same currency at the same time. Thus, there would be a profit to the operate without risk, assuming there were no transaction costs.

An American company has exported in Jan. of the current year to a India client. The payments of Rs 10 Lacs are due in March. The American company wants to cover itself against the risk of a depreciation of Rs. The Rs March future contracts are quoted at US $ .022/Rs 1. The spot rate in Jan. is US$ 0.022 per Rs.

- In Jan. the American company deposits the guarantee with the clearing House and sells 8 Rs future contracts, each of 1.25 Lacs. The total amount covered is Rs 10 Lacs = (8 × 1.25000).
- During all this period up to the maturity date the American company will pay maintenance margins if Rs rises and conversely will have its a/c credited if Rs slips. In March, this company repurchases (or closes) the contract at a rate of 0.020 $ per Rs. It makes a gain of 2000 $ =[(0.022–0.020) × 8 × 1.25000]. This gain is equal to the loss of opportunity on the spot market, that is 2000$. The spot rate on the date of closure or repurchase of the contract is 0.020$ per Rs.

6.16.2 Foreign Exchange Options Market

It is an instrument that permits its holder (buyer or owner) to take advantage of a favourable evolution of exchange rate. It is taken recourse to by companies to cover the exchange rate risk. There are two types of options: call and put options. These are bought or sold at a premium, which is paid to the writer of the option, usually in local currency per unit of foreign currency.

6.16.2.1 Call option

The holder of a call option acquires a right but not an obligation to buy a certain quantity of foreign currency at a predetermined price (also called exercise or strike price). A writer (or seller) of a call option has an obligation to sell a certain amount of foreign currency at a predetermined price.

6.16.2.2 Put option

The holder of a put option acquires a right but not an obligation to sell a certain quantity of foreign currency at a predetermined strike price. The writer of a put option has an obligation to buy a certain amount of foreign currency at a predetermined price. Thus, it is the holder (buyer or owner) of an option who has a choice to use or abandon the exercise of the option where as the seller of an option should be ready to sell (in case of call) or buy (in case of put) the amount agreed upon. The latter has no choice of his own.

Example: A french importer has bought an equipment from a US firm for US $1 million on 1 March in the current year to be paid for in 3 months. The importer fears an appreciation of the US dollar. He decides to cover himself in the 'Option Market'. The data are

Exchange Rate FFr 5.00/US $ or US$ 0.20/FFr. He is considering call option for the purpose as he will be required to buy foreign exchange (i.e. US$)

The characteristics of call option are:

Strike Price : FFr. 5.05/US$
Maturity date : 1 June
Premium : 3%

The buyer of the call option i.e. the importer pays the premium amount of US$ 30,000 = (1 million × 0.03) or FFr 150, 000 = (30,000 × 5).

On 1 June there are three possibilities:

1st Possibility: The US currency has appreciated and the spot rate is FFr 5.5/US$. In this situation the holder of the call option will exercise his option and buy US dollars at the strike price of FFr. 5.05/US$. He will pay thus,

FFr 5.05 million = (5.05 × 1.0 million)
Total cost = (5,050,000 + 150,000) FFr
= 5.20 million FFr.

Thus, his net price is FFr 5.20/US$ instead of FFr 5.5/US$.

2nd Possibility: The US currency has depreciate and on 1 June, it is at FFr 4.75/US $.

In this situation, he abandons his call options and buys dollars from the market at FFr. 4.75/US $. His total payment is thus,

(4.75 × 1.0 million + 0.15 million) FFr. = 4.90 million FFr.

Thus, his net Price is FFr 4.9/US$ instead of FFr 4.75/US$.

3rd Possibility: The US dollar is at FFr 5.05/US$. Here, he can afford to be indifferent to either the market option or the call option. He will pay the same price whether he resorts to one or the other. He pays (5,050,000 + 1,50,000) FFr.

= 5.20 million FFr, this is, the same amount as in the Ist possibility.

This means he has never to pay more than FFr 5.20 million, whatever be the level of appreciation of the US dollar.

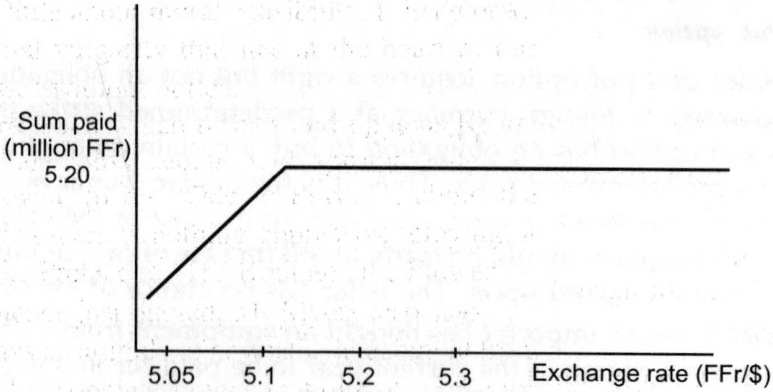

6.16.3 Covering Interest Rate Risk in Options Market

Options on interest rate may be used:

- For covering against interest rate variations; in effect, purchase of a option enables the buyer to ensure that he would not have to play more than a certain rate of interest on his borrowing, or would not receive less than a certain minimum rate on his lending;
- For speculations
- For arbitrage operations.

6.16.3.1 Organized markets of interest rate options

Interest rate options were first of all negotiated on the Stock Exchange of Amsterdam. In 1982, an options market developed in Chicago (Chicago Board of Trade), Thereafter, the markets of Sydney, London, Singapore, Paris, Copenhagen, Montreal etc. were developed. Assets traded on interest rate options market are either fixed-rate financial securities or an interest rate guarantee: 3–months LIBOR, 3-months Euro–DM, 3-months Euro–dollar etc.

6.16.3.2 Mechanism of interest rate options

Purchase of a call option gives a right to the holder to buy a financial asset at a fixed price and purchase of a put option gives him a right to sell a financial asset at a fixed price, called exercise price, on payment of a premium to the seller of the option. Interest rate options have certain characteristics:

- Contracts are standardized from the viewpoints of amount, maturity and period (March, June, September, December);
- Exercise Prices are given at intervals of 0.25 dollar for Euro–dollar contracts, for example, 92.25, 92.50, 92.75 etc;
- Quotations, for example, for Euro–dollar contracts are made in index points and 1 index point corresponds to 25 dollars. Thus, if an option on Euro–dollar is quoted at 0.30, this means that the option has a price of 0.30 × 100 × 25 = 750 dollars. Minimum function is 25 dollar.
- Contracts are easily negotiable;
- The clearing house ensures the regularity of operations.

6.16.3.3 *Purchase of a put option*

A put option is also called a borrowing option. In order to cover against a rise in the interest rate, an operator (for example, an enterprise that has to borrow shortly by issuing bonds or a portfolio manager who has to shortly liquidate his bonds) purchases put options. Let us say, a treasury manager estimates in January that he would need to borrow in March. The current interest rate on bonds is 6 per cent, but it is likely to go up in March. So he buys a put option by paying a price. If in March the rate goes up he exercises his put option and sells his bonds at 6 per cent. And if the rate remains at 6 per cent or goes down, he abandons his put option.

Similarly, a portfolio manager knows that he would liquidate his debenture/ bonds in the three months. Suppose the bond rate presently 77. But, if the interest rate swings upward, then the bond rate forced to comedown, say 74 in March. So, in order to compulsate this risk he may buys put options. On the other hand, suppose the interest does not increase than the investor would liquidate his bond at the price of 77. On the other hand, if the interest rate decreases which means the bond price will increase, say to 82, the investor will liquidate its bonds at the price of Rs 82.

6.16.3.4 *Purchase of a call option*

A call option is used when one fears a fall in interest rates. For instance, a treasury manager has to place in a month's time dollars for three months. He had a doubt that the interest rate may decrease from the current rate of 6.5% to 4.0%. So, he may buys a call option. If the interest rate decrease so as to ensure a return of 6.5% or more on his placement and cell the bond. In the reverse condition, he will have enough option and place his dollars at the prevailing market rate, say at 8.0%.

CHAPTER 7

Foreign Exchange Market in India

7.1 INTRODUCTION

India is the place where the concept of coinage developed at its earliest in around 6th century BC which later on built the base for other currencies of the world. According to the historians, the Indian currency i.e. rupee was brought into existence by Sher Shah Suri in the 16th century and it was evaluated as equal to 40 copper coins per rupee. The dominance of Mughals over India started diminishing when the British arrived in the country. The paper money was introduced under their reign in the latter part of the 18th century. Bank of Hindostan made the earliest rupee notes issues in the year 1770.

It was followed by some more issues of the currency notes by private and presidency banks. For 100 odd years, the issue of bank notes by the private and presidency banks continued but with the formation of The Paper Currency Act in 1861, the issue of notes was monopolized by the Government of India. The government of India (British India) initially appointed the presidency banks as their agents to help it with the circulation of bank notes as it was a tough job to promote the use of common note over a wide stretch of area. The notes had to be made a legal tender due to the problem arising from the redemption of these notes.

In 1867, the presidency banks were dismantled from the positions as the agents to the Government of India and the responsibility of the management of the currency was given to the mint masters, account generals and the controller of the currency. The first series of notes that was issued by the government of India was the Victoria portrait series. The notes in the series were uni-faced and were issued in 5 denominations. This series was replaced by the under print series of notes in 1867 which was kept in use for than 50 years. This long duration of time observed many positive changes in the bank note quality and introduction of a few security features as well. The need to issue small denominations note arose with the beginning of the World War I and Rs 1 note was issued for the first time.

In 1923, the under print series was replaced by the king's portrait series and they were continued to be used till 1935. The reserve bank of India took over the authority to print and circulate banknotes from the government of India. The notes bearing the portrait of George V were replaced by the notes bearing the portrait of George VI in 1938. In 1940, the one rupee note was re-launched due to the emergence of Second World War. The notes with the portrait of George VI were in circulation till 1947 and where taken off the money market with the independence of India. The Indian rupee was adopted as a sole currency of the country and the use of all other domestic coinage was put to an end. The country adopted the decimalization standards in the year 1957. The current Mahatma Gandhi's portrait series was introduced in the year 1996.

In India, the RBI had always played an active role in the foreign exchange market. However, since the country faced a severe balance of payments (BOP) crisis in the early 1990s, there was a greater understanding of the importance of the rupee–dollar exchange rate on the economy. With reserve down to only around $ 1 billion in mid-1991, caused partly due to a fall in exports and also due to a decline in remittances (following the Gulf war), the country was close to defaulting on its debt repayments. The Indian government then negotiated with the IMF for SDR of around $ 2 billion to stave off any external debt crisis.

Factors affecting the exchange rates between two countries. The volatility in the foreign exchange rate depends upon a numerous macro economic factors that have different degrees of importance to different economies of the world. Some special and exceptional factors affecting the rates may also exist in the case of different countries. Following are shown the common factors on which the foreign exchange rate depends.

- Flow of imports and exports between the countries
- Flow of capital between the countries
- Relative inflation rates
- Fluctuation limits on exchange rate imposed by the governments of the countries
- Merchandise trade balance
- Rate of inflation in the country
- Flow of funds between the countries for the payment of stock and bond purchases
- Relative growth
- Short term and long term interest rate differentials
- Cost of borrowings

7.2 FOREIGN EXCHANGE MARKET IN INDIA

Foreign exchange market in India works under the Central Government in India and executes wide powers to control transactions in foreign exchange. The foreign exchange Mgmt. Act, 1999 regulates the whole foreign exchange market in India. Before this act the foreign exchange market in India was regulated by the Reserve Bank of India through the exchange control department by the FERA, 1947. With the economic and Industrial development, the need for conservation of foreign exchange currency was urgently felt and on the recommendation of the Public Accounts Committee, the Indian government passed the Foreign Exchange Regulation Act, 1973 and gradually, this act became famous as FEMA.

In the year 1992 all foreign investments in India and the repatriation of foreign capital required previous approval of the government. The FERA rarely allowed foreign majority holdings for foreign exchange in India. In July 1991, a new foreign investment policy announced, which declared the automatic approval for foreign exchange in India for thirty-four industries. These industries were designated with high priority, up to an equivalent limit of 51 per cent.

In the year 1994 foreign and non-resident Indian investors were permitted to repatriate not only their profits but also their capital for foreign exchange in India. From the year 1975 to 1992 the rupee was coupled to a trade–weighted basket of currencies. In Feb. 1992, the Indian government started to make the rupee convertible, and in March 1993 a single floating exchange rate in the market of foreign exchange in India was implemented. In July 1995, Rs 31.81 was worth US$1 as compared to Rs 7.86 in 1980 Rs 12.37 in 1985 and Rs 17.50 in 1992.

Since adoptation of liberalisation foreign exchange markets in India have witnessed explosive growth in trading capacities The importance of the exchange rate of foreign exchange in India for the Indian economy has also been for greater than ever before. While the Indian government has clearly adopted a flexible exchange rate regime, in practice the rupee is one of most resourceful trackers of the US dollar.

The foreign exchange market India is growing very rapidly since, the annual turnover of the market is more than $ 400 billion. This foreign exchange transaction in India does not include the inter-banks transactions. According to the record of foreign exchange in India, RBI released these transactions. The average monthly turnover in the merchant segment was $ 40.5 billion in 2003-04 and the inter-bank transaction was $ 134.2 for the same period. The average total monthly turnover in the sector of foreign exchange in India was about $ 174.7 billion for the same period. The transactions are made on spot and also on forward bases, which include currency swaps and interest rate swaps.

Indian foreign exchange market is made up of the buyers, sellers, market mediators and the monetary authority of India. The main center of foreign exchange in India is Mumbai. There are several other centers for foreign exchange transaction in India including the major cities of Kolkata, New Delhi, Chennai, Bangalore, Pondicherry and Cochin. With the development of technologies, all the foreign exchange markets of India work collectively and in much easier process.

The foreign exchange market in India is a flourishing ground of profit and higher initiatives are taken by the central government in order to strengthen the foundation. In past years, currency market has reflected the strong growth globally. In India, government efforts to ease capital movement have led the country recording the fastest rise in its turnover growth in the segment over the last three years.

- India's share in worldwide foreign exchange market turnover has grown to 0.9% in the year 2007, marking a three times jump from 0.3% in the year 2004.
- During this period of time, it is the fastest increase in market share of India for any other country in the world.
- India is the 16th largest foreign exchange market in the world in terms of total daily turnover which was US$ 34 billion in 2007.
- Average daily turnover of global forex market rose to $ 3.2 trillion in April 2007, an increase of 69% at current exchange rates and 63% at constant exchange rates.
- Daily global trading volumes would likely reach US$ 5 trillion by 2010.
- Emerging market currencies are estimated to be on atleast one side of almost 20% of all transactions, compared to less than 15% in April 2004 and less than 17% in April 2001.

There were many commercial and cooperative banks in India who are authorised to deal in foreign exchange. These commercial and cooperative banks are called Authorised Dealers and are eligible to operate in the foreign exchange market. These banking institutions cover their open positions in currencies London (UK) through their branches abroad or in India in the inter–bank market. Thousands of crores were financed by these banks.

The foreign department of every bank draws up a position sheet for each currently in which purchases and sales of the currency are recorded. The general tendency of the banks to avoid from taking any exchange rate risk by keeping uncovered balance and are not permitted to do so under the previous regulations, these banks tries to cover their position by the end of the day. When the purchases of currency exceed to the sales of the currency, the credit balance is positive and are overbought. This is to be covered by equal sales of that currency. When the sales of currency exceed with the purchases of currency. The debit balance is negative, short or oversold position and is to be covered by equivalent purchases. Both sales and purchases of currency would include spot and forward, import bills or export bills purchased.

7.3 EXCHANGE RATE SYSTEM IN INDIA

Since, September 1939 to June 1972, India was the member of the sterling area, during this period the external value of the rupee i.e. exchange rate was kept stable in terms of sterling. After the inception of the IMF, of which India was the founder member, the external value of the rupee was declared in terms of gold and US dollar as Rs 1 = 0.268601 grams of five gold and Rs 1 = US$ 0.3022 and its value was maintained stable in terms of £ pound by purchases and sales of sterling by the Reserve Bank of India. At that time the value of £ was Rs 1 = 15. 6d.

The Indian Rupee was devalued twice, first in the year Sept, 1949 by 30.5% and in June 1966 by 36.5%. In the last month of the year 1966 the value of rupee became Re 1 : 13.3 US cents. This link with sterling which was maintained by keeping the rupee stable in terms of sterling and using the sterling an intervention currency was justified on the ground that the bulk of India's trade was with the sterling area and that India's foreign interests lie with sterling which was considered at that time a stable and strong reserve currency.

As the Bretton woods system was breakdown in August 1971, the flotations of various major currencies of the country including Indian Rupee was temporarily kept pegged to the US dollar at Rs 7.5/$1, and this rate was kept stable by intervention in the market by purchases and sales of sterling. The exchange rate of rupee and dollar was used to determine the exchange rate of rupee-sterling. This position continued up to December 1971, when under the smithsonian agremeent, the exchange rate of sterling was fixed in terms of US dollar and the rupee was again linked to sterling thereafter. This problem continues to June 1972 and there after major currencies including sterling started floating. In between June 1972 & September 1975, rupee was kept stable in terms of sterling but was allowed to fluctuate against all other currencies. During this period, rupee was effectively devalued against all major currencies other than £ pound by as much as 18 to 20%. The impact of such depreciation was not favourable to India with her inelastic supplies of experting goods and increasing debt burden, along with the high rising in the import bills, India had delink itself with £ completely in Sept. 1975. Since then, the external value of rupee was determined by the market value.

Since September 1975, the value of rupee has been maintained stable within a wider margin of 2.25% on either side up to 30th Jan. 1970 and 5% thereafter. A middle rate, as between selling and buying rates is fixed in terms of sterling which continued to be an intervention currency. The cross rates for the rupee against other currencies are calculated and fixed by banks in terms of the cross quotations. Whenever there is a change in the market value of the rates of the currencies in the basket by more than 2.25% against the standard unit of account, namely, SDR, which helps in altering the exchange rate between rupee–sterling. The external value of rupee was kept stable within the permitted band of 5% on either side of the middle rate. Minor fluctuation on either side evidence the fact that India does not need the support of any currency, namely sterling or dollar.

With the introduction of the new economic policy new change occurs in the foreign exchange policy and exchange rate management. FERA was diluted and commercial banks allowed greater freedom of lending and their deposits and lending rates have also been freed to a large extent. Foreign exchange release is mostly left to the banks. Rupee was made partially convertible first in the year 1992. In the next year, *i.e.* 1993 the rupee was fully converted on trade account and thereafter full convertibility on current account, inclusive of invisible account in 1994. The era of decontrol on foreign exchange has started with these reforms. RBI had adopted a new mechanism for the Management of Foreign Exchange Rate in the year 1994. In this context the Foreign Exchange Regulation Act (FERA) was replaced by Foreign Exchange Management Act (FEMA) in the year 2000.

7.3.1 Currency Deals

Nowadays the currency are dealed in the form of quotations. In India the direct quotations are used for the currency dealing. The banks follow two way quotas–based on "gire less and take more". The difference between the buying and selling rates are the banks profit. The interest component for any period is shown separately from the currency position. The deviation depends on the cable cost, brokerage cost and administrative cost leaving only a small margin of profit to the banker.

If suppose the quotation is US$ 1 = Rs 45–Rs 46 then the banker is prepared to buy dollars at Rs 45 and sell it at Rs 46. Here the principle is buy low and sell high. For instance, taken a quotation of dollar to pounds say 1 £ = US$ 1.630 US 1.645 quoting bank wants to sell sterling at US 1.645 and buy at US 1.63. The price of dollar to D.M at US$ 1.5800/30 means that for every dollar, the quoting bankwill pay 1.5800 DM and would receive 1.5830 DM for US dollar. The banks always wants profit from the quotation.

7.3.2 Trading by Banks

In India, these banks are situated also in Chennai and Bangalore. The foreign banks mostly concentrate on the trading with Indian Banks mostly situated in Mumbai. The major player banks are SBI, Punjab National Bank etc. The central dealing room of SBI is situated at Kolkata. Mostly the inter bank market operations is concentrated in the Indian commercial capital at Mumbai. In India, the spot and forward trading operation is done through bank. The spot trading is settled on the same day, value on tomorrow. The maximum extent of the spot trading is two days (Sat & Monday). The forward rate of trading operation is made beyond to the period of the spot trading. The trading operations in India are done as:

Table 7.1

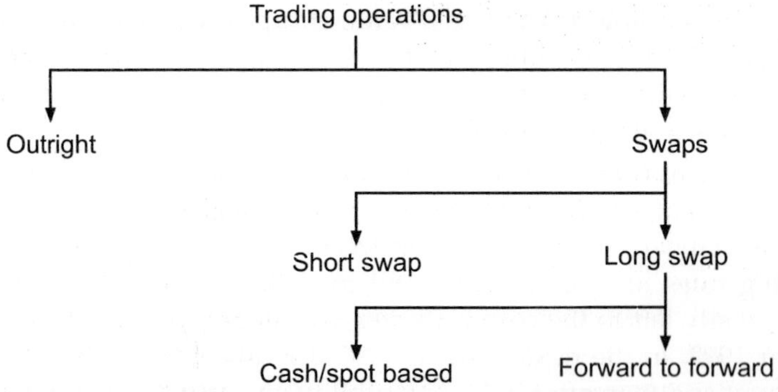

RBI Policy towards Banks: RBI has been publishing the Reference Rate of exchange of rupee against dollar and other currency on a daily basis. As it announced the new forex rate at every morning at 9:00 O'clock at regular basis.

RBI deals with the buying and selling of Rupee for the dollar on spot as well as forward rate of exchange. On the basis of which RBI refinance the rate, Foreign Exchange Dealers Association (FEDAI) is giving the rates for banks, but banks are free to adjust their rates depending upon their currency positions.

The rate of RBI and FEDAI is made in terms of rupee to dollar. The FEDAI determined the rate of Forex of Rupee to dollar on the basis of speculation in the exchange market. For instance, in March, 1994 the RBI rate for Rs/$ was 31.3800 whereas the FEDAI rate was 31.3790, it was 0.0010 differ to each other this rate change in the year Dec. 1999 as 48.4900 of RBI where as the FEDAI rates was 43.5100 the difference increased to 0.0100.

In the forward exchange market, RBI allowed free functioning following the current account convertibility of the rupee since March 1994, specially after the deregulation of lending rates in Oct. 1994. RBI has been persuading banks to develop forward market in India by dealings with interbank and in foreign market. There is however need to established foreign exchange derivatives for providing hedge through forward contracts, swaps and cross currency options. It is possible to develop Rupee based options if international quotes for rupee are available which is not the case at present.

Toward the end of 2006, foreign exchange inflows, especially of dollars, into India started rising sharply. This put upward pressure on the rupee's exchange rate against the dollar. India's steady economic growth offered several opportunities for foreign companies. Between April 2006 and March 2007, FDI of $ 16 billion flowed into India. The rupee's appreciation against the dollar was seen to be beneficial to the Indian economy in some ways, and detrimental in other ways. The rise in the value of rupee meant that inflation was curbed. The inflation rate in India declined from 6.73 per cent in February 2007 to 4.10 per cent in August 2007.

In June, 2007, the Economist Intelligence Unit estimated that for the year 2007, the rupee's average annual exchange rate against the dollar would be 41.3 (a 13.5 per cent real appreciation year on year), and for the year 2008, it would be 40 (6 per cent). The Indian rupee weakened further by about ten paisa to 46.60 against the dollar in early trade today amid steady trend in local stocks and higher dollar in overseas markets.

The domestic currency resumed steady at 11-11-2009 overnight closing level of 46.50/51 a dollar but later touched a low of 46.60 before being quoted at 46.5750/5850 a dollar in late morning deals. At the Inter bank Foreign Exchange (Forex) market, the domestic unit traded 2 paise lower at 46.52 a dollar in early trade. Yesterday, the rupee ended five paise lower at 46.50/51 against the US currency after the benchmark Sensex slipped by 58.16 points at 16,440.56. The main reason is the demand for the US currency from refiners and importers mainly put some pressure on the Indian rupee.

A brief detail of the Foreign exchange of India with the major nations of the world is described below.

Table 7.2

Foreign Exchange Rate-Indian Rupees (as on 14th January 2009)

Currency	INR per unit	Unit per INR
USD–United States Dollars	48.9100173589	0.0204457094
EUR–Euro	64.3953830872	0.0155290636
UKP–United Kingdom Pounds	70.8721807402	0.0141099087
JPY – Japan Yen	0.5491529797	1.8209862041
AUD – Australia Dollars	32.3622146341	0.0309002338
BDT – Bangladesh Taka	0.7150587174	1.3984865518
CAD – Canada Dollars	39.8228462559	0.0251112136
CNY – China Yuan	7.1557133201	0.1397484716
HKD – Hong Kong Dollars	6.3053039850	0.1585966358
IDR – Indonesia Rupiahs	0.0043909749	227.7398567158
MYR – Malaysia Ringgits	13.6424287504	0.0733007310
MUR -- Mauritius Rupees	1.5260535837	0.6552849852
NZD – New Zealand Dollars	26.8574552546	0.0372336095
PKR – Pakistan Rupees	0.6257678489	1.5980367189
RUB – Russia Rubles	1.5619965735	0.6402062699
SAR – Saudi Arabia Riyals	13.0419771044	0.0766754911
SGD – Singapore Dollars	32.8232411919	0.0304662173
SAR – South Africa Rand	4.8841142828	0.2047454138
LKR – Sri Lanka Rupees	0.4297633083	2.3268622070
CHF – Switzerland Francs	43.6725272791	0.0228976902

Source: www.businessnews.com

In the above table, the maximum value of foreign currency is of £ pound, who, had Rs 70.87 to 1 £ . The second appreciated value is of Euro-dollar, followed by US $. Some countries like Japan, Bangladesh, Sri Lanka, Pakistan whose value in terms of rupee is less, otherwise mostly the other countries valuation in terms of rupees is high.

7.4 INTERNATIONAL RISK MANAGEMENT

International business and financial decision-making require an understanding and consideration of risk factors. In fact, both domestic and international business involve risk due to uncertainty of amount of gains that will be available from a business project. Added to this, foreign investment involves a number of unique risks which would affect international finance immediately and international business at a later stage. These risks include:

- Political risks.
- Commercial risks.
- Exchange control restrictions on remittances.

- Exchange rate fluctuation.
- Different stages and rates of inflation.

7.4.1 Political Risks

Political risks are the hurdles or hindrances created by the host country. These hurdles include

1. Remittances of profits.
2. Restrictions on the types of activities of MNC.
3. Restrictions on transfering activities.
4. Imposing quotas on imports.
5. Restrictions on employing expartriates.
6. Nationalising the assets of the business. For example, Zimbabwe recently nationalised the assets of foreign companies.
7. Looting of the stock during internal disturbances. For e.g. Stocks of India firms were looted in recent internal disturbances in Fiji.

These political risks enhance the risk of foreign investment due to degree of uncertainty of return. Hence, business houses prefer to invest in friendly countries.

7.4.2 Commercial Risk

The business houses estimate demand for products and services in foreign countries before actually making investment. For example, whirlpool estimated the demand for its washing machines in Indian market are started marketing the product in India after liberalisation. But, at a later stage it found that the actual sales volume is far less than the estimated demand. Same is the case with Pepsi & Coca-Cola in India. Such risks are called the commercial risks. These risks are due to

1. Decline in demand due to decline in income.
2. Decline in demand due to the cultural variation.
3. Decline in demand due to patronage of the domestic products.
4. Due to change in the customer taste.

7.4.3 Risks Due to Exchange Control Restrictions on Remittances

Eritrean Government during 1998 initially imposed the restriction that Coca-Cola company should not remit more than 50% of its profits to its parent company. Similarly, the Taiwan government imposed the restriction that the MNC's should not take more than 75% of their assets back. Such restrictions are called exchange control restrictions on remittances. The parent company should consider these issue while investing in foreign countries.

7.4.4 Risks Due to Exchange Rate Fluctuations

It is quite common that the exchange rates fluctuate quite after. The fluctuation are mostly in favour of hard currencies and the advanced countries. And the risk is more in case of developing countries. Therefore the MNC's should take into consideration the risks of exchange rate fluctuations while investing in developing countries.

7.4.5 Risks of Different Stages and Rates of Inflation

Inflation stages and rates vary from country to country. Normally, the inflation is in the first stage in underdeveloped countries and it is in growth stage in developing countries while it is in boom stage in advanced countries. Inflation was in boom in UK during 1975 whereas it was in the initial stage in India. But the impact of UK's inflation on India pushed India's inflation to the growth stage. Then, we delinked our Rupee from UK's pound. This rate of inflation affects global business.

7.4.6 Techniques of Assessing Risk Management

The MNCs has to manage risks in order to reduce the consequences and the risks.

Techniques of risk management include:

1. Maintaining sound diplomatic relations with other countries.
2. Avoiding investment in enemy countries.
3. Estimating the demand for the product in foreign countries
4. Insuring the various business operations.
5. Getting the benefits from the institutions like Export Credit Guarantee Corporation.
6. Getting refinance facility.

CHAPTER 8

International Institutions

8.1 UNITED NATIONS CONFERENCE ON TRADE AND DEVELOPMENT (UNCTAD)

Established in 1964, UNCTAD promotes the development-friendly integration of developing countries into the world economy. UNCTAD has progressively evolved into an authoritative knowledge-based institution whose work aims to help shape current policy debates and thinking on development, with a particular focus on ensuring that domestic policies and international action are mutually supportive in bringing about sustainable development. In 1961 UNO World Trade and Development Conference from March 31, 1964 to June 16, 1964. A world-wide international trade policy was determine in this conference. Various issues related to extension of international trade of developing countries were also discussed in that Conference. The Conference came to be known as UNCTAD. Presently, UNCTAD has become a permanent organization for promoting international trade.

8.1.1 Objectives of UNCTAD

1. To promote international trade especially with a view to accelerating the economic development of underdeveloped countries.
2. To determine policies and principles for international trade and economic development.
3. To promote the strategy for implementing pre-approved principles and policies.
4. To assist economic and social council of the UNO.
5. To provide a suitable platform for trade dialogues.

The organization works to fulfill this mandate by carrying out three key functions:

- It functions as a forum for intergovernmental deliberations, supported by discussions with experts and exchanges of experience, aimed at consensus building.

- It undertakes research, policy analysis and data collection for the debates of government representatives and experts.
- It provides technical assistance tailored to the specific requirements of developing countries, with special attention to the needs of the least developed countries and of economies in transition. When appropriate, UNCTAD cooperates with other organizations and donor countries in the delivery of technical assistance.

The Secretary-General of UNCTAD is Dr. Supachai Panitchpakdi (Thailand), who took office on 1 September 2005.

In performing its functions, the secretariat works together with member Governments and interacts with organizations of the United Nations system and regional commissions, as well as with governmental institutions, non-governmental organizations, the private sector, including trade and industry associations, research institutes and universities world wide.

8.1.2 Overview of the Main Activities

8.1.2.1 Trade and commodities

- **Commodity diversification and development:** Promotes the diversification of production and trade structures. Helps Governments to formulate and implement diversification policies and encourages enterprises to adapt their business strategies and become more competitive in the world market.
- **Competition and consumer policies:** Provides analysis and capacity building in competition and consumer protection laws and policies in developing countries. Publishes regular updates of a Model Law on Competition.
- **Trade negotiations and commercial diplomacy:** Assists developing countries in all aspects of their trade negotiations.
- **Trade Analysis and Information System (TRAINS):** Comprehensive computer-based information system on trade control measures that uses UNCTAD's database. The CD-ROM version includes 119 countries.
- **Trade and environment:** Assesses the trade and development impact of environmental requirements and relevant multilateral agreements and provides capacity-building activities to help developing countries participate in and derive benefits from international negotiations on these matters.

8.1.2.2 Investment and enterprise development

- **International investment and technology arrangements:** Helps developing countries to participate more actively in international investment rule making at the bilateral, regional and multilateral levels. These arrangements include the organization of capacity-building seminars and regional symposia and the preparation of a series of issues papers.
- **Investment policy reviews:** Intended to familiarize Governments and the private sector with the investment environment and policies of a

given country. Reviews have been carried out in a number of countries, including Ecuador, Egypt, Ethiopia, Mauritius, Peru, Uganda and Uzbekistan.

- **Investment guides and capacity building for the LDCs:** Some of the countries involved are Bangladesh, Ethiopia, Mali, Mozambique and Uganda.
- **Empretec:** Promotes entrepreneurship and the development of small and medium-sized enterprises. Empretec programmes have been initiated in 27 countries, assisting more than 70,000 entrepreneurs through local market-driven business support centres.

8.1.2.3 Macroeconomic policies, debt and development financing

- **Policy analysis and research:** On issues concerning global economic interdependence, the international monetary and financial system, and macroeconomic and development policy challenges.
- **Technical and advisory support:** To the G24 group of developing countries (the Intergovernmental Group of 24) in the World Bank and the International Monetary Fund; advisory services to developing countries for debt rescheduling negotiations under the Paris Club.
- **DMFAS programme:** Computer-based debt management and financial analysis system specially designed to help countries manage their external debt. Started in 1982, and now installed in 62 countries.

8.1.2.4 Technology and logistics

- **ASYCUDA programme:** Integrated customs system that speeds up customs clearance procedures and helps Governments to reform and modernize their customs procedures and management. Installed in over 80 countries, ASYCUDA has become the internationally accepted standard for customs automation.
- **ACIS programme:** Computerized cargo tracking system installed in 20 developing countries of Africa and Asia.
- **E-Tourism initiative:** Linking sustainable tourism and Information and communication technologies (ICTs) for development, UNCTAD has developed this Initiative to help developing countries' destinations to become more autonomous by taking charge of their own tourism promotion by using ICT tools.
- **Technology:** Services the UN Commission on Science and Technology for Development and administers the Science and Technology for Development Network; carries out case studies on best practices in transfer of technology; undertakes Science, Technology and Innovation Policy Reviews for interested countries, as well as capacity-building activities.
- **Train for trade programme:** Builds training networks and organizes training in all areas of international trade to enable developing countries to increase their competitiveness. Currently developing distance learning programmes focusing on the LDCs.

8.1.2.5 Africa, least developed countries, landlocked developing countries and small island developing states

- **Africa:** Provides analytical work aimed at increasing the understanding of problems faced by African countries in their development efforts, and facilitating a better integration of Africa into the world economy. Particular emphasis is placed on supporting the New Partnership for Africa's Development (NEPAD).
- **Least Developed Countries (LDCs):** It Provides analytical work and technical assistance aimed at enabling relevant States, to make the best possible use of LDC status in the framework of the Programme, of Action for the Least Developed Countries for the Decade 2001-2010, and to better understand the policy-related issues that are specially relevant to LDCs, notably with a view to developing productive capacities and reducing poverty in these countries.
- **Landlocked Developing Countries (LLDCs):** Provides analytical work and technical assistance to LLDCs in support of the implementation of the 2003 Almaty Programme of Action, which deals with the special needs of LLDCs within a new global framework for transit transport cooperation for landlocked and transit developing countries.
- **Small Island Developing States (SIDS):** Provides analytical work and technical assistance to SIDS in support of the implementation of the 2005 Mauritius Strategy for the Further Implementation of the Programme of Action for the Sustainable Development of Small Island Developing States, with particular emphasis on issues of economic vulnerability and specialization.

8.1.3 UNCTAD Conferences

The highest decision-making body of UNCTAD is the quadrennial conference, at which member States assess current trade and development issues, discuss policy options and formulate global policy responses. The conference also sets the organization's mandate and work priorities. The conferences serve an important political function: they allow intergovernmental consensus building regarding the state of the world economy and development policies, and they play a key role in identifying the role of the United Nations and UNCTAD in addressing economic development problems.

UNCTAD-I	Cairo	March-June 1964
UNCTAD-II	New Delhi	February-March 1968
UNCTAD-III	Santiago (Chili)	April-May 1972
UNCTAD-IV	Nairobi	May 1976
UNCTAD-V	Manila	May-June 1979
UNCTAD-VI	Belgrade	June-July 1983
UNCTAD-VII	Geneva	1987

Contd...

UNCTAD-VIII	Cartegina de Indias (Columbia)	1992
UNCTAD-IX	Midrand	April-May 1996
UNCTAD-X	Bangkok	February 2002
UNCTAD-XI	Sao Paulo, Brazil	June 2004

Source: Compiled from www.unctad.org

8.1.4 UNCTAD XI Yields Some Positive Achievements

The 11th session of the United Nations Conference on Trade and Development (UNCTAD XI) ended on 18 June in a rather good spirit with some useful results for developing countries. UNCTAD XI concluded with some encouraging results. The most important of these was the recognition, the first by a multilateral conference involving both North and South, of developing countries' need, in formulating their developmental plans, for 'policy space', which is increasingly being whittled away by trade agreements and loan conditionalities.

The conference adopted a declaration called the Sao Paulo Consensus, which contains analyses of globalisation, trade and development issues, proposes policy responses and spells out the role of UNCTAD.

Significant events on the sidelines of UNCTAD XI included the launching of a new round of South-South trade talks (under the Global System of Trade Preferences Among Developing Countries (GSTP)), the Ministerial meeting of the Group of 20 developing countries on agriculture issues and a special Ministerial meeting of the Group of 77 and China on the 40th anniversary of its founding.

The highlight at the closing session was a long and emotional farewell speech by the outgoing UNCTAD Secretary-General, Rubens Ricupero, which ended with a standing ovation.

UN Secretary-General Annan, at the inaugural session, had announced that Ricupero would soon complete his term and paid tribute to his impact on global policy-making and advocacy against hypocrisy and people in need.

Another highlight of the closing session was an attempt by the United States to have its closing statement is part of the record of the conference. Jamaica, for the G77 and China, asked for clarification if statements could be so record. After the UNCTAD legal officer clarified that only statements of position and reservations (and not general statements) could be reflect in the conference report, Jamaica requested that the G77 statement also be included in the report.

The US had referred to some contentious issues in the Sao Paulo Consensus and the G77 and China made a detailed statement expressing disappointment that its views on some specified issues had not been fully accepted.

UNCTAD XI's most important achievement was the inclusion in the Sao Paulo Consensus of a section on the need for developing countries to have 'policy space', which has been increasingly eroded by trade agreements and loan conditions.

It was the first time a multilateral conference involving North and South had recognised this idea and it will be useful to developing countries' negotiators when they argue their case in the World Trade Organisation (WTO), at the International Monetary Fund and in regional and bilateral trade agreements.

There had been much heated debate over eight months on this issue, which the developing countries were pushing as their biggest issue, and which the developed countries had been resisting and eventually trying to dilute the language.

As a compromise, the Sao Paulo Consensus (paragraph 8) now states: 'The increasing interdependence of national economies in a globalising world and the emergence of rule-based regimes for international economic relations have meant that the space for national economic policy, i.e. the scope for domestic policies, especially in the areas of trade, investment and industrial development, is now often framed by international disciplines, commitments and global market considerations.

'It is for each Government to evaluate the trade-off between the benefits of accepting international rules and commitments and the constraints posed by the loss of policy space. It is particularly important for developing countries, bearing in mind development goals and objectives, that all countries take into account the need for appropriate balance between national policy space and international disciplines and commitments.'

Developing-country diplomats were also able to ward off attempts by the major developed countries to constrain UNCTAD's future activities through the ongoing UN reform process by placing some of UNCTAD's future work into the framework of other organisations and processes. The final language in the Sao Paulo Consensus retains UNCTAD's present independence.

Another issue, governance, was resolved by reference in the final text (para 21) to both national and international aspects. But the issue of corporate responsibility and accountability, pushed by developing countries, was much watered down to only a recognition that existing voluntary international instruments could be improved, and that UNCTAD should carry out analytical work to enhance corporate contributions to development in host developing countries, and draw lessons as far as the trade and development dimension is concerned.

A last-minute attempt by developing countries to include a provision that national and international 'innovative financial mechanisms' supportive of developing countries should be supported in the end yielded a very much diluted text that 'voluntary financial mechanisms' should be 'explored'.

A significant development at UNCTAD XI was the political impetus from leaders of the South for South-South trade and cooperation to build solidarity among developing countries and reduce their dependence on the North.

This had been the main theme in the inaugural session's keynote speeches of Brazil's President Lula da Silva and Thai Prime Minister Thaksin Shinawatra, and supported by Annan who said that 'a new round of talks to expand the GSTP holds promises, and it could be a new global trade geography, which would help give the South a rightful place in international relations.'

As a concrete initiative to promote South-South trade, on 16 June at a well-attended side event, Ministers of the 44-member GSTP launched a new round of negotiations, which will start in November and is scheduled to take two years to complete.

All members of the G77 and China were invited to join the GSTP scheme, which provides trade preferences to developing countries without extending them to developed countries, and thus is a potentially significant instrument for South-South trade promotion.

The reactivation of the GSTP is seen by its main proponents as a concrete manifestation of South-South cooperation as well as a reply to the pressures put by major developed countries (especially the US and EU) on the developing countries to agree to drastically lower their industrial tariffs in the WTO on the ground that the developing countries themselves would most benefit as this would increase South-South trade.

8.1.5 Commodities Crisis

Another interesting decision at UNCTAD XI was the establishment of an international task force on commodities. The commodities crisis was one of the main themes at UNCTAD XI, being highlighted by the President of the UN General Assembly (Saint Lucia Foreign Minister Julian Hunte), other leaders and a well-attended UNCTAD-Common Fund for Commodities side event on commodities.

The decision is contained in an Annex to the Sao Paulo Consensus, entitled UNCTAD XI Multi-Stakeholder Partnerships. The section on commodities states that there is at present no comprehensive and systematic consultative framework to share information and use expertise among key actors in reviewing the commodity situation, and efforts of all interested stakeholders should thus be put together and focus on breaking the cycle of poverty in which commodity producers are now locked.

'An independent task force on commodities will be established in consultation with interested stakeholders to address the above set of issues,' says the Annex. 'The task force will function in an informal and flexible manner, with partners cooperating in a spirit of voluntary enterprise.'

Partners will include member states, international organisations (FAO, IMF, ITC, UNDP, the Common Fund for Commodities, the World Bank), commodity-specific bodies (international commodity organisations and study groups), the private sector (in particular major corporations engaged in production, marketing and distribution of commodities), NGOs promoting action on commodity issues and the academic community researching into commodity problems and solutions.

The issues mentioned for the task force to address include: facilitating collaboration among the stakeholders and achieving greater coherence in integrating commodity issues in development portfolios; collecting and sharing best practices and lessons learnt and maximising the mobilisation of resource flows; commodity sector vulnerability and risks; facilitating participation of developing-country farmers in international markets; distribution of value added in the commodity value chain; promotion of economically, socially and environmentally sustainable approaches to production and trade of individual commodities of interest to developing countries; mining and sustainable economic development; promoting business networks; and commodity information and knowledge management.

The establishment of the task force and the cautious list of issues it is to cover is a far cry from the first two decades of UNCTAD, when initiatives to attain fair prices for commodities and negotiations for establishing and maintaining commodity agreements were the bread and butter of UNCTAD's work.

Nevertheless, despite its mild and limited agenda, the decision for setting up the task force on commodities at UNCTAD XI is a positive step forward, given the severity of the commodities crisis and the absence of a venue or mechanism in the international system to discuss the crisis, let alone address it.

At the closing session, UNCTAD Secretary-General Ricupero urged the international community to prioritise actions to help the least developed countries.

The dark side of globalisation is the lack of supply capacity, or the inability of developing countries to produce competitively, he said.

'Many developing countries fear trade negotiations as in their hearts they know they are not competitive, and they depend on only two or three commodities, so how can we expect them to be enthusiastic about negotiations?' he said. 'UNCTAD has to help them in their supply problems and in negotiations.'

In present world, the prime mover of the global economy is the trade. Trade cannot be continuing until the developing countries are not prosperous. These Countries are not having the various skill of International Trade as the Developed Nation has therefore UNCTAD will look after the trade interest of the developing countries. The libralisation and growth and given some opportunity to these countries to grow their economy for which UNCTAD will help them.

8.1.6 Membership of UNCTAD

The following 193 countries are members of UNCTAD. The members of the Trade and Development Board are marked with an "*".

Afghanistan*	Germany*	Oman*
Albania*	Ghana*	Pakistan*
Algeria*	Greece*	Palau
Andorra	Grenada*	Panama*
Angola*	Guatemala*	PapuaNewGuinea*
Antigua and Barbuda	Guinea*	Paraguay*
Argentina*	Guinea-Bissau	Peru*
Armenia*	Guyana*	Philippines*
Australia*	Haiti*	Poland*
Austria*	Holy See	Portugal*

Azerbaijan*
Bahamas
Bahrain*
Bangladesh*
Barbados*
Belarus*
Belgium*
Belize
Benin*
Bhutan*
Bolivia*
Bosnia and Herzegovina
Botswana*
Brazil*
Brunei Darussalam
Bulgaria*
Burkina Faso*
Burundi*
Cambodia*
Cameroon*
Canada*
Cape Verde
Central African Republic*
Chad*
Chile*
China*
Colombia*
Comoros
Congo*
Costa Rica*
Côte d´Ivoire*
Croatia*
Cuba*
Cyprus*
Czech Republic*
Democratic People´s Republic of Korea*
Democratic Republic of the Congo*
Denmark*
Djibouti*
Dominica*
Dominican Republic*
Ecuador*
Egypt*
El Salvador*
Equatorial Guinea*
Eritrea
Estonia*
Ethiopia*
Fiji
Finland*
France*
Gabon*
Gambia
Georgia*
Honduras*
Hungary*
Iceland*
India*
Indonesia*
Iran (Islamic Republic of)*
Iraq*
Ireland*
Israel*
Italy*
Jamaica*
Japan*
Jordan*
Kazakhstan*
Kenya*
Kiribati
Kuwait*
Kyrgyzstan*
Lao People´s Democratic Republic
Latvia*
Lebanon*
Lesotho*
Liberia*
Libyan Arab Jamahiriya*
Liechtenstein*
Lithuania*
Luxembourg*
Madagascar*
Malawi
Malaysia*
Maldives
Mali*
Malta *
Marshall Islands
Mauritania*
Mauritius*
Mexico*
Micronesia (Federated States of)
Moldova*
Monaco
Mongolia*
Montenegro*
Morocco*
Mozambique*
Myanmar*
Namibia*
Nauru
Nepal*
Netherlands*
New Zealand*
Nicaragua *
Niger
Nigeria*
Norway*
Qatar*
Republic of Korea*
Romania *
Russian Federation*
Rwanda*
Saint Kitts and Nevis
Saint Lucia
Saint Vincent and the Grenadines
Samoa
San Marino
Sao Tome and Principe*
Saudi Arabia*
Senegal*
Serbia*
Seychelles
Sierra Leone *
Singapore*
Slovakia*
Slovenia*
Solomon Islands
Somalia*
South Africa*
Spain*
Sri Lanka*
Sudan *
Suriname*
Swaziland
Sweden *
Switzerland*
Syrian Arab Republic*
Tajikistan
Thailand*
The Former Yugoslav Republic of Macedonia*
Timor-Leste
Togo*
Tonga
Trinidad and Tobago*
Tunisia*
Turkey *
Turkmenistan
Tuvalu
Uganda*
Ukraine*
United Arab Emirates*
United Kingdom of Great Britain and Northern Ireland*
United Republic of Tanzania*
United States of America*
Uruguay *
Uzbekistan
Vanuatu
Venezuela*
Viet Nam *
Yemen*
Zambia*
Zimbabwe*

Source: www.unctad.org

8.1.7 UNCTAD´s Main Publications

8.1.7.1 Trade and Development Report (TDR)

The Trade and Development report analyses current economic trends and major policy issues of international concern, and makes suggestions for addressing these issues at various levels.

8.1.7.2 World Investment Report (WIR)

The *World Investment report* focuses on trends in foreign direct investment (FDI) worldwide and at the regional and country levels, as well as emerging measures to improve FDI´s contribution to development.

8.1.7.3 Economic Development in Africa Report

The *Economic Development in Africa report* analyses selected aspects of Africa´s development problems and major policy issues confronting African countries.

8.1.7.4 Least Developed Countries report (LDC)

UNCTAD´s *Least Developed Countries Report* provides a comprehensive and authoritative source of socio-economic analysis and data on the world´s most impoverished countries. Each *Report* contains a statistical annex, which provides basic data on the LDCs.

8.1.7.5 Development and Globalization: Facts and Figures (DGFF)

With economic globalization challenging much of our traditional wisdom, this brief synopsis of data and information explains new and emerging economic trends.

8.1.7.6 Information Economy Report (IER) and E-Commerce and Development Report (ECDR)

The *Information Economy Report* focuses on trends in information and communications technologies (ICT), such as e-commerce and e-business, and on national and international policy and strategy options for improving the development impact of these technologies in developing countries. It replaces the *E-commerce and Development Report* published by UNCTAD from 2001 to 2004.

8.1.8 Relationship with Other International Organizations

As the focal point for the integrated treatment of trade and development, UNCTAD interacts and cooperates with a variety of other organizations within and outside the United Nations system. These include the following:

8.1.8.1 World trade organization

UNCTAD and WTO have been joining forces to ensure a better functioning of the multilateral trading system. In April 2003, the organizations signed a Memorandum of Understanding providing for cooperation and consultations on their technical assistance activities and for the conduct of joint studies on selected issues. UNCTAD and WTO interact frequently, and the same Government representatives often attend the intergovernmental processes in both organizations.

8.1.8.2 International trade centre

The ITC is jointly sponsored by UNCTAD and WTO for operational, enterprise-oriented aspects of trade development, with an emphasis on trade promotion. In contrast to UNCTAD, whose technical assistance is primarily tailored to Governments, ITC's technical assistance focuses on assisting businesses in developing countries. Both UNCTAD and WTO are represented in the Joint Advisory Group supervising ITC's work, and UNCTAD has a number of joint technical assistance activities with ITC.

8.1.8.3 UN regional commissions and UNDP

UNCTAD cooperates with these international entities on a project-by-project basis, be it in relation to research projects, joint workshops and seminars, or technical assistance. Since UNCTAD has no representatives in the field, the UNDP country offices are also used to support UNCTAD activities in various countries.

8.1.8.4 Bretton woods institutions (International Monetary Fund and World Bank)

The World Bank and UNCTAD cooperate in the delivery of some technical assistance and capacity-building programmes. The UNCTAD secretariat, through the Debt Management–DMFAS programme, is also an active member of the Inter-Agency Task Force on Finance Statistics, which is chaired by the IMF. The three agencies also cooperate in organizing seminars. UNCTAD attends the biannual meetings of the IMF and the World Bank, and both institutions participate in UNCTAD's intergovernmental meetings.

Evaluation at UNCTAD The **UNCTAD Evaluation and Planning Unit** coordinates the oversight activities within the organization that serve to both ensure and enhance the quality and resonance of its programmes and projects.

The main activities of the unit to cover this mandate include:

- Conducting an annual in-depth evaluation of an UNCTAD programme for the Trade and Development Board;
- Organizing and overseeing programme and project evaluations at the request of donor agencies;
- Participating in joint evaluations with other international organizations;
- Overseeing and coordinating UNCTAD's involvement in the United Nations results-based management framework;
- Providing guidance and assistance to programme managers in using results-based management methodologies;
- Participating and contributing to inter-agency initiatives on evaluation, such as setting up evaluation standards or joint country-level evaluations; and

- Acting as the focal point for UNCTAD on all oversight matters, such as external evaluations, inspections and audits.

8.1.9 Dynamics of Trade and Development

The Trade and Development Report, 2007 reflects and tacitly endorses the growing phenomenon of regional pacts and arrangements. "In the absence of an appropriate multilateral framework, regional cooperation is likely to be a viable second-best solution.' As the fastest growing region, East and South Asia led by China and India, continues to drive the world economy; developing countries recorded almost 30 per cent rise in per capita GDP between 2003 and 2007 versus 10 per cent in the G-7 countries. Per capita GDP in Africa, West Asia and Latin America increased by more than 15 per cent over the past five years, a rate not seen in these regions since the early 1980s. The transition economies of South-East Europe and the CIS (Commonwealth of Independent States) have been the most rapidly growing sub-regions since 1999-2000, with an accumulated increase in per capita income of almost 75 per cent. The dynamics of overall growth in developing countries have been stimulated by strong growth in export revenues: developing economies more than doubled their real exports during 1998-2006, whereas those of the G-7 rose by less than 50 per cent. The share of the developing countries in global trade raised from 29 per cent in 1996 to 37 per cent in 2006. For developing countries in particular a stable external sector is crucial. For a safeguard against manipulation of exchange rates, wage rates, taxes or subsides, it is argued that the globalised economy needs a new code of conduct to govern overall competition between nations and thus avoid the fight for market shares. It is further suggested that changes in the real exchange rate should be subject to multilateral oversight and disciplines. Realising that such a solution at the global level has indeed a dim prospect; initiatives for monetary cooperation at the regional level have received increasing attention in recent years. Regional cooperation between developing countries has to extend beyond trade liberalisation to include policy areas which strengthen the potential for growth and structural change in these countries. Regional economic cooperation can provide means to help countries cope better with globalisation. A marked tendency to give priority to market forces in determining factor allocation is reflected in the increasing number of regional and bilateral RTAs (regional trade agreements), FTAs (free trade agreements) or PTAs (preferential trade agreements) especially during the last 20 years. The number of such trade agreements notified to the GATT/WTO shot up from 20 in 1990 to 86 in 2000 and to 159 in 2007. The WTO in its the Future of the WTO decries this proliferation of RTAs and FTAs, as in its view they render the MFN (most-favoured nation) principle the exception rather than the rule, and lead to increased discrimination in world trade. The trend labelled as "new regionalism' denotes a departure from multilateralism; it has grown out of a sense of frustration at the slow progress in satisfactory multilateral trade negotiations. Logistics Over the past 20 years, intra-regional trade in all developing regions has expanded faster than extra-regional trade. In East Asia, it represents almost half of that region's total trade; in Latin America excluding Mexico, it is 30 per cent. Intraregional trade among the economies in transition that are members of the CIS accounted for about a quarter of the group's total trade in 2005. In the case of ASEAN (Association of Southeast Asian Nations), intraregional trade on weighted average is 25 per cent of its total trade. Developing countries in East and Southeast Asia accounted for almost 50 per cent of total ASEAN trade in 2005 compared to 30 per cent in 1990. In addition to better market access that the FTAs/RTAs provide, they may also attract more FDI to the developing country partner. Overall, the Report strongly brings out that the developing countries would serve their interests better by advancing multilateral trade negotiations, of course, with a stronger development dimension built into international trade rules. The growing importance of logistics attracts attention today as never before. High transport costs and poor connectivity are detrimental to a country's development; for landlocked countries, they pose a particular challenge. Enhancing trade with partners outside the region would require an emphasis on measures such as pre-arrival customs clearance at seaports, joint border operations, mutual recognition of trade and transport-related documents and licences, and customs automation at border crossings. It is maintained, "More trade leads to better and less expensive transport services, which in turn results in more intraregional trade'; so also in regard to regional management and investment projects in the areas of energy and water supply. An efficient energy infrastructure is a precondition for economic development in general, and for industrial development and diversification in particular. "Regional energy cooperation can leverage the necessary external support for the huge public investment needed to develop the energy infrastructure.

8.2 WORLD TRADE ORGANISATION (WTO)

World Trade is a dynamic phenomenon and a highly complex process. There has a need to develop of fair system of International Trade in which the developed countries, developing countries and the least developed countries all have equal opportunity for market access, discriminatory trade barriers are dismantled and unjust government support to export eliminated. WTO is borne out of such a desire.

The establishment of World Trade Organisation is an important landmark in the history of International Trade in both goods and services, it also contains the single most important set of governing rules. On January 1, 1995 WTO was officially constituted which took the place of GATT as an effective formal organisation. GATT was an informal organisation which regulated world trade since 1948. WTO is a permanent organisation on the contrary that GATT was temporary in nature. WTO was established on the basis of an international treaty approved by participating countries. The Uruguay round of GATT (1986–93) gave birth to WTO. The members of the GATT signed on an agreement of Uruguay round in April 1994 in Morocco for establishing a new organisation named WTO.

8.2.1 Administration of WTO

A General council is made in WTO for its administration. It includes one permanent representative of each member nation. Generally, one meeting will held in a month at Geneva. In every two years the WTO's ministerial conference would be held. The Director General is the highest official of WTO to look after the day to day working. The General Council of WTO elects Director General for four years. Four Deputy Director Generals are also elected to assist the Director General.

Presently the Director General of WTO is Pascal Lamy.

8.2.2 Headquarter and Members of WTO

The headquarter of WTO is also at Geneva. At the time of inception of WTO there were 132 member nations in which 90 were developing country, 27 were least develop country and 08 were developed country. According to the WTO Report 2003, at the end of April 2003, 146 countries were the members of WTO In Cancun conference held in Maxico on 10–14 Sept. 03 Nepal and Combodia also got the membership of WTO which increased the present membership of WTO to 148. Presently there were 153 members countries. The official language of WTO is English, French, Spanish.

8.2.3 Objectives of WTO

The following are the basic objective of WTO

1. To improve standard of living of people in the member countries.
2. To ensure full employment and broad increase in effective demand.
3. To enlarge production and trade of goods and services.
4. To ensure optimum utilisation of world resources.
5. To accept the concept of sustainable development.
6. To protect the world environment.

8.2.4 Functions of WTO

1. To provide facilities for implementation, administration and operation of multilateral and bilateral agreements of the world trade.
2. To provide a platform to member countries to decide future strategies related to trade and tariff.
3. To administer the rules and processes related to dispute settlement.
4. To implement rules and provisions related to trade policy review mechanism.
5. To assist IMF and IBRD for establishing coherence in universal economic policy determination.
6. To ensure the optimum use of world resources.

8.2.5 Ministerial Conference of WTO

8.2.5.1 First ministerial conference of WTO

The First Ministerial Conference of WTO was held in Singapore on December 9–13, 1996. In this conference developed and developing countries both having conflicting interest were found engaged in strengthening their interests.

Important Issues of the conference

- Labour Standards
- Investment
- Competition in International Trade
- Textiles in International Trade
- Information Technology

Developing countries including India were opposing the attempts of linking labour standards with International Trade but developed countries under the leadership of USA were advocating for the link. Developing countries were arguing that Labour standard is not the jurisdiction of WTO but this matter is concerning with International Labour Organisation (ILO). They also opposed against the issue of investment in International Trade.

Developing nations succeed in getting labour standards approved as a subject matter of International Labour Organisation only. On the other hand, developed nations got success in correlating issues of investment and competition with International Trade. The issues related to investment with International Trade will be solved under 'TRIMs' i.e. Trade Related Investments Measures, for which a working group was constituted. A separate working group for issues related to anti-competitive practices was also recommended and accepted for constituting it. The other achievement of the first conference was in the field of Computer and Information technology.

8.2.5.2 Second ministerial conference of WTO

The Second Ministerial Conference of WTO was held on May 18–20, 1998 at Geneva (Switzerland). 132 member countries participated in this meeting. The Geneva meeting is known for the multilateral trading system. In this meeting the previous agenda of the first conference was not included although it was the part of discussion. On India side, it was attended by then commerce Minister Mr. Ram Krishna Hedge. India's point was clerified by him as he said. "The less developed countries could not get the proper benefit because of lack of clear direction about the Uruguay Round Talk of GATT.

The important issues and decisions which was made in the meeting was

To ensure the faithful implementation of existing multilateral agreements a new mechanism have to set up.

Rejection of the measure of projectionist and accepting a new one for open and transparent rule based trading system.

The second ministerial conference was highly emphasised by its multilateral trading system and its effective implementation for entire world. The basic objective was to increase the global trade, enhancing new set up trading system that could help in expanding the world trade. This expanding of the trade definately help in creating new and more job opportunity to world. It would also help in improving the living standards of the people in the entire world. It was also stated that this trend of the multilateral trading system must flow to the developing needs of the developing countries.

8.2.5.3 Third ministerial conference of WTO

The Third Ministerial Conference of WTO was held at Seatal in USA on Nov. 30 to Dec. 03, 2000. This meeting was comprises of 137 member countries. This meeting was a failure as the developing countries jointly protested against the lack of transparency and imposition of the views of the developed on the developing nations in the negotiations. The main objections raised by the developing nations were the issues of human rights and preservation of ecology. The protestors countries raised the voice against the violation of these issues by the WTO and they named the WTO as "Wrong Trade Organisation". Another issue of the protesting was the inclusion of labour standards in the list. The Indian side was represented by Murasoli Maran, the Commerce Minister. He represented his stand forcefully and successfully in the conference. The member countries of WTO could not reach on consensus regarding market access, agreements about the trade of agricultural services etc.

This conference was failure because of the highly protested by the developing nations. They criticised the WTO that it cared little for the views of the Asian, African and Latin American countries and highly cared to developed nations. They also argued that it exploits the developing nations for the benefit of advanced countries under the slogan of 'glabalisation'. Another reason was the inclusion of labour standards. As the developing nations have the competitive advantage due to cheap labour, which leads to low production costs. So, they feel that the talks about labour standards as a play to prevent their products from entering the western countries.

8.2.5.4 Fourth ministerial conference of WTO

The Fourth Ministerial Conference of WTO was held at Doha (capital of Qatar) from 9–14 November 2001. In this conference 142 member countries were participated. In this conference the developed nations wanted a new round of multilateral trade negotiation to be launched soon, which included investment competition policy, trade facilitation, transparency in government procurement, environment, agricultural and trade related aspects of intellectual property rights (TRIPs). Developing countries including India wanted that the implementation issues should be resolved before a new Round. India had almost single–handedly fought against the developed nations. The issue points of Doha ministerial conference are as follows.

- Implementation Issues
- Special and Differential Treatment
- Agriculture
- Rules & Regulation
- Negotiation on Market Access for other than Agricultural Products

- Services
- TRIPs
- Dispute Settlement Understanding
- Trade and Environment
- Labour Standards
- Work Programme
- Singapore issues

In this conference the future work programme of the WTO was decided. While there were strong pressures to launch a comprehensive round of negotiations including multilateral regimes on investment, competition policy, trade facilitation, government procurement and environment. India underlined the need for resolving the implementation issues arising from the current agreements in a time bound manner before addressing new issues for negotiations.

The substantial outcome of the Doha ministerial is the work programme aimed at reduction in custom's tariffs and opening up of agriculture and services. Exporters of farm goods can expect to benefit from the reduction of domestic support and export subsidies in Europe and the USA.

In this conference India made significant gains on public health concerns in the trips agreement. The agreement over amendment to TRIPs, which would allow countries access to low price patented drugs in case of a public health emergency, was a victory for India.

8.2.5.5 Fifth ministerial conference of WTO

The Fifth Ministerial Conference of WTO was held at Cancun (Mexico) on September 10, 2003. In this conference 148 member countries were participated. The Cancun Ministerial conference was meant mainly to be a forum to review the progress of negotiations under the Doha work Programme mandated at Doha and give directions wherever required, and a specific decision on the status of the Singapore issues. The conference also provided ample opportunity to test the seriousness of developed countries with regard to the development dimension of the Doha work programme. However, the Cancun Ministerial conference became complex in view of the serious differences in the ambition levels of WTO members on the two most contentious issues, namely agriculture and Singapore issues.

This conference was heavily loaded against the interests of developing countries and opposed strongly from the developing nations which resulted in the failure of the conference. The Cancun Ministerial conference recognised that more work needed to be done in some key areas to make the member countries to proceed towards the conclusion of the negotiations unfulfillment of commitments taken at Doha.

One positive outcome of this ministerial conference was that the developing nations strongly expressed for protecting their interests and their unity inspite of pressures exerted by developed countries to break the coalitious. A new path created for a more decisive and impressive role could be made by developing nations. This ministerial conference had certainly boost up the developing nations for putting strong points for their issues as well as on the agenda and in negotiating outcomes. Another positive development was the role of G–20 in effectively placing, the viewpoints of the world community dependent on agriculture for livelihood before the Cancun ministerial conference.

8.2.5.6 Sixth ministerial conference of WTO

The Sixth Ministerial Conference of WTO was held in Hongkong, during 13–18 December 2005. In this conference WTO ministers had agreed to establish modalities for agricultural and Non-Agricultural Market Access (NAMA), submit the Draft schedules and conclude the negotiations across all areas of the Doha Round by the end of 2006. Some important points of the Agreement of this conference are as follows:

The ministerial agreed to ensure the parallel elimination of all forms of export subsidies and disciplines on all export measures with equivalent effect to be completed by the end of 2013.

It was agreed to resolve the Doha work programme and to conclude negotiations in 2006.

It was also resolve that domestic subsidies must be cut, but the cut will extent is to be negotiated in 2006.

The minister were agreed for reduction or appropriate elimination of tariffs, including particular reduction or elimination of tariff peaks, high tariffs and tariff escalation in certain product's of export interest to developing countries, taking fully consideration the specific needs and interests of developing nations.

It was agreed to make amendment on the TRIPs agreement concerning to the public health of the developing nations.

It was also agreed to establish a modalities in agricultural and non-agricultural market access (NAMA) by the end of 30th April, 2006 and prepare draft schedules by 31st July, 2006.

The Ministers were also agreed to adopt the policy of Swiss formula, which means that countries who had highest protective level must cuts the largest.

This conference reaffirmed the Declarations and Decisions adopted at Doha, as well as the Decision adopted by the General Council on 01 August 2004. And the Ministerial conference declared its full commitment to give effect to them. It was agreed to resolve all Doha work Programme fully and to conclude the negotiations launched at Doha successfully in 2006. It was agreed by all the ministers to cut the domestic subsidies but to the level of negotiated in 2006. The understanding on domestic support is to have three bands for reduction of the support, based on the levels of trade distorting domestic support to farmers given by different countries. It has been agreed that the three largest subsidisers namely, the European community, the United states and Japan, will attract the highest levels of cuts in their trade–distorting domestic support entitlements and that these cuts must be effective one. The ministerial adopted four bands on Non-Agricultural Market Access (NAMA), for structuring tariff cuts, recognising the need to agree on the relevant their hold- including those applicable for developing countries.

India with other developing nations got the flexibility to designate some products as 'Special' or Sensitive on which there will be no eats. Moreover, the duty cuts by developing nations will be based on less than full reciprocity i.e. that it will be less than the developed nations. India and other developing nations were exempt from making any cuts in domestic agricultural subsidies and concessions on export subsidies. Another benefits was the special and differential treatment clause provides flexibility on tariff reductions on certain sensitive items less than fully reciprocity in reduction commitment.

In this ministerial conference an important grievance of the developing nations has been that the Doha decisions have not been earnestly implemented. They were of the opinion that any further trade negotiations are uncalled for when the Doha decisions remained unfulfilled.

8.2.6 Benefits of WTO

- It helps promote peace and prosperity across the globe.
- Disputes are settling amicably.
- Rules bring about greater discipline in trade negotiations, thereby reducing inequalities largely.
- Free trade reduces the cost of living and increases household income.
- Companies have greater access to markets and consumers have wider range of products to choose from.
- Good governance accelerates economic growth.

8.2.7 India and WTO

India is one of the founding members of WTO along with 134 other countries. India's participation in an increasingly rule based system in governance of International trade, would ultimately lead to better prosperity for the nation. Various trade disputes of India with other nations have been settled through WTO. India has also played an important part in the effective formulation of major trade policies. By being a member of WTO several countries, is now trading with India, thus giving a boost to production, employment, standard of living and an opportunity to maximize the use of the world resources?

India is proud to have been a founder Member both of GATT and of WTO. Over the years, the negotiators, which India has played a prominent role in shaping the multilateral trading system as it, exists today. Indian contribution is significant to the successful conclusion of all trade negotiations. India participated effectively in the formulation of all major trade agreements. Since the formation of WTO, our delegation has been active at all times in all deliberations and has played a part in concluding difficult negotiations.

Another issue of deep concern is the trend towards unilateral action by certain developed countries in total disregard of provisions laid down in the Uruguay Round Agreements. India had deeply force to a great expense and considerable difficulty, to take such issues to the dispute settlement mechanism. Distinguished delegates are aware that developing countries and least-developed countries have to battle against resource constraints and shortage of skills and expertise in these areas.

At the Singapore Conference, India had drawn the attention of Members to the adverse impact on India's exports of actions taken under this Agreement, such as the series of transitional safeguard measures, which were subsequently found to be inconsistent even with the provisions of the Agreement. India has taken careful note of the First Major Review of the Agreement conducted by the Council for Trade in Goods earlier this year. It is a matter of deep concern to us to note that, in spite of the provisions negotiated by us to ensure a commercially meaningful phasing out of restrictions maintained under the MFA regime, the review confirmed that the bulk of restrictions would get integrate into the GATT 1994 only at the end of the transition period. In the context of the Agreement on Textiles and Clothing, the use of anti-dumping measures on textile and clothing exports which are already under a quota regime, is a clear case of protectionism and needs to be deplored in the strongest terms. The Member nations have decided to entrust the Council for Trade in Goods with the task of keeping the implementation of the ATC under regular review. India reaffirms its commitment to fulfill this mandate given to the Council, especially in the process be initiating with respect to evaluating the overall implementation of WTO Agreements. The textiles and clothing sector is an extremely significant part of our own economy accounting for 20% of national industrial output and providing means of living to 30 million people. Any restriction of market access for our exports of textiles and clothing products would, therefore, have very serious implications for us in terms of income and employment and jeopardize the very credibility of the multilateral trading system.

The Agreement on Agriculture will come up for review in the year 2000. India had the opportunity to have a fresh look at this area, keeping in view the development perspective and the needs of developing countries. There remain a number of inequities as far as the implementation of the Agreement is concerned. For instance, while the majority of developing countries are prohibit from providing export subsidies, the developed countries are permit to resort to such subsidies provided their budgetary outlays are within their reduction commitment. This is obviously unfair in the sense that countries, which have been distorting the market in the past, can continue to maintain subsidy regimes, while others are prohibit from using such measures in the future. This Agreement is base on the rationale of open international trade in the agricultural sector. It presupposes the supremacy of an open price based system, thereby implying that a country should import agricultural products if they are produce cheaper elsewhere. India and certain other developing countries have been stressing the need for the multilateral trading system to recognize the importance of food security. A country may not have the resources to buy agricultural products from international markets even if they are easily available. The exemptions given for direct payments to farmers and deficiency payments from the ambit of reduction commitments in respect of production subsidies also need to careful study. There is also the issue of the possible negative effects of the reform programme on least-developed and net-food-importing developing countries which has not been effectively addressed as yet, despite a Ministerial Decision during the Uruguay Round negotiations.

India however, deeply committed to the success of the multilateral trading system. As it believe that the WTO and the multilateral trading system must be effective instruments for serving the needs of the weakest section of the society in all parts of the world. No single pattern, no single package of measures considered universally applicable. Recently, the G-8 leaders along with the G-5 members — China, India, Brazil, South Africa and Mexico — had called for concluding the Doha Round in 2010. New Delhi will host a G-20 ministerial meeting on September 3 and 4 to provide a direction to the world leaders when they meet in Pittsburgh, US.

8.2.8 Dispute Settlement System in the World Trade Organisation (WTO)

The dispute settlement system in the WTO is similar to a 'court of law' in a civil society. It consists of multilaterally agreed rules and procedures that provide member countries the means to settle their trade disputes.

Trade disputes arise when one country violates any of the agreed provisions of any WTO agreement and this violation impairs or nullifies the benefit that would have otherwise come to another country. For example, if country A imposes a tariff rate on country B that is more than the rate that it imposes on all other member countries of the WTO (Most Favoured Nation rate), then A is violating the Most Favoured Nation rule (which requires that a member country of the WTO should extend equal treatment to all member countries) and is impairing the benefits to B by illegally restricting its exports. This will result in a trade dispute between B and A.

B can therefore use the dispute settlement system to settle this dispute. Settling the dispute, in this case, will mean ensuring that A starts complying with the Most Favoured Nation rule and hence imposing the same tariff rate on B that it is imposing on other member countries. This will stop the restriction of exports of B to A and hence restore the benefits to B, which were earlier impaired because of higher tariff being imposed by country A.

8.2.8.1 Significance of the dispute settlement system

The dispute settlement system is significant in many ways:

1. **Guarantor of rights and obligations:** By providing the means to countries to settle their trade disputes, it acts as a guarantor for the rights and obligations of countries in the WTO. Countries in the WTO engage in international trade for mutual benefit and gain based on agreed rules and procedures. For country A to enjoy its right, country B has to fulfil its obligation, and vice versa. In case of a country not fulfilling its obligation, other member countries can challenge the action of this country in the dispute settlement body (DSB). The DSB will then ask this country to change its action and bring it in accordance with the agreed rules and procedures.

Hence, the DSB enforces the rules of the WTO and maintains the sanctity of 'rule of law' that is the bedrock of the multilateral trading regime embodied in the WTO.

2. **Provides stability and predictability:** The DSB gives stability and predictability to the multilateral trading regime as countries know that if their rights are infringed, an effective recourse is available. This keeps countries interested in the system. Without an effective dispute resolution machinery and proper enforcement mechanism, a rule-based system will not work properly and countries will not have adequate faith in the system.

3. **Protection against unilateral action:** Since the DSB in the WTO comprises multilaterally agreed rules and procedures to settle disputes, every trade dispute has to be settled according to the procedure established by law. No country can act unilaterally against any other country without going through the DSB.

8.2.8.2 DSB disputes settlement method

There are several stages in resolving disputes:

First Stage—Consultation: The first stage in settling the dispute is consultations. In this stage, the complaining country notifies the DSB and makes a representation requesting the other country to enter into consultations. Such representation and request has to be made in writing giving the reasons for the consultation including the identification of the issues involved in the dispute.

The country that gets the request for consultations should sympathetically consider the request for consultations and reply within 10 days after the date of the receipt of the request. It is also required to enter into consultations within 30 days after the date of the receipt of the request. If the consultations fail to settle the dispute within 60 days of receipt of the request, the complaining party may request the establishment of a panel.

The rationale behind having consultations is to provide adequate opportunity to the disputing countries to settle their disputes by talking to each other. The primary role of the DSB is not to function as a judicial court that passes judgements but to settle disputes. Hence it first allows countries to settle their differences without moving the judicial machinery. It is only if disputing countries are not able to resolve their differences by talking to each other that they move to the second stage, which is a judicial process.

Second Stage—Panel: Failure of consultations leads to the formation of a panel. If the consultations fail, the complaining party may make a written request to the DSB to form a panel. The DSB, after receiving such a request, will form a panel. A panel is like a tribunal that examines the evidence and decides who is right and who is wrong. The panel is required to make findings that will assist the DSB in making recommendations or rulings to decide the dispute.

A panel shall comprise three to five members, who could be well-qualified individuals either from government or non-government agencies, or someone who has served or presented a case to a panel, or who has taught or published on international trade law or policy, or served as a senior trade policy official of a member country. The members of a panel are chosen in consultation with the countries involved in the dispute. If the parties to the dispute do not agree on the members of the panel, then the Director General of the WTO appoints the members of the panel.

The panel, after consultations with the parties to the dispute, will fix the timetable for the entire panel process. This timetable should be such that it accords sufficient time for the parties to make submissions to the panel. The panel shall issue its final report within six months from the date the panel was formed. In cases of urgency the panel will issue its reports within three months.

Once the panel has given its report to the DSB, it shall not be considered for adoption until 20 days after the date of circulation of the report. Within 60 days after the circulation of the report amongst the member countries, the report shall be adopted. Non-adoption of the report within 60 days can only happen because of two reasons. First, the DSB decides by consensus not to adopt the report. Second, either party to the dispute decides to appeal against the report. In such a case, the panel report shall not be considered for adoption by the DSB till the appeal is heard and decided.

Third Stage—Appellate Body (AB): Appealing against the findings of the panel by a party to the dispute implies moving to the third stage of dispute resolution. In case of an appeal, the dispute comes to the AB. The AB is a permanent judicial body in the WTO established by the DSB. The main function of the AB is to hear the appeals from the panel cases. It comprises seven members with not more than three members hearing a particular appeal. Members of the AB are people who have recognised authority and demonstrated expertise in law, international trade and different WTO agreements. They should not be affiliated to any government.

The appeal to the AB should be on the interpretation of the law and not mere facts or requests to re-examine the evidence. The AB has to complete its proceedings on the appeal within 60 days from the date the appealing country notifies its intention to appeal. If the AB thinks that it is not possible for it to submit its report within the 60-day time period, it will have to inform the DSB about it in writing. However, in no case can the AB proceedings exceed 90 days. The AB has the right to reverse, uphold, change or modify the findings of the panel.

The AB report will be adopted by the DSB and has to be unconditionally accepted by the parties to the dispute. In other words, the findings of the AB are final and there cannot be any appeal against its findings (AB in the WTO is like the apex court in any country or society). The only situation where the AB report cannot be adopted by the DSB is when there is a consensus against adopting the report. In other words, only if all the member countries (including the country winning the dispute) reject the report, it will not be adopted by the DSB. The report will be adopted even if one member wants it to be adopted.

If the panel or the AB comes to the conclusion that a particular action of a country is in violation of a WTO provision, it will recommend that this particular country bring its action into conformity with the WTO provisions. The adoption of the panel or the AB report by the DSB implies that the dispute has been settled.

8.2.8.3 Country fails to comply with the rulings of the DSB

If the country at fault fails to comply with the ruling, and then the other disputing country has the right to seek compensation from the non-complying country. One of the ways of compensating could be by providing access to the markets of the losing country at lower tariff rates. For instance, there could be a dispute where country A is found guilty of imposing higher tariff rates on pens coming from country B. In such a case, the DSB will ask country A to remove its excess tariff rate on pens coming from B. If A expresses its inability to remove the excess tariff rates, then it may compensate B by providing access to, say, tea coming from B at a lower tariff rate. However, this compensation will be given only if it is acceptable to the winning country; acceptance of the winning country is therefore of paramount importance.

In case no satisfactory compensation is worked out within 20 days after entering into negotiations for compensation, the country seeking the compensation may request the DSB to authorise it to retaliate against the non-complying country. Retaliation in the WTO is like inflicting a punitive action. However, it is important to bear in mind that the retaliatory mechanism is not meant to punish any country but only to urge countries to comply with the ruling and the covered agreement. It is supposed to act as a deterrent against flouting the rulings of the DSB. The DSU agreement states that countries can retaliate by suspending the concessions (not honouring the obligations towards the non complying country under the WTO agreements that would have otherwise been honoured in normal practice) to the flouting country.

This suspension of concessions can take place in three ways:

1. **In the same sector:** The complaining or the country that has won the dispute shall first suspend concessions in the same sector in which the other country has been found guilty of not fulfilling its obligations under the covered agreement. So, if there is a dispute involving the telecommunication sector under the General Agreement on Trade in Services (GATS), then the retaliation has to be in the telecommunication sector only. Retaliation in such a case by the country that has won the dispute could be to limit the foreign direct investment (FDI) for the flouting country to 25 per cent as against an upper limit of 51 per cent for all other member countries in the WTO.

2. **Across different sectors:** If retaliating in the same sector is impracticable or will be ineffective, then the complaining country can retaliate in another sector. Retaliating in the same sector can be impracticable if there is a possibility that the retaliating country will suffer harm. For instance, there may be a case where the flouting country is the only country that has invested in the telecommunication sector in the complaining country and the entire telecommunication services in the complaining country is due to the FDI of the flouting country. In such a case, it will not be in the interest of the complaining country to restrict the FDI from the flouting country; it will hurt the interests of the complaining country more than that of the flouting country.

Retaliating in the same sector i.e. telecommunications in this case may also be ineffective if the flouting country does not invest in telecommunications in the complaining country, or if it has a meagre commercial interest in the telecommunications sector in the complaining country. In such a case, even if the complaining country suspends concessions in the telecommunication sector under the GATS agreement, there will not be any effect on the flouting country and hence retaliation will be ineffective. The complaining country can therefore suspend concessions in some other sector, such as the distributional sector in this case.

3. **Across different agreements:** If suspending concessions in other sectors is also found to be impracticable or ineffective, then the complaining country can suspend concessions under any other agreement of the WTO. For instance, if the dispute involved GATS agreement and retaliating under GATS is impracticable or ineffective, then the complaining country can retaliate under, say, the TRIPS agreement. Retaliation under the TRIPS agreement could be by de-recognising product patenting on pharmaceuticals or by not extending copyright protection to the products of the flouting country in the territory of the complaining country.

Before retaliating or suspending concessions, the complaining country will seek authorisation from the DSB. This authorisation will be granted unless all the member countries of the WTO are against such authorisation. Further, the retaliation or suspension of concessions should be equivalent to the injury caused by the distortion of the flouting country. So, if the wrong action of the flouting country is causing a harm of, say, five units to the complaining country, then the complaining country will retaliate or suspend concessions only to the extent that impairs benefits worth five units to the flouting country, and not more.

8.2.8.4 Effectiveness of DSB in settlement of trade disputes

DSB has been quite successful in settling disputes. In the last 10 years of its existence it has received more than 300 complaints. The countries involved in the disputes settled many of these complaints or disputes mutually. An interesting case in this regard was the anti dumping dispute between India and Bangladesh. This dispute was settled at the consultation stage itself. About 100 disputes have reached the panel or the AB stage. The number of disputes is a clear pointer to the fact that countries have great faith in the DSB as the guarantor of their rights and obligations unlike the previous dispute resolution mechanism under GATT.

There have also been cases where smaller countries have won disputes against big and powerful countries, which generally does not happen in international disputes of any nature. In a recent case, the two small Caribbean islands of Antigua and Barbuda successfully challenged the trade restrictive actions of the US on gambling services.

However, this is not to say that the DSB of the WTO is a perfect dispute resolution mechanism. There are certain inadequacies in it and this has often acted as a deterrent for smaller countries to realise complete gains from the DSB.

The inadequacies in the functioning of the DSB were taken on board during the fourth ministerial conference of the WTO at Doha . As a part of the larger negotiating round on the multilateral trading regime, negotiations were also launched on improving and clarifying the DSB. This review process was to be completed by May 2003. However, this deadline was missed and it was extended to May 2004. Even this deadline was missed as member countries failed to reach any agreement. The Hong Kong (HK) Declaration adopted at the sixth ministerial conference of the WTO at HK in December 2005 only states that countries will work towards the rapid conclusion of the DSB negotiations and does not specify any end date. Negotiations on improving and clarifying the DSB are underway and many proposals have been made in this regard.

8.2.8.5 Crucial negotiation Issues handle by DSB

Some of the most important issues from the perspective of developing countries are the following:

1. **Notifying mutually agreed solutions:** As we have seen above, the first stage in settling the dispute is by the countries to the dispute undertake consultations. If the consultations succeed, it implies that the dispute has been settled. This settlement of the dispute through successful consultations is to be notified to the DSB. However, the flaw in the present regime is that there is nothing that tells which country will notify the result of the consultation to the DSB. Also, there is no time frame within which the countries are required to notify, nor are they required to provide sufficient information that would enable others to understand the reasons behind the mutually agreed solution.

This non-timely and inadequate notification comes in the way of boosting transparency in the functioning of the DSB. It may also obscure the rights and interests of other countries who may be significantly interested in the dispute and may never come to know the exact reasons behind the dispute being settled through consultations. Therefore, some countries such as India and Japan have proposed that once a satisfactory agreement is reached the same should be notified with sufficient information to the DSB within 60 days.

2. **Amicus Curiae submissions:** One of the controversial aspects of the functioning of the DSB is the discretion of a panel to seek information from any source in order to settle the dispute. In this regard, many non-governmental organisations and other bodies based in the North submit *amicus curiae* briefs to the court (amicus *curiae* means friend of the court). The opportunities to submit *amicus curiae* briefs gives an added advantage to developed countries as the organisations based in these countries have better access to all kinds of information and resources.

Developing countries such as India have argued against the submission of these *amicus* briefs as it puts developing countries in a disadvantageous position.

3. **Burden of legal costs:** Initiating a dispute in the DSB of the WTO requires a huge amount of expenditure for developing and least developed countries. This huge expenditure is mainly on account of excessive reliance on foreign legal experts since most of these countries do not have adequate domestic capacity to fight cases in the DSU on their own. This high litigation cost in initiating a dispute often acts as a deterrent for many developing and least developed countries.

In this regard developing countries such as India have proposed that in disputes that involve a developing country and a developed country and where the dispute is decided in the favour of the developing country, the developed country should pay the litigation costs to the developing country.

4. **Retaliatory mechanism:** As discussed above, the present system in the DSB allows the complaining country to retaliate by following a sequence. Many developing countries have argued that there should not be any sequence while taking retaliatory measures. In other words, countries should be free to explore any of the three options without having to prove the impracticability or ineffectiveness of any other options. This will provide greater deterrence powers to the DSB and make it more credible and stronger in getting the losing country to comply with the DSB ruling.

8.2.9 Present Scenario of WTO in International Trade

The year 2008 saw a lot of development as well as a number of setbacks in the Doha Round of WTO talks. Much as all wanted to be unable to conclude the Agriculture and NAMA modalities. It has been successful in July 2008. It has been well scheduling a Ministerial meeting of the WTO around this time to conclude the Doha Round. There are various views that the global economic crisis does not promise well for the successful completion of this Round. It is believe that the Doha Development Round is a part of the solution to the crisis. A fair and satisfactory outcome to the trade negotiations can actually provide impetus to the combined international effort to break out of the economic crisis.

The momentum of DOHA round talks could not sustained post July 2008 due to two reasons:

(*i*) The contagion of the financial crisis spread across the world and preoccupied policy makers and

(*ii*) The US positions may take the negotiating table given the political compulsion in some countries. But it provides all with a much needed pause to reflect before to engage again. Even though it could not reach final agreement as it had intended, on many specific issues that seemed intractable in the past, have made considerable progress.

In the agricultural space it stands on the special safeguard mechanism for farmers has been consistent. It can have consistently sought measures that will insulate the farmers from the sudden decline in international prices or surge in import volumes of agricultural commodities. India is not the US, where, 2 per cent of the labour force is in agriculture, and this labour force feeds the entire nation. In India, agriculture accounts for 18 per cent of GDP, and accounts for 56 per cent of the workforce. Most of the members of this workforce are subsistence farmers, working on land holdings less than 2 acres; many are not even landowners, and mere sharecroppers. Even an incremental surge in agricultural imports could affect the lives of millions of farmers. We cannot jeopardize their lives in the name of global trade.

In NAMA, the modalities for tariff cuts must reflect the mandate of "less than full reciprocity in reduction commitments" and "comparability in ambition between NAMA and Agriculture". Flexibilities must be both adequate and appropriate and without undue constraints for defending sensitive tariff lines. On Sectoral Initiatives, have always said that India would be willing to participate in negotiating the terms of sectoral initiatives provided it is on a good faith basis without any prejudging of the final participation or outcome.

In the areas of Agriculture and NAMA most of the technical work has been completed, what now require is political will to move ahead. If such political can be garnered in the next few weeks with the active participation of the world leaders, the negotiations can be resumed and can think about implementation the 'modalities' in agriculture and NAMA before summer. If that happens, it would be on course to finishing the Round by the end of the year.

Growing protectionism is emerging as a problem for the global trading system. While it is alright to talk about a 'standstill,' it needs to be clear what it means. It cannot ask developing countries to exercise restraint on tariffs while developed countries continue to pile up huge subsidies to their industries and agriculture. Completion of the Doha Round would help to reduce protectionist pressures while at the same time strengthening the global trading system.

At last it could be said that the Doha Round has a future and can be concluded this year. But for the Doha Round to finish off, the development mandate has to be treasured. The developed countries had demonstrated statesmanship and a greater willingness to appreciate the concerns of the developing countries. India's confidence in the multilateral trading system and in the institution of the WTO remains intact. India has always been and will continue to be an ardent supporter of a rule-based, transparent multilateral trading system.

8.3 INTERNATIONAL MONETARY FUNDS (IMF)

8.3.1 Introduction

During the Great Depression of the 1930s, countries attempted to shore up their failing economies by sharply raising barriers to foreign trade, devaluing their currencies to compete against each other for export markets, and curtailing their citizens' freedom to hold foreign exchange. These attempts proved to be self-defeating. World trade declined sharply and employment and living standards plummeted in many countries.

This breakdown in international monetary cooperation led the IMF's founders to plan an institution charged with overseeing the international monetary system—the system of exchange rates and international payments that enables countries and their citizens to buy goods and services from each other. The new global entity would ensure exchange rate stability and encourage its member countries to eliminate exchange restrictions that hindered trade.

8.3.2 Organization and Purpose

The International Monetary Fund (IMF or Fund) and the International Bank for Reconstruction and Development (IBRD or World Bank) were both establishes at the United Nations Monetary and Financial Conference, held at Bretton Woods, New Hampshire, on July 1-22, 1944. The two were create to oversee stability in international monetary affairs and to facilitate the expansion of world trade. Membership in the World Bank requires membership in the IMF, and they are both specialized agencies of the United Nations. The International Monetary Fund was created in July of 1944, originally with 45 members, with a goal to stabilize exchange rates and assist the reconstruction of the world's international payment system. Countries contributed to a pool which could be borrowed from, on a temporary basis, by countries with payment imbalances.

The World Bank was given domain over long-term financing for nations in need, while the IMF's mission was to monitor exchange rates, provide short-term financing for balance of payments adjustments, provide a forum for discussion about international monetary concerns, and give technical assistance to member countries. These functions are still generally true of both organizations, although the policies determining how they are carried out have been modified and amplified over time.

The Fund's legal authority is base on an international treaty called the Articles of Agreement (Articles or the Agreement) which came into force in 27 December 1945. The first Article in the Agreement outlines the purposes of the Fund and, although the Articles have been amended three times in the course of the last 47 years prior to 1998, the first Article has never been altered.

The IMF started financial operations on March 1, 1947. Drawings on Fund reserves were made by 11 countries between 1947 and 1948, although there were no drawings in 1950 and very few in the following years. During this time, the Fund worked on its drawings policies. One outcome was the stand-by arrangements, established in 1952, modified in 1956, and reviewed periodically since then. Stand-by arrangements provide a procedure for drawing on Fund resources with conditions based on a structural adjustment program for the borrower country. Stand-by arrangements became the model for other lending procedures designed by the Fund to meet the needs of its members.

By the early 1960s, the US dollar's fixed value against gold, under the Bretton Woods system of fixed exchange rates, was seen as overvalued. A sizable increase in domestic spending on President Lyndon Johnson's Great Society programs and a rise in military spending caused by the Vietnam War gradually worsened the overvaluation of the dollar.

8.3.3 Objectives of IMF

According to 'Articles of Agreement' of the IMF, its main objectives are as follows:

1. To promote international monetary cooperation.
2. To ensure balanced international trade.
3. To ensure exchange rate stability.
4. To eliminate or to minimize exchange restrictions by promoting the system of multilateral payments.
5. To grant economic assistance to member countries for eliminating the adverse imbalance in balance of payments.
6. To minimize imbalances in quantum and duration of International Trade.

8.3.4 Board of Governors

The Board of Governors is the highest decision-making body of the IMF. It consists of one governor and one alternate governor for each member country. The governor is appointed by the member country and is usually the minister of finance or the head of the central bank.

While the Board of Governors has delegated most of its powers to the IMF's Executive Board, it retains the right to approve quota increases, special drawing right (SDR) allocations, the admittance of new members, compulsory withdrawal of members, and amendments to the Articles of Agreement and By-Laws.

The Board of Governors also elects or appoints executive directors and is the ultimate arbiter on issues related to the interpretation of the IMF's Articles of Agreement. Voting by the Board of Governors usually takes place by mail-in ballot.

The Boards of Governors of the IMF and the World Bank Group normally meet once a year, during the IMF-World Bank Spring and Annual Meetings, to discuss the work of their respective institutions. The Meetings, which take place in September or October, have customarily been held in Washington for two consecutive years and in another member country in the third year.

The Annual Meetings usually include two days of plenary sessions, during which Governors consult with one another and present their countries' views on current issues in international economics and finance. During the Meetings, the Boards of Governors also make decisions on how current international monetary issues should be addressed and approve corresponding resolutions.

The Annual Meetings are chaired by a Governor of the World Bank and the IMF, with the chairmanship rotating among the membership each year. Every two years, at the time of the Annual Meetings, the Governors of the Bank and the Fund elect Executive Directors to their respective Executive Boards.

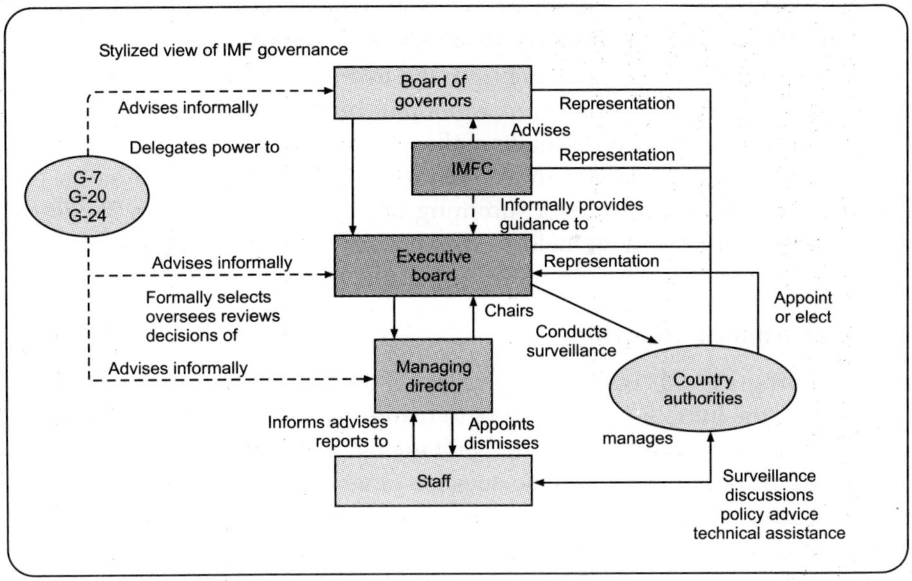

Source: Martines-Diaz, 2006

8.3.5 Ministerial Committees

Two ministerial committees, the International Monetary and Financial Committee (IMFC) and the Development Committee, advise the IMF Board of Governors.

The IMFC has 24 members, drawn from the pool of 185 governors. Its structure mirrors that of the Executive Board and its 24 constituencies. As such, the IMFC represents all the member countries of the Fund.

The IMFC meets twice a year, during the Spring and Annual Meetings. The Committee discusses matters of common concern affecting the global economy and also advises the IMF on the direction its work. At the end of the Meetings, the Committee issues a joint communiqué summarizing its views. These communiqués provide guidance for the IMF's work program during the six months leading up to the next Spring or Annual Meetings. There is no formal voting at the IMFC, which operates by consensus.

The Development Committee is a joint committee, tasked with advising the Boards of Governors of the IMF and the World Bank on issues related to economic development in emerging and developing countries. The committee has 24 members (usually ministers of finance or development). It represents the full membership of the IMF and the World Bank and mainly serves as a forum for building intergovernmental consensus on critical development issues.

8.3.6 The Executive Board

The IMF's 24-member Executive Board takes care of the daily business of the IMF. Together, these 24 board members represent all 186 countries. Large economies, such as the United States and China, have their own seat at the table but most countries are grouped in constituencies representing 4 or more countries. The largest constituency includes 24 countries.

The Board discusses everything from the IMF staff's annual health checks of member countries' economies to economic policy issues germane to the global economy. The board normally makes decisions based on consensus but sometimes formal votes are taken. At the end of most formal discussions, the Board issues what is known as a summing up, which summarizes its views. Informal discussions may be held to discuss complex policy issues still at a preliminary stage.

8.3.7 Governance Reform

Important progress was made in the reform of the Fund's governance in 2006-08, including the initiation of a process to realign members' voting power (see Country Representation). However, enhancing the Fund's legitimacy and effectiveness must also deal with the question of whether the significant changes since the establishment of the Fund require reform of the institutional framework through which members' voting power is actually exercised. Among other things, this requires careful consideration of the respective roles and responsibilities of the Board of Governors, the IMFC, the Executive Board, and IMF management.

Managing Director Dominique Strauss-Kahn appointed in September 2008 a committee of eminent persons to assess the adequacy of the IMF's current framework for decision making and advise on any modifications that might enable the institution to fulfill its global mandate more effectively. The eight-person committee, chaired by Trevor Manuel, Minister of Finance of South Africa, reported its findings in March 2009.

8.3.8 Functions of IMF

The IMF's fundamental mission is to help ensure stability in the international system. It does so in three ways: keeping track of the global economy and the economies of member countries; lending to countries with balance of payments difficulties; and giving practical help to members.

8.3.9 Surveillance

When a country joins the IMF, it agrees to subject its economic and financial policies to the scrutiny of the international community. It also makes a commitment to pursue policies that are conducive to orderly economic growth and reasonable price stability, to avoid manipulating exchange rates for unfair competitive advantage, and to provide the IMF with data about its economy. The IMF's regular monitoring of economies and associated provision of policy advice is intended to identify weaknesses that are causing or could lead to financial or economic instability. This process is known as surveillance.

8.3.9.1 Country surveillance

Country surveillance is an ongoing process that culminates in regular (usually annual) comprehensive consultations with individual member countries, with discussions in between as needed. The consultations are known as "Article IV consultations" because they are required by Article IV of the IMF's Articles of Agreement. During an Article IV consultation, an IMF team of economists visits a country to assess economic and financial developments and discuss the country's economic and financial policies with government and central bank officials. IMF staff missions also often meet with parliamentarians and representatives of business, labor unions, and civil society.

The team reports its findings to IMF management and then presents them for discussion to the Executive Board, which represents all of the IMF's member countries. A summary of the Board's views is subsequently transmitted to the country's government. In this way, the views of the global community and the lessons of international experience are brought to bear on national policies. Summaries of most discussions are released in Public Information Notices and are posted on the IMF's web site, as are most of the country reports prepared by the staff.

In June 2007 the IMF's Executive Board adopted a comprehensive policy statement on surveillance. The 2007 Decision on Bilateral Surveillance over Member's Policies, complements Article IV of the IMF's Articles of Agreement and introduces the concept of external stability as an organizing principle for bilateral surveillance. This means that the main focus of the discussions between the IMF and country officials is whether there are risks to the economy's domestic and external stability that would call for adjustments to that country's economic or financial policies.

8.3.9.2 Regional surveillance

Regional surveillance involves examination by the IMF of policies pursued under currency unions–including the euro area, the West African Economic and Monetary Union, the Central African Economic and Monetary Community, and the Eastern Caribbean Currency Union. Regional economic outlook reports are also prepared to discuss economic developments and key policy issues in Asia Pacific, Europe, Middle East and Central Asia, Sub-Saharan Africa, and the Western Hemisphere.

8.3.9.3 Global surveillance

Global surveillance entails reviews by the IMF's Executive Board of global economic trends and developments. The main reviews are based on the *World Economic Outlook* reports and the *Global Financial Stability Report*, which covers developments, prospects, and policy issues in international financial markets. Both reports are published twice a year, with updates being provided on a quarterly basis. In addition, the Executive Board holds more frequent informal discussions on world economic and market developments.

The IMF also has the option of holding multilateral consultations, involving smaller groups of countries, to foster debate and develop policy actions designed to address problems of global or regional importance. In 2006, multilateral consultations brought together China, euro area countries, Japan, Saudi Arabia, and the United States to discuss global economic imbalances.

The IMF shares its expertise with member countries by providing technical assistance and training in a wide range of areas, such as central banking, monetary and exchange rate policy, tax policy and administration, and official statistics. The objective is to help improve the design and implementation of members' economic policies, including by strengthening skills in institutions such as finance ministries, central banks, and statistical agencies. The IMF has also given advice to countries that have had to reestablish government institutions following severe civil unrest or war.

In 2008, the IMF embarked on an ambitious reform effort to enhance the impact of its technical assistance. The reforms emphasize better prioritization, enhanced performance measurement, more transparent costing and stronger partnerships with donors.

8.3.9.4 Beneficiaries of technical assistance

Technical assistance is one of the IMF's core activities. It is concentrated in critical areas of macroeconomic policy where the Fund has the greatest comparative advantage. Thanks to its near-universal membership, the IMF's technical assistance program is informed by experience and knowledge gained across diverse regions and countries at different levels of development.

About 80 per cent of the IMF's technical assistance goes to low- and lower-middle-income countries, in particular in sub-Saharan Africa and Asia. Post-conflict countries are major beneficiaries. The IMF is also providing technical assistance aimed at strengthening the architecture of the international financial system, building capacity to design and implement poverty-reducing and growth programs, and Helping Heavily Indebted Poor Countries (HIPC) in debt reduction and management.

8.3.9.5 Types of technical assistance

The IMF's technical assistance takes different forms, according to needs, ranging from long-term hands-on capacity building to short-notice policy support in a financial crisis. Technical assistance is delivered in a variety of ways. IMF staff may visit member countries to advise government and central bank officials on specific issues, or the IMF may provide resident specialists on a short- or a long-term basis. Technical assistance is integrated with country reform agendas as well as the IMF's surveillance and lending operations.

The IMF is providing an increasing part of its technical assistance through regional centers located in Gabon, Mali, and Tanzania for Africa; in Barbados for the Caribbean; in Lebanon for the Middle East; and in Fiji for the Pacific Islands. As part of its reform program, the IMF is planning to open four more regional technical assistance centers in Africa, Latin America and Central Asia. The IMF also offers training courses for government and central bank officials of member countries at its headquarters in Washington, D.C., and at regional training centers in Austria, Brazil, China, India, Singapore, Tunisia and the United Arab Emirates.

8.3.10 Members' Quotas and Voting Power, and Board of Governors

Table showing the top 20 member countries in terms of voting power (2, 216, 193 votes in total):

IMF member country	Quota: Millions Of SDRs	Quota: percentage of total	Governor	Alternate Governor	Votes: number	Votes: percentage of total
United States	37149.3	17.09	Timothy F. Geithner	Ben Bernanke	371743	16.79
Japan	13312.8	6.13	Kaoru Yosano	Masaaki Shirakawa	133378	6.02
Germany	13008.2	5.99	Axel A. Weber	Peer Steinbrück	130332	5.88
France	10738.5	4.94	Christine Lagarde	Christian Noyer	107635	4.86
United Kingdom	10738.5	4.94	Alistair Darling	Mervyn King	107635	4.86
China	8090.1	3.72	Zhou Xiaochuan	Hu Xiaolian	81151	3.66
Italy	7055.5	3.25	Giulio Tremonti	Mario Draghi	70805	3.2
Saudi Arabia	6985.5	3.21	Ibrahim Al-Assaf	A. Hamad Al-Sayari	70105	3.17
Canada	6369.2	2.93	Jim Flaherty	Mark Carney	63942	2.89
Russian Federation	5945.4	2.74	Aleksei Kudrin	Sergey Ignatiev	59704	2.7
Netherlands	5162.4	2.38	Nout Wellink	L.B.J. van Geest	51874	2.34
Belgium	4605.2	2.12	Guy Quaden	Jean-Pierre Arnoldi	46302	2.09
India	4158.2	1.91	Pranab Mukherjee	D. Subbarao	41832	1.89
Switzerland	3458.5	1.59	Jean-Pierre Roth	Hans-Rudolf Merz	34835	1.57
Australia	3236.4	1.49	Wayne Swan	Ken Henry	32614	1.47
Mexico	3152.8	1.45	Agustín Carstens	Guillermo Ortiz	31778	1.43
Spain	3048.9	1.40	Pedro Solbes	Miguel Fernández Ordóñez	30739	1.39
Brazil	3036.1	1.40	Guido Mantega	Henrique de Campos Meirelles	30611	1.38
Korea, South	2927.3	1.35	Okyu Kwon	Seong Tae Lee	29523	1.33
Venezuela	2659.1	1.22	Gastón Parra Luzardo	Rodrigo Cabeza Morales	26841	1.21
Remaining 165 countries	60081.4	29.14	Respective	Respective	637067	28.78

Note: The 27 member states of the European Union have a combined vote of 710,786 (32.07%).

Source: www.imf.org

8.3.11 Special Drawing Rights (SDRs)

The SDR, or Special Drawing Right, is an international reserve asset that member countries can add to their foreign currency and gold reserves and use for payments requiring foreign exchange. Its value is set daily using a basket of four major currencies: the euro, Japanese yen, pound sterling, and U.S. dollar.

The IMF introduced the SDR in 1969 because of concern that the stock and prospective growth of international reserves might not be sufficient to support the expansion of world trade. (The main reserve assets at the time were gold and U.S. dollars.) The SDR was introduced as a supplementary reserve asset, which the IMF could "allocate" periodically to members when the need arose, and cancel, as necessary.

IMF member countries may use SDRs in transactions among themselves, with 16 "institutional" holders of SDRs, and with the IMF. The SDR is also the IMF's unit of account. A number of other international and regional organizations and international conventions use it as a unit of account, or as the basis for a unit of account. The SDR is an international reserve asset, created by the IMF in 1969 to supplement its member countries' official reserves. Its value is based on a basket of four key international currencies, and SDRs can be exchanged for freely usable currencies. With a general SDR allocation taking effect on August 28 and a special allocation on September 9, 2009, the amount of SDRs will increase from SDR 21.4 billion to SDR 204.1 billion (currently equivalent to about $317 billion).

8.3.11.1 The role of the SDR

The SDR was created by the IMF in 1969 to support the Bretton Woods fixed exchange rate system. A country participating in this system needed official reserves—government or central bank holdings of gold and widely accepted foreign currencies—that could be used to purchase the domestic currency in foreign exchange markets, as required to maintain its exchange rate. But the international supply of two key reserve assets—gold and the U.S. dollar—proved inadequate for supporting the expansion of world trade and financial development that was taking place. Therefore, the international community decided to create a new international reserve asset under the auspices of the IMF.

However, only a few years later, the Bretton Woods system collapsed and the major currencies shifted to a floating exchange rate regime. In addition, the growth in international capital markets facilitated borrowing by creditworthy governments. Both of these developments lessened the need for SDRs.

The SDR is neither a currency, nor a claim on the IMF. Rather, it is a potential claim on the freely usable currencies of IMF members. Holders of SDRs can obtain these currencies in exchange for their SDRs in two ways: first, through the arrangement of voluntary exchanges between members; and second, by the IMF designating members with strong external positions to purchase SDRs from members with weak external positions. In addition to its role as a supplementary reserve asset, the SDR, serves as the unit of account of the IMF and some other international organizations.

8.3.11.2 Basket of currencies determines the value of the SDR

The value of the SDR was initially defined as equivalent to 0.888671 grams of fine gold—which, at the time, was also equivalent to one U.S. dollar. After the collapse of the Bretton Woods system in 1973, however, the SDR was redefined as a basket of currencies, today consisting of the euro, Japanese yen, pound sterling and U.S. dollar. The U.S. dollar-value of the SDR is posted daily on the IMF's website. It is calculated as the sum of specific amounts of the four currencies valued in U.S. dollars, on the basis of exchange rates quoted at noon each day in the London market.

The basket composition is reviewed every five years by the Executive Board to ensure that it reflects the relative importance of currencies in the world's trading and financial systems. In the most recent review (in November 2005), the weights of the currencies in the SDR basket were revised based on the value of the exports of goods and services and the amount of reserves denominated in the respective currencies which were held by other members of the IMF. These changes became effective on January 1, 2006. The next review will take place in late 2010.

8.3.11.3 The SDR interest rate

The SDR interest rate provides the basis for calculating the interest charged to members on regular (non-concessional) IMF loans, the interest paid and charged to members on their SDR holdings, and the interest paid to members on a portion of their quota subscriptions. The SDR interest rate is determined weekly and is based on a weighted average of representative interest rates on short-term debt in the money markets of the SDR basket currencies.

8.3.11.4 SDR allocations to IMF members

Under its Articles of Agreement, the IMF may allocate SDRs to members in proportion to their IMF quotas. Such an allocation provides each member with a costless asset. However, if a member's SDR holdings rise above its allocation, it earns interest on the excess; conversely, if it holds fewer SDRs than allocated, it pays interest on the shortfall.

There are two kinds of allocations:

8.3.11.5 General allocations of SDRs.

General allocations have to be based on a long-term global need to supplement existing reserve assets. Decisions to allocate SDRs have been made three times. The first allocation was for a total amount of SDR 9.3 billion, distributed in 1970-72 in yearly installments. The second allocation, for SDR 12.1 billion, was distributed in 1979–81 in yearly installments.

The third general allocation was approved on August 7, 2009 for an amount of SDR 161.2 billion and will take place on August 28, 2009. The allocation would mean a simultaneous increase in eligible members' SDR holdings and in their cumulative SDR allocation by about 74.13 per cent of their quota.

8.3.11.6 Special allocations of SDRs.

A proposal for a special one-time allocation of SDRs was approved by the IMF's Board of Governors in September 1997 through the proposed Fourth

Amendment of the Articles of Agreement. Its intent is to enable all members of the IMF to participate in the SDR system on an equitable basis and correct for the fact that countries that joined the Fund after 1981—more than one-fifth of the current IMF membership—have never received an SDR allocation. This allocation would increase members' cumulative SDR allocations by SDR 21.5 billion using a common benchmark ratio as described in the amendment.

The Fourth Amendment became effective for all members on August 10, 2009 when the Fund certified that at least three-fifths of the IMF membership (112 members) with 85 per cent of the total voting power accepted it. On August 5, 2009, the United States joined 133 other members in supporting the Amendment. The special allocation will be implemented on September 9, 2009.

8.3.12 India's Relations with the International Monetary Fund

I. Membership Status: Joined: December 27, 1945; *Article VIII*

II. General Resources Account:	**SDR Million**	**%Quota**
Quota	4,158.20	100.00
Fund holdings of currency	3,364.27	80.91
Reserve Tranche Position	794.00	19.09
Lending to the Fund		
Holdings Exchange Rate		
III. SDR Department:	**SDR Million**	**%Allocation**
Net cumulative allocation	681.17	100.00
Holdings	0.33	0.05

India and the IMF has a positive relationship. The IMF has provided financial assistance to India, which has helped in boosting the country's economy. The IMF praised the country for it was able to avoid the Asian Financial Crisis in 1999 and was also able to maintain the average rate of growth of its economy. The Managing Director of International Monetary Fund Rodrigo De Rato visited India in May 2005. In 2005, the IMF said that the budget of India is very positive for it points that the economy of the country will grow at the rate of 6.7%.

IMF has played an important role in Indian Economy. IMF has provided economic assistance from time to time to India and has provided appropriate consultancy in determination of various policies in the country. Till 1970, India was among the first five nations having the highest quota with IMF and due to this status India was allotted a permanent place in Executive Board of Directors. India has taken loans in foreign currencies from IMF for improving its balance of payments imbalances. India has also taken technical consultancy for solving its internal economic problems. The expert groups of the IMF have visited India on various times.

International Monetary Fund said that the reasons behind the economy growth of India are that the RBI has been able to control inflation and has handled its monetary policies very skillfully. The IMF has suggested that India can become a financial super power by bringing in more reforms in its economic policies that will increase its growth rate to 8%.

8.3.13 The Current Relationship between IMF and India

The relationship between the IMF and India has grown strong over the years. In fact, the country has turned into a creditor to the IMF and has stopped taking loans from it. India and IMF must continue to boost their relationship this way, as it will prove to be advantageous for both. INDIA'S CURRENT QUOTA IN THE IMF IS SDR (SPECIAL DRAWING RIGHTS) 4,158.20 MILLION IN THE TOTAL QUOTA OF SDR 213 BILLION, GIVING IT A SHARE HOLDING OF 1.91 %. HOWEVER, BASED ON VOTING SHARE, INDIA (TOGETHER WITH ITS CONSTITUENCY COUNTRIES VIZ. BANGLADESH, BHUTAN AND SRI LANKA) IS RANKED 21st IN THE LIST OF 24 CONSTITUENCY.

The break-up of SDR 4158.2 million quota of India is given below:

8.3.13.1 India's quota position in the fund (as of June 30, 2007)

	SDR MILLION	% QUOTA
QUOTA	4,158.20	100.00
FUND HOLDING OF CURRENCY	3,852.36	92.64
RESERVE POSITION	305.87	7.36

8.4 INTERNATIONAL BANK FOR RECONSTRUCTION AND DEVELOPMENT (IBRD)

8.4.1 Introduction

IBRD was established in 1945 and has 185 members at present. IBRD aims to reduce poverty in Middle Income countries and creditworthy poorer countries by promoting sustainable developments through loans, guarantees and non-lending services which include analytical advisory services. The IBRD is owned by the member countries whose voting power is linked to its capital subscription based on the country's relative economic strength. IBRD funds are semi-concessional and are of longer maturity and therefore, cheaper than commercial external borrowings. Government of India utilizes IBRD loans primarily for infrastructure projects. The International Bank for Reconstruction and Development (IBRD) aims to reduce poverty in middle-income and creditworthy poorer countries by promoting sustainable development through loans, guarantees, risk management products, and analytical and advisory services. Established in 1944 as the original institution of the World Bank Group, IBRD is structured like a cooperative that is owned and operated for the benefit of its 186 member countries.

IBRD raises most of its funds on the world's financial markets and has become one of the most established borrowers since issuing its first bond in 1947. The income that IBRD has generated over the years has allowed it to fund development activities and to ensure its financial strength, which enables it to borrow at low cost and offer clients good borrowing terms.

Each institution plays a different but collaborative role to advance the vision of an inclusive and sustainable globalization. The IBRD focuses on middle income and creditworthy poor countries, while IDA focuses on the poorest countries in the world. Together we provide low-interest loans, interest-free credits and grants to developing countries for a wide array of purposes that include investments in education, health, public administration, infrastructure, financial and private sector development, agriculture, and environmental and natural resource management.

At its Annual Meeting in September 2006, the World Bank – with the encouragement of its shareholder governments – committed to make further improvements to the services it provides its members. To meet the increasingly sophisticated demands of middle-income countries, IBRD is overhauling financial and risk management products, broadening the provision of freestanding knowledge services and making it easier for clients to deal with the Bank.

Shareholding: India holds 44,795 shares amounting to US $ 5,403.8 million out of the total IBRD subscription of 15,72,661 shares amounting to US $ 1,89,718 million. The voting power of India is 2.78%.

Sectors: The commitments by IBRD are against projects in various sectors like transport, energy, urban infrastructure (including water & sanitation) etc.

Terms of lending: On September 27, 2007 the World Bank Board has approved reduction and simplification in IBRD (International Bank for Reconstruction and Development) loan pricing which would be applicable to all new loans signed on or after May 16, 2007. India presently borrows from IBRD as Variable Spread Loans (VSL).

The new conditions of VSLs are as follows:

(*i*)	Current Interest rate	LIBOR FLAT
(*ii*)	Contractual spread	0.30%
(*iii*)	Front-end fee	0.25%
(*iv*)	Commitment fee	NIL
(*v*)	Repayment period	20 YEARS INCLUSIVE OF GRACE PERIOD OF 5 YEARS

The change in loan pricing for IBRD loans is for all loans given by the World Bank to member countries, and not India-specific. Government of India has advocated a review of IBRD loan pricing and chose to support the above pricing option out of the three options made available by the World Bank management to all member countries.

8.4.2 Objectives of IBRD

According to the Clause-I of the Agreement made at the time of establishment of World Bank. The basic objectives of IBRD are:

- To provide long-run capital to its member countries for economic reconstruction and development
- To rehabilitate war ruined economics
- To finance productive efforts according to peacetime requirements
- To develop resources and production facilities in underdeveloped countries

- To induce long-run capital investment for assuring balanced development of International Trade
- To promote capital investment in member countries by providing guarantee on private loans or capital investment
- If private capital is not available even after providing guarantee, then World Bank provides loans for productive activities on considerate conditions
- To provide guarantee for loans granted to small and large units and other projects of member countries
- To ensure the implementation of development projects so as to bring about a smooth transference from a war-time to peace economy.

8.4.3 Functions of IBRD

The IBRD, also called the World Bank, performs the following functions:

1. To assist in the reconstruction and development of territories of its members by facilitating the investment of capital for productive purpose, and the encouragement of the development of productive facilities and resources in less developed countries.
2. To promote private foreign investment by means of guarantees on participation in loans and other investment made by private investors, and when capital is not available on reasonable terms, to supplement private investment by providing finance for productive purpose out of its own resources or from borrowed funds.
3. To promote the long-range balanced growth of international trade and the maintenance of equilibrium in the balance of payments of member countries by encouraging international investment for the development of their productive resources, thereby assisting in raising productivity, the standard of living and conditions of workers in their territories.
4. To arrange the loans made or guaranteed by it in relation to international loans through other channels so that more useful and urgent small and large projects are .dealt with first.

8.4.4 Memberships

The members of the International Monetary Fund are the members of the IBRD. It had 181 members in June 1996. If a country resigns its membership, it is required to pay back all loans with interest on due dates. If the Bank incurs a financial loss in the year in which a member resigns, it is required to pay its share of the loss on demand.

8.4.5 Organisation of IBRD

Like the IMF, the IBRD has a three-tier structure with a President, Executive Directors and Board of Governors. At present, Lewis Preston is the President of the World Bank Group (IBRD, IDA and IFC). He was elected by the Bank's Executive Directors whose number is twenty-one. Of these, 5 are appointed by the five largest shareholders of the World Bank. They are the US, UK, West

Germany, France and Japan. The remaining 16 are elected by the Board of Governors. There are also Alternate Directors. The first five belong to the same permanent member countries to which the Executive Directors belong. But the remaining Alternate Directos are elected from among me group of countries who cast their votes to choose the 16 Executive Directors belonging to their regions.

The President of the World Bank presides over the meetings of the Board of Executive Directors regularly once a month. The Executive Directors decide about policy within the framework of the Articles of Agreement. They consider and decide on the loan and credit proposals made by the President. They also present to the Board of Governors at its annual meetings audited accounts, an administrative budget, and the Annual Report on the operations and policies of the Bank. The President has a staff of more than 6,000 persons who carryon the working of the World Bank. He is assisted by a number of Senior Vice-Presidents and Directors of various departments and regions. The Board of Governors is the supreme body. Every member country appoints one Governor and an Alternate Governor for a period of five years. The voting power of each Governor is related to the financial contribution of its government.

8.4.6 Capital Structure

The IBRD started with an authorised capital of $ 10 billion divided' into 1,00,000 shares of $ 1,00,000. Of this, $ 9,400 million was actually subscribed. On 30 June 1985 the authorised capital stock of the IBRD comprised 7,16,500 authorise 4 shares of the par.value of SDR 1,00,000 each. In July 1992, the total authorised Bank capital was $ 184.1 billion with a capital increase of $ 9.3 billion or 77,159 shares provided to the republics of the former Soviet Union.

8.4.7 Funding Strategy

The IBRD's funding strategy has the following four basic objectives: The first is to ensure the *availability of funds* to the Bank. For this purpose, the IBRD seeks to maintain unutilised access to funds in the markets in which it borrows. The second objective is to *minimise the effective cost* of those funds to its borrowers. This is done through the currency mix of its borrowings and the time of borrowings. In the former case, it tends to maximise borrowings in currencies with low nominal interest rates. The time of borrowings is manipulated in two ways:

(A) When interest rates are expected to rise, the Bank seeks to increase its borrowings, and

(B) When interest rates are expecting to fall, it seeks to defer borrowings. The third objective is to *control volatility in net income and overall* loan *charges.* For this purpose, the Bank started in July 1982 a pool-based variable lending rate system that uniformly adjusts interest charges applicable to the outstanding balance on all loans made under it. The existing loans were not affects by this lending system. When the majority of loans and borrowir.gs are incorporating into the new lending rate system in future, the volatility of interest rates will be much reduces. The fourth objective of the funding strategy is to provide an

appropriate degree of *maturity transformation* between its borrowing and lending. Maturity transformation refers to the Bank's capacity to lend at longer maturities than it borrows. At the same time, it provides its borrowers with a modest degree of maturity transformation.

8.4.8 Borrowing and Lending Activities

The IBRD is a corporate institution whose capital is subscribe by its members. It finances its lending operations primarily from its own medium and long-term borrowings in the international capital markets, and currency swap agreements (CSA). Under the CSA proceeds of a borrowing country are converted into a different currency, and simultaneously, a forward exchange agreement is ex-ecuted providing for a schedule of future exchanges of the two currencies in order to recover the currency converted. The effect of currency swaps is to transform the cost of original borrowing to a cost, which reflects the market yield of the currency obtained in the conversion.

The Bank also borrows under the Discount-Note Programme. First, it places bonds and notes directly with its member governments, government agencies and central banks. Second,. it offers issues to investors and in the public markets through investing banking firms, merchant banks and commercial banks.

The IBRD has evolved two new borrowing instruments. First, Central Bank Facility (CBF) is a one-year, US dollar dominated facility for borrowing from official sources, particularly central banks. It is design to reverse the declining trend in the IBRD's borrowings from such sources since the 1970s. In 1984, the Executive Directors authorised the Bank to borrow under the Facility up to $ 750 million with a one-year maturity plus funds maturity within a month under the Facility. Second, borrowings in Floating Rate Notes (FRNs) are mean to help the IBRD to meet some of the objectives of its funding strategy. The FRN market enables the Bank to gain access to a set of investors like commercial banks and certain other financial institutions, which have not traditionally bought IBRD notes. The FRNs carry a medium/long-term maturity. A substantial amount of its resources also comes from its retained earnings and the flow of payments on its loans.

The Bank lends to member countries in any of the following ways:

- by marketing or participating in loans out of its own funds;
- by making' or participating in direct loans out of funds raised in the market of a member or otherwise borrowed by the Bank;
- by guaranteeing in whole or in part loans made by private investors through the usual investment channels.

The total amount outstanding of participating in loans', direct loans and guarantees should not exceed 100 per cent of its unimpaired subscribed capital, reserves and surplus. It guarantees, participates in or makes loans to its members on the following conditions:

(*i*) If it is satisficd that in the prevailing market conditions the borrower would' be unable to obtain the loan under conditions which in the opinion of trt; Bank are reasonable to the borrower.

(*ii*) Loans are for specific projects of reconstruction or development, except in special circumstances.

(*iii*) If the member in whose territory the project is located is not itself the borrower, the member or its central bank fully guarantees the repayment of the principal, the payment of interest and other charges on the loan.

(*iv*) The project for which the loan is required has been recommended by a competent committee in the form of a written report after a careful study of the proposal.

(*v*) The borrower or the guarantor is in a position to meet its obligations' under the loan.

In 1981, the Executive Board of the Bank approved modifications in IBRD repayment terms which' include shifting repayment of new loans for low income countries to annuity, extension of grace period through fiscal year 1991 on new loans to middle income countries from 3 to 5 years and review of repayment terms for middle income countries within 3 years.

8.4.9 Facilities Provided by IBRD to its Member Countries

The bank provides the following facilities to member countries:

8.4.9.1 Structural Adjustment Facility (SAF)

Since 1985, the IBRD has introduced SAF to borrowing countries in order to reduce their balance of payments deficits while maintaining or regaining their economic growth. SAF funds are used to, finance general imports with a few agreed exceptions such as luxury and military imports. SAFs are released in two parts and are based on stiffer conditions laid down by the Bank. The Bank aims at providing support to programmes running from 5 to 7 years through a series of up to five SAFs to a borrowing country.

8.4.9.2 Enhanced Structural Adjustment Facility (ESAF)

In December 1937, the Bank has set up the ESAF to increase the availability of concessional resources to low-income member countries. It provides new concessional resources totaling SDR 6 billion which will be finance by special loans and contributions from developed and OPEC countries. Like the SAP, ESAF is meant to help the borrowing countries reduce their balance of payments deficits and encourage growth. Its financial terms are similar to the SAP. The interest rate is 0.5 per cent with repayments in ten semi-annual installments beginning after 5-1/2 years of disbursements.

The Bank makes medium and long-term loans unusually running up to the completion 10 of the project. Loans generally have a grace period of 5 years and repayable over 20 years or less. The interest rate charged on loans by the Bank calculating in accordance with a guideline dated to its cost of borrowing. Therefore, loans are at variable interest rates. It charges an annual commitment charge of 0.75 per cent on undistributed balances and a one-time front-end fee on the amount of loan.

The Bank's lending operations for two decades since its inception were concentrated heavily upon capital infrastructural projects such as power generation and distribution, railways and roads, ports, telecommunications, major irrigation works; etc. Since the 1970s, loans for infrastructural investments have come down. Instead, it has begun to finance changes in the educational system in the developing countries, to establish institutions for the financing of industrial investments and provision of technical assistance in the selection and appraisal of industrial projects, and to help in the preparation of agricultural projects. Its present development strategy lays more emphasis on investments that can directly affect the welfare of the poor people of the developing countries by increasing their productivity and standard of living. Towards this loan, it has been financing projects for agriculture and rural development, education, family planning, nutrition, low-cost housing, drinking water and sewerage. The distribution of IBRD funds is made by the country-income group and by sector to the developing countries.

8.4.9.3 *Special Action Programme (SAP)*

The Special Action Programme (SAP) has started in 1983 to strengthen the IBRD's ability to assist member countries in adjusting to the current economic environment. It has four major elements:

1. An expansion in lending for high-priority operations that support structural adjustment, policy' changes, production for export, fuller use of existing capacity, and the maintenance of crucial infrastructure.
2. The Bank accelerates disbursements under existing and new investment commitments to ensure timely implementation of high priority projects.
3. The Bank Expand advisory services on the design and implementation of appropriate policies include reviews of state enterprises studies to strengthen development-orientation and project implementation capabilities, studies to increase the mobilization of domestic resources, reviews of Incentives for export diversification, and exploration of ways to strengthen debt- management capabilities.
4. The Bank makes efforts by other donors for fast disbursing assistance in support of programmes of the Bank and IMP.

8.4.9.4 *Other activities*

The other activities of the IBRD include training, technical assistance, inter-organizational cooperation, economic research and studies, operations evaluation, and settlement of investment disputes of its members.

The Bank set up a staff college in 1956, known as the Economic Development Institute (EDI) for training senior officials of the member developing countries. It helps them to improve the management of their economies and to increase the efficiency of their investment programmes. Its training material ranges from macroeconomic planning, pricing, and development policies to management of agricultural research, rural health care, industrial policy, energy policy, railway management, etc. The EDI also organizes seminars in

Washington and in different regions of the world in cooperation with regional institutes.

Technical assistance has been an integral part of the Bank operation since its inception. It consists of two broad categories: (*i*) engineering-related, such as feasibility studies, engineering design, and construction supervision; and (*ii*) institution-related, such as diagnostic policy and institutional studies, management support and training. The primary way of providing technical assistance is through loans made for specific sectors and in components of loans made for capital infrastructures. Such technical assistance includes fund for supervision, implementation and engineering services, energy, power, transportation, water supply, industry, etc. To meet gaps in project preparation and for institution building, the bank advances funds to prospective buyers through Project Preparation Facility (PPF) created in 1975. The Bank also serves as executing agency for projects financed by the United Nations Development Programme (UNDP). Further, it provides such technical assistance as short-term training, advisers of technology service on evaluation and monitoring panels, and demographic, economic advice on project preparation.

The IBRD is also engaged in inter-organizational cooperation. The IBRD and other international organizations cooperation between them is based on the formal agreements such as the Cooperative Programmes between it and the FAO, the UNESCO, the WHO, the GATT, the UNCTAD, the United Nations Environment Programme (UNEP), the UNDP, the United Nations Industrial Development Organisation (UNIDO), the International Fund for Agricultural Development (IFAD), the ILO, the African Development Bank, the Asian Development Bank, etc.

The Bank devotes roughly 3 per cent of its administrative budget to economic and social research. The research programme was started in 1971. Since then 165 research projects have been completed, while 180 are in progress. In addition, there are more than 100 generally smaller research studies undertaken at the discretion of the Bank departments. In 1983, the Bank established a Research Department for the purpose of review of the projects and allocation of optimised budget for economic and social research.

The Bank helps borrowers in the post-evaluation of their Bank assisted projects. It has set up the Operations Evaluation Department (OED) for this purpose. Projects reviewed are also subject to performance audit by the OED staff. Members of borrowers' staff visit this Department for seeking help in the preparation of project completion report. The EDI also includes a course devoted to monitoring and evaluation by borrowers which is conducted by it in collaboration with EDI staff.

The Bank has set up the International Centre of Settlement of Investment Disputes (ICSID) between States and Nationals of other States. All members of the Bank have signed and deposited their instruments of ratification pertaining to this. The Bank has successfully mediated in solving many international investment disputes such as the River Water Dispute between India and Pakistan, and of the Suez Canal between Egypt and the UK.

The Bank's overall performance must be judged not just on its lending but on its success in providing advice and technical assistance: The Bank is laying greater emphasis on developing human resources such as education, population, health and nutrition, and on environment. The Bank also provides assistance to the private sector in such areas as financial, power, telecommunications, information technology, oil and gas, and industry and mining.

The World Bank conditionality for lending are:

1. An unflinching commitment towards economic stability so as to reduce inflation and elicits;
2. An efficient regulatory mechanism ensuring transparent policies and depoliticized environment;
3. Adequate risk management;
4. Provision for long term finance; and
5. Increase in the share of the private sector in the country's GDP in the Bank meeting of 1996, the Bank President declared that countries plagued by corruption would not be liable to receive Bank assistance in future. In the fiscal year 1996, the World Bank disbursements totaled $ 13.4 billion and the IDA disbursements were $ 5.9 billion.

8.4.10 Critical Appraisal

The IBRD has been quite successful in achieving its principal objective of reconstruction and development. It helped in the reconstruction of Europe after its destruction in the Second World War. It has also been helping the developed and developing countries alike in the process of growth. Since the 1970s, it has been lending more to developing countries not only for infrastructure investment but also for raising the productivity and standard of living of the poor people of the total IBRD loans of $ 13.4 billion in the fiscal year 1996, member countries. In Latin America and Caribbean received 15 per cent, in Asia 33 per cent, in Africa 15 per cent and in Europe, Middle East Moreover, and North America 2.9 per cent.

8.4.11 India Relationship with IBRD

India is one of the founder members of the Bank and held a permanent seat on its' Board of Executive Directors for a number of years. The Bank has been assisting India in its planned economic development by granting loans, conducting field surveys, rendering expert advice, sending missions, study teams, and training Indian personnel at the EDI. In addition, a Chief Mission of the Bank at New Delhi represents it for monitoring and consultations on its aided projects in India. India has been the largest receiver of the World Bank assistance since August 1949. The Bank's disbursements to India during fiscal year 1996 amounted to $ 1,309 million. Against it, India paid the Bank $ 1,149 million for past loans and $ 884 million as interest, making the net receipts as minus (–) $ 723 million from the World Bank. The World Bank has been assisting India in such projects as development of ports, oil exploration including the Bombay High and gas power projects, aircrafts, coal, iron, aluminum, fertilizers, railway modernization, technical assistance, industrial development finance corporations, etc.

India Development Forum has replaced the Aid India Consortium of twelve developed countries, which was giving aid to India for its development plans at the instance of the World Bank, since 1995. The Bank also helped India to solve amicably its river water dispute with Pakistan.

India has thus gained much for being the member of the World Bank for the development of agricultural, industry, energy and transport. However, with reduced availability from the IDA, India will have to borrow more from the Bank in future. This will entail a heavy burden on India's resources for the terms of World Bank loans are much harder than of the IDA credits.

8.4.12 Recent Development

The World Bank Group extended loans, credits, grants, equity investments, and guarantees totaling over US$5.5 billion to South Asia in fiscal year 2008. The funding supports 79 new projects designed to overcome poverty and boost growth through practical plans enhancing the business and investment environment and empowering poor people. Contributing to this strong support was: US$1.491 billion from the International Bank for Reconstruction and Development (IBRD), which provides financing, risk management products and other financial services; US$2.756 billion from the International Development Association (IDA), which provides interest-free loans and grants; US$1.26 billion from the International Finance Corporation (IFC), which makes equity investments and provides loans, guarantees, and advisory services to private-sector business in developing countries; and US$36.6 million from the Multilateral Investment Guarantee Investment Agency (MIGA), the group's political risk insurance agency.

Globally, the World Bank Group committed US$38.2 billion in fiscal year 2008, up 11 per cent from fiscal year 2007. An important contribution during the fiscal year was the Bank Group's response to the food price crisis. It created a US$1.2 billion rapid financing facility with the first grants approved in FY08. More funds have subsequently been approved in the current financial year, including a US$8 million grant for Afghanistan, which supports the rehabilitation of around 500 small, traditional irrigation schemes, which are impart of the banks providing financial assistance scheme for the development and rehabilitation schemes for the countries.

India was the largest borrower from IBRD and IDA, accounting for US$2.154 billion, or nearly 10 per cent of total lending from these two institutions. IBRD in the year 2007-08 provides 1317.0 million of US dollars of assistance to India. Within South Asia, Bangladesh was the second largest borrower with US$753 million (IDA), followed by Pakistan at US$545 million (IDA/IBRD), and Nepal at US$380 million (IDA).

Many of the Bank's projects in the last fiscal year supported existing programs that are delivering results. Looking ahead the Bank will focus on crosscutting reforms such as governance and fiscal management, and continue addressing deficiencies in the region's investment climate, such as weak infrastructure, red tape, and corruption. It will also deepen its engagement in states where poverty is increasingly concentrated, such as Orissa and Bihar in India.

IBRD lending in the past year focused on helping India close its infrastructure gap, often cited as the greatest constraint to foreign investment. To help address the problem, the Bank provided a US$400 million loan for the Rampur Hydropower Project in the state of Himachal Pradesh that will provide renewable, low-carbon energy to India's overstretched northern electricity grid. It also extended a US$600 million loan to the Power Grid Corporation of India, backed by a guarantee from the Government of India, designed to increase reliable power exchange between states.

CHAPTER 9

Regional Economic Integration

9.1 INTRODUCTION

Economic integration is the integration of some countries who create opportunities among the member countries and to avoid the unnecessary competition. In this type of regional economic integration some countries make the integration to make free trade among the member countries so that flow of goods, services, labour, capital, technology etc. circulate easily among the member countries. These countries discriminate against the other nations of the world, which are not parties to the agreement, through imposition of tariff custom duties etc. The motive behind making regional economic integration differ from region to region and country to country. In the year 2003 there were 265 regional trade agreement had been notified to WTO.

C. Shiells* suggests some motives behind formulating the regional economic integration. These are:

1. To obtain economic benefits from achieving a more efficient production structure by exploiting economics of scale through spreading fixed costs over larger regional market, increased economic growth from foreign direct investment, learning from experience, etc.
2. To ensure increased security of market access for smaller countries by forming regional trading blocs with larger countries.
3. To pursue non-economic objectives such as strengthening political ties and managing migration flows.
4. To improve members bargaining strength in multilateral trade negotiations or to protest against the slow pace of trade negotiations.
5. To promote regional infant industries which cannot be viable without a protected regional market.
6. Finally, to prevent further damage to their trading strength due to further trade diversion from third countries.

(*Regional Trading Blocs; 'Trade Creating or Diverting', Finance and Development, 32 (1) 1995).

Briefly, it can be said that the regional integration is formulated to promote free trade within regions will produce benefits from trade to the party countries of regional integration. The different types of regional economic integration scheme differ among the party countries because they represent different levels of economic integration.

Generally, the integration is formulated among the countries who are neighbouring or similar economy, like SAARC etc. The reason behind is that due to neighbour of the country the transportation cost for goods will be less, the consumer taste and preferences may be similar etc. However, it is not the necessary to have specific geographical boundary.

9.2 DIFFERENT TYPES OF ECONOMIC INTEGRATION

The different types of economic integration generally formed by the different nations of the world. They are:

1. **Free Trade Area (FTA):** Under this type of economic integration the member countries make a free arrangement of trade among themselves. There were no restriction applied for the movement of goods and services among the member countries. The member countries impose high tariff against other nations who are not the member of the economic integration. For example, NAFTA (North American Free Trade, Associations), LAFTA (Latin American Free Trade Association) etc.
2. **Customs Union:** A custom union is that integration were the member countries abolish all the restrictions and barriers on trade among themselves and also charge a uniform tariff to the rest of the world. The member countries through 'Trade Creation' and 'Trade Diversion' favoured the member countries in trade. For example 'European Union'.
3. **Common Market:** The common market can be called as the extention of custom union. Under this the member countries not only remove the barrier among themselves but also they allows the factors of production to move freely among the member countries. A common market demands establish a significant degree of harmony and cooperation on monetary, fiscal employment, wages etc. For example, the MERCOSUR, of the south American grouping of Brazil, Argentina, Paraguay and Uruguay.
4. **Economic Union:** The economic union is the integration of some countries who mutually agreed for making a uniform policy regarding monetary and fiscal policy. The other feature of this type of integration is the similar of the common market. For example 'European Union'.
5. **Economic Integration:** The economic integration is characterised by the common external policy among the member countries. Under it a full economic union requires a common currency, harmonization, tax rates and a common monetary and fiscal policy. All the members bound by decisions of a supernational authority consisting of executive, judicial and legislative branches.

9.3 EUROPEAN UNION (EU)

The first step to form a group in Europe was begin with the establishment of European Coal and Steel Community (ECSC) on 10 August, 1952 on the basis of Paris agreement made on 18 April, 1951. The six nations sign for this agreement. These were: Belgium, France, West Germany, Italy, Luxemburg and Netherlands. The objectives of establishing ECSC was to improve employment and better living conditions among member countries by ensuring cooperative attitude for coal and steel trading. ECSC has played a very important role in establishing a common international market for coal and steel.

9.3.1 European Economic Community (EEC)

The six European countries who constituted the ECSC made a treaty in the year 1957 known as Rome Treaty. On the basis of this treaty they constitute the European Economic Community (EEC). It comes into existence on 1 January 1958. The aim of EEC was to ensure complete free trade among the member countries.* On 1 January 1973, Britain, Denmark Ireland, Greece, Spain and Portugal became its members. On 1 January 1995, Austria, Finland and Sweden join this organisation and the number of members countries increased to 15. In the Year 2005 ten nations officially joined world's largest regional economic community. They are Czech Republic, Slovakia, Hungary, Poland, Slovenia, Lithuania, Latvia, Estonia, Cyprus and Malta. The number of member increased to 25. The European Union now world's biggest trading entity. Its share about one-fourth of the global GDP. Its head quarter is at Brussels (Belgium).

- According to Article 2 of the Rome Treaty of 1957 the main object of EEC is:

"The community shall have its task, by setting up a common market, to promote throughout the community a harmonious development by economic activities, a continuous and balanced expansion an increase in stability and accelerated raising of the standard of living and closerive relations between the member states belonging to it."

9.3.2 European Free Trade Association (EFTA)

This trade association was established on 3 May, 1960 by seven countries at Stockholm (Sweden). These countries were Britain, Austria, Denmark, Norway, Sweden, Switzerland and Portugal. This free Trade Association was established with the view to curtail custom duties and other tariffs among member countries. The tariff was totally removed from the member countries till 31 December 1996. Another view point of this association was to establish a market in the West Europe by making an agreement with EEC. This was fulfilled in the year 1972. Another objective was to promote the World trade. The founder member countries of this association were known as 'outer seven'. The constitutes of EEC were known as 'Inner Six'. The Headquarter of the EFTA is at Geneva.

9.3.3 Constitution of European Union

The European Union was formally established when the Maastricht Treaty came into force on 1 November, 1993 and in 1995 Austria, Sweden and

Finland joined the newly established EU. In 2002, euro notes and coins replaced national currencies in twelve of the member states. Since then, the eurozone has increased to encompass sixteen countries, with Slovakia joining the eurozone on 1 January, 2009. In 2004, the EU saw its biggest enlargement to date when Malta, Cyprus, Slovenia, Estonia, Latvia, Lithuania, Poland, the Czech Republic, Slovakia, and Hungary joined the Union.

On 1 January, 2007, Romania and Bulgaria became the EU's newest members and Slovenia adopted the euro. In December of that year European leaders signed the Lisbon Treaty which was intended to replace the earlier, failed European Constitution, which never came into force after being rejected by French and Dutch voters. However, uncertainty clouds the prospects of the Lisbon Treaty's coming into force as result of its rejection by Irish voters in June, 2008. On 17 July, 2009, the Parliament of Iceland agreed to formally apply for EU membership and to begin talks for an agreement to be put to a referendum to the Icelandic voters. On 23 July, 2009 the Icelandic foreign minister formally submitted Iceland's application for membership to his Swedish counterpart.

The European Union is composed of 27 sovereign member states: Austria, Belgium, Bulgaria, Cyprus, the Czech Republic, Denmark, Estonia, Finland, France, Germany, Greece, Hungary, Ireland, Italy, Latvia, Lithuania, Luxembourg, Malta, the Netherlands, Poland, Portugal, Romania, Slovakia, Slovenia, Spain, Sweden, and the United Kingdom.

There are three official candidate countries, Croatia, Macedonia and Turkey, and Albania, Bosnia and Herzegovina, Montenegro, Serbia and Iceland are officially recognised as potential candidates. Kosovo is also listed as a potential candidate but the European Commission does not list it as an independent country because not all member states recognise it as an independent country separate from Serbia.

9.3.4 Criteria of Joining European Union

To join the EU a country must meet the Copenhagen criteria, defined at the 1993 Copenhagen European Council. These require a stable democracy that respects human rights and the rule of law; a functioning market economy capable of competition within the EU; and the acceptance of the obligations of membership, including EU law. Evaluation of a country's fulfilment of the criteria is the responsibility of the European Council. The current framework does not specify how a country could exit the Union, but the proposed Treaty of Lisbon contains a formal procedure for withdrawing.

Four Western European countries that have chosen not to join the EU have partly committed to the EU's economy and regulations: Iceland, Liechtenstein and Norway are a part of the single market through the European Economic Area, and Switzerland has similar ties through bilateral treaties. The relationships of the European microstates, Andorra, Monaco, San Marino and the Vatican include the use of the euro and other areas of co-operation.

9.3.5 European Union Governance

The presidency of the Council, which rotates twice per year, is currently held by Sweden.

The EU is often described as being divided into three areas of responsibility, called pillars. The original European Community policies form the first pillar, while the second consists of Common Foreign and Security Policy. The third pillar originally consisted of Justice and Home Affairs, however owing to changes introduced by the Amsterdam and Nice treaties, it currently consists of Police and Judicial Co-operation in Criminal Matters. Broadly speaking, the second and third pillars can be described as the intergovernmental pillars because the supranational institutions of the Commission, Parliament and the Court of Justice play less of a role or none at all, while the lead is taken by the intergovernmental Council of Ministers and the European Council. Most activities of the EU come under the first, Community pillar. This is mostly an economically oriented pillar and is where the supranational institutions have the most influence. Presently the Commission President is Mr. José Manuel Barroso.

The activities of the EU are regulated by a number of institutions and bodies. They carry out the tasks and policies set out for them in the treaties. The EU receives its political leadership from the European Council, which is composed of one representative per member state—either its head of state or head of government—plus the President of the Commission. Each member state's representative is assisted by its Foreign Minister. The Council uses its leadership role to sort out disputes which have arisen between member states and the institutions, and to resolve political crises and disagreements over controversial issues and policies.

The Council is headed by a rotating presidency, with every member state taking the helm of the EU for a period of six months during which that country's representatives chair meetings of the European Council and the Council of Ministers. The member state holding the presidency typically uses it to drive a particular policy agenda such as economic reform, reform of the EU itself, enlargement or furthering European integration. The Council usually meet four times a year at European Summits.

The European Council should not be mistaken for the Council of Europe, an international organisation independent from the EU.

9.3.6 European Union Structure

The European Commission acts as the EU's executive arm and is responsible for initiating legislation and the day-to-day running of the EU. It is intended to act solely in the interest of the EU as a whole, as opposed to the Council which consists of leaders of member states who reflect national interests. The commission is also seen as the motor of European integration. It is currently composed of 27 commissioners for different areas of policy, one from each member state. The President of the Commission and all the other commissioners are nominated by the Council. Appointment of the Commission President, and also the Commission in its entirety, have to be confirmed by Parliament.

The European Parliament forms one half of the EU's legislature. The 785 Members of the European Parliament (MEPs) are directly elected by EU citizens every five years. Although MEPs are elected on a national basis, they sit according to political groups rather than their nationality. Each country has a set number of seats. The Parliament and the Council form and pass legislation jointly, using co-decision, in certain areas of policy. This procedure will extend to many new areas under the proposed Treaty of Lisbon, and hence increase the power and relevance of the Parliament. The Parliament also has the power to reject or censure the Commission and the EU budget. The President of the European Parliament carries out the role of speaker in parliament and represents it externally. The president and vice presidents are elected by MEPs every two and a half years.

The Council of the European Union (sometimes referred to as the Council of Ministers) forms the other half of the EU's legislature. It consists of a government minister from each member states and meets in different compositions depending on the policy area being addressed. Notwithstanding its different compositions, it is considered to be one single body. In addition to its legislative functions, the Council also exercises executive functions in relations to the Common Foreign and Security Policy.

The judicial branch of the EU consists of the European Court of Justice (ECJ) and the Court of First Instance. Together they interpret and apply the treaties and the law of the EU. The Court of First Instance mainly deals with cases taken by individuals and companies directly before the EU's courts, and the ECJ primarily deals with cases taken by member states, the institutions and cases referred to it by the courts of member states. Decisions from the Court of First Instance can be appealed to the Court of Justice but only on a point of law.

9.3.7 European Union Legal System

The EU is based on a series of treaties. These first established the European Community and the EU, and then made amendments to those founding treaties. These are power-giving treaties which set broad policy goals and establish institutions with the necessary legal powers to implement those goals. These legal powers include the ability to enact legislation which can directly affect all member states and their inhabitants. Under the principle of supremacy, national courts are required to enforce the treaties that their member states have ratified, and thus the laws enacted under them, even if doing so requires them to ignore conflicting national law, and (within limits) even constitutional provisions.

The main legal acts of the EU come in three forms: regulations, directives and decisions. Regulations become law in all member states the moment they come into force, without the requirement for any implementing measures, and automatically override conflicting domestic provisions. Directives require member states to achieve a certain result while leaving them discretion as to how to achieve the result. The details of how they are to be implemented are left to member states. When the time limit for implementing directives passes, they may, under certain conditions, have direct effect in national law against Member States. Decisions offer an alternative to the two above modes of legislation. They are legal acts which only apply to specified individuals, companies or a particular Member State. They are most often used in Competition Law, or on rulings on State Aid, but are also frequently used for procedural or administrative matters within the institutions. Regulations, directives and decisions are of equal legal value and apply without any formal hierarchy.

One of the complicating features of the EU's legal system is the multiplicity of legislative procedures used to enact legislation. The treaties micro-manage the EU's powers, indicating different ways of adopting legislation for different policy areas and for different areas within the same policy areas. A common feature of the EU's legislative procedures, however, is that almost all legislation must be initiated by the Commission, rather than member states or European parliamentarians. The two most common procedures are co-decision, under which the European Parliament can veto proposed legislation, and consultation, under which Parliament is only permitted to give an opinion which can be ignored by European leaders. In most cases legislation must be agreed by the council.

National courts within the Member States play a key role in the EU as enforcers of EU law, and a "spirit of cooperation" between EU and national courts is laid down in the Treaties. National courts can apply EU law in domestic cases, and if they require clarification on the interpretation or validity of any EU legislation related to the case it may make a reference for a preliminary ruling to the ECJ. The right to declare EU legislation invalid however is reserved to the EU courts.

9.3.8 European Union Foreign Relations

Foreign policy cooperation between member states dates from the establishment of the Community in 1957, when member states negotiated as a bloc in international trade negotiations under the Common Commercial Policy. Steps for a more wide ranging coordination in foreign relations began in 1970 with the establishment of European Political Cooperation which created an informal consultation process between member states with the aim of forming common foreign policies. It was not, however, until 1987 when European Political Cooperation was introduced on a formal basis by the Single European Act. EPC was renamed as the *Common Foreign and Security Policy* (CFSP) by the Maastricht Treaty.

The Maastricht Treaty gives the CFSP the aims of promoting both the EU's own interests and those of the international community as a whole. This includes promoting international co-operation, respect for human rights, democracy, and the rule of law.

The Amsterdam Treaty created the office of the High Representative for the Common Foreign and Security Policy (currently held by Javier Solana) to co-ordinate the EU's foreign policy. The High Representative, in conjunction with the current Presidency, speaks on behalf of the EU in foreign policy matters and can have the task of articulating ambiguous policy positions created by disagreements among member states. The Common Foreign and Security Policy requires unanimity among the now 27-member states on the appropriate policy to follow on any particular issue. The unanimity and difficult issues treated under the CFSP makes disagreements, such as those which occurred over the war in Iraq, not uncommon.

Besides the emerging international policy of the European Union, the international influence of the EU is also felt through enlargement. The perceived benefits of becoming a member of the EU act as an incentive for both political and economic reform in states wishing to fulfil the EU's accession criteria, and are considered an important factor contributing to the reform of former Communist countries in Central and Eastern Europe. This influence on the internal affairs of other countries is generally referred to as opposed to military "hard power"

Besides the CFSP, the Commission also has its own representation in international organisations. This is primarily through the European Commissioner for External Relations, who works alongside the High Representative. In the UN, as an observer and working together, the EU has gained influence in areas such as aid due to its large contributions in that field (see below). In the G8, the EU has rights of membership besides chairing/ hosting summit meetings and is represented at meetings by the presidents of the Commission and the Council. In the World Trade Organisation (WTO), where all 27-member states are represented, the EU as a body is represented by Trade Commissioner Catherine Ashton.

9.3.9 European Union's Single Market Concept

Since its origin, the EU has established a single economic market across the territory of all its members. Currently, a single currency is in use between the 16 members of the eurozone. If considered as a single economy, the EU generated an estimated nominal gross domestic product (GDP) of US$18.39 trillion (15.247 trillion international dollars based on purchasing power parity) in 2008, amounting to over 22% of the world's total economic output in terms of purchasing power parity, which makes it the largest economy in the world by nominal GDP and the second largest trade bloc economy in the world by PPP valuation of GDP. It is also the largest exporter, and largest importer of goods and services, and the biggest trading partner to several large countries such as India and China.

170 of the top 500 largest corporations measured by revenue (Fortune Global 500) have their headquarters in the EU. In May, 2007 unemployment in the EU stood at 7% while investment was at 21.4% of GDP, inflation at 2.2% and public deficit at –0.9% of GDP. There is a great deal of variance for annual per capita income within individual EU states, these range from US$7,000 to US$69,000.

EU member states have a standardised passport design with the words "European Union" given in the national language(s) at the top; in this case that of the United Kingdom.

Two of the original core objectives of the European Economic Community were the development of a common market, subsequently renamed the single market, and a customs union between its member states. The single market involves the free circulation of goods, capital, people and services within the EU, and the customs union involves the application of a common external tariff on all goods entering the market. Once goods have been admitted into the market they can not be subjected to customs duties, discriminatory taxes or import quotas, as they travel internally. The non-EU member states of Iceland, Norway, Liechtenstein and Switzerland participate in the single market but not in the customs union. Half the trade in the EU is covered by legislation harmonised by the EU.

Free movement of capital is intended to permit movement of investments such as property purchases and buying of shares between countries. Until the drive towards Economic and Monetary Union the development of the capital provisions had been slow. Post-Maastricht there has been a rapidly developing corpus of ECJ judgements regarding this initially neglected freedom. The free movement of capital is unique insofar as that it is granted equally to non-member states.

The free movement of persons means citizens can move freely between member states to live, work, study or retire in another country. This required the lowering of administrative formalities and recognition of professional qualifications of other states.

The free movement of services and of establishment allows self-employed persons to move between member states in order to provide services on a temporary or permanent basis. While services account for between sixty and seventy percent of GDP, legislation in the area is not as developed as in other areas. This lacuna has been addressed by the recently passed Directive on services in the internal market which aims to liberalise the cross border provision of services. According to the Treaty the provision of services is a residual freedom that only applies if no other freedom is being exercised.

9.3.10 Euro Currency

The creation of a European single currency became an official objective of the EU in 1969. However, it was only with the advent of the Maastricht Treaty in 1993 that member states were legally bound to start the monetary union no later than 1 January, 1999. On this date the euro was duly launched by eleven of the then fifteen member states of the EU. It remained an accounting currency until 1 January, 2002, when euro notes and coins were issued and national currencies began to phase out in the eurozone, which by then consisted of twelve member states. The eurozone has since grown to sixteen countries, the most recent being Slovakia which joined on 1 January, 2009.

Fifteen of the 27 European Union's member countries are participating in the common currency. They are:

- Belgium
- Germany
- Greece

- Spain
- France
- Ireland
- Italy
- Luxembourg
- The Netherlands
- Austria
- Portugal
- Finland
- Slovenia (since 1st January, 2007)
- Cyprus (since 1st January, 2008)
- Malta (since 1st January, 2008)

All other EU member states, except Denmark and the United Kingdom, are legally bound to join the euro when the economic conditions are met, however only a few countries have set target dates for accession. Sweden has circumvented the requirement to join the euro area by not meeting the membership criteria.

The euro is designed to help build a single market by, for example: easing travel of citizens and goods, eliminating exchange rate problems, providing price transparency, creating a single financial market, price stability and low interest rates, and providing a currency used internationally and protected against shocks by the large amount of internal trade within the eurozone. It is also intended as a political symbol of integration and stimulus for more.

The euro, and the monetary policies of those who have adopted it in agreement with the EU, are under the control of the European Central Bank (ECB). There are eleven other currencies used in the EU. A number of other countries outside the EU, such as Montenegro, use the euro without formal agreement with the ECB.

Euro (1 Euro is ...)

Currency Name	Currency rate
Indian Rupees	70.06
Australian Dollar	1.7106
Canadian Dollar	1.5672
Danish Kroner	7.4447
Hong Kong Dollar	11.0805
Indonesian Rupiah	14398.2737
Japanese Yen *	133.218
New Zealand Dollar	2.096
Norwegian Kroner	8.6209
Pound Sterling	0.8814

Singapore Dollar	2.0635
South Korean Won	1772.8239
Swedish Kroner	10.225
Swiss Franc	1.5158
Thai Baht	48.6238
US Dollar	1.4297
Chinese Yuan	9.7715
Arab Emirates Dirham	5.252

* for 100 units

Source: www.thehindu.com (01 Sept. 2009 Edition)

9.3.11 European Union Regional Development

There are substantial economical disparities across the EU. Even corrected for purchasing power, the difference between the richest and poorest regions (NUTS-2 and NUTS-3 of the Nomenclature of Territorial Units for Statistics) is about a factor of ten. On the high end Frankfurt has • 71,476 PPP per capita, Paris • 68,989, and Inner London • 67,798, while the three poorest NUTS, all in Romania, are Vaslui County with • 3,690 PPP per capita, Boto Şani County with • 4,115, and Giurgiu County with • 4,277. Compared to the EU average, the United States GDP per capita is 35% higher and the Japanese GDP per capita is approximately 15% higher.

There are a number of Structural Funds and Cohesion Funds to support development of underdeveloped regions of the EU. Such regions are primarily located in the new member states of East-Central Europe. Several funds provide emergency aid, support for candidate members to transform their country to conform to the EU's standard (Phare, ISPA, and SAPARD), and support to the former USSR Commonwealth of Independent States (TACIS). TACIS has now become part of the worldwide EuropeAid programme. The EU Seventh Framework Programme (FP7) sponsors research conducted by consortia from all EU members to work towards a single European Research Area.

North American Free Trade Agreement (NAFTA) Regional Economic Integration in USA

The success of European Union encourage the other parts of the world for making regional cooperations between them. This wave also effect the American continents for building regional economic integration. The big effect was seen in the developing nations of the south-American continents. The Latin American free Trade Association (LAFTA) was established by south American countries like Argentina, Brazil, Chile, Mexico, Paraguay, Peru, Uruguay, Colombia, Ecuador, Venezuela and Bolivia in the year, 1960. With the view of more integration among member countries and for broads from free trade integration a new association established in the year, 1980 by these members countries by these name Latin American Integration Association (LAIA). The main objective of this new association was to eliminate restrictions on trade among the member countries and to reduce the customs and tariffs to eliminate them gradually. The another association was established by five countries of south American continental like Bolivia, Colombia, Ecuador, Peru, Venezuela, for making more cooperation among these five countries named as Andean pact in the year, 1969. It was revived in the year, 1991. Four strong nations of South-American continent Argentina, Brazil, Paraguay, Uruguay formed a new association for mutual integration and cooperation in the year, 1991 as Southern care common market (MER COSUR). Some central American countries like El Salvador, Guatemala, Honduras, Nicaragua, Costa Rica formed a central American Economic integration as Central American Common Market (CACM). The main objective of this association was to develop a mutual trust and copulation between the member countries by eliminating restrictions on tariff and custom union.

The impact of all these regional economic integration of south and central American countries influence the north American countries to form their regional economic integration. The first, impact was the bilateral trade agreement between USA and Canada in the year, 1988. Second both the developed nation realises that their pact was not profitable for both the countries as their product had similar price and lost. On realising that they convinced the Maxico to join their association to get physical resources easily and cheaply from it. This new association is known as North American Free Trade Agreement (NAFTA).

9.4 NORTH AMERICAN FREE TRADE AGREEMENT (NAFTA)

9.4.1 Introduction

The **North American Free Trade Agreement (NAFTA)** is an agreement signed by the governments of Canada, Mexico, and the United States, creating a trilateral trade blocks in North America. The agreement came into force on 1 January, 1994. The main reason of creating a trade block in this economic region was to grasps the opportunity availability in Maxico regarding their cheaper physical and human resources. It superseded the Canada-United States Free Trade Agreement between the U.S. and Canada. In terms of combined purchasing power parity GDP of its members, as of 2007 the trade block is the largest in the world and second largest by nominal GDP comparison.

In 1988, Canada and the United States signed the Canada-United States Free Trade Agreement after which the US Congress approved implementing legislation. The American government then entered into negotiations with the Mexican government for a similar treaty, and Canada asked to join the negotiations in order to preserve its perceived gains under the 1988 deal.

On 1 January, 1994, the North American Free Trade Agreement between the United States, Canada, and Mexico (NAFTA) entered into force. Implementation of the North American Free Trade Agreement (NAFTA) began on 1 January, 1994. This agreement will remove most barriers to trade and investment among the United States, Canada, and Mexico. The Agreement has brought economic growth and rising standards of living for people in all three countries. In addition, NAFTA has established a strong foundation for future growth and has set a valuable example of the benefits of trade liberalization.

Under the NAFTA, all non-tariff barriers to agricultural trade between the United States and Mexico were eliminated. In addition, many tariffs were eliminated immediately, with others being phased out over periods of 5 to 15 years. This allowed for an orderly adjustment to free trade with Mexico, with full implementation beginning 1 January, 2008. All remaining duties and quantitative restrictions were eliminated, as scheduled, on 1 January, 2008.

The Major Functions of NAFTA are

- Eliminate trade barriers in various service sectors belonging to its member nations.
- Reduce high Mexican tariffs and help to promote agricultural exports.
- Assist firms spanning the three nations to bid on government contracts.
- Assure fair market value to investors by reducing risk and offering the same legal rights that are enjoyed by local investors.
- Help investors to claim against a government by offering legal help.

The Challenges for NAFTA are

- Resolve current trade disputes pertaining to sugar, softwood lumber and trucking, just to mention a few.
- Address the issue of 10 million illegal Mexican immigrants in the US.
- Include Mexico in important provisions relating to investments.
- Enable funding and adequate mandates for key institutions like NAD Bank (North American Development Bank).
- Resolve the trade deficit of the US with Canada and Mexico, which grew from $9.1 billion in 1993 to $138.5 billion in 2007.

Promoting economic integration is not easy for any treaty but NAFTA rose to do just that. In 1994, NAFTA was established with a $6 trillion economy. By 2004, NAFTA grew to an economy of $12.5 trillion.

NAFTA created the world's largest free trade area, which now links 444 million people producing $17 trillion worth of goods and services.

Trade between the United States and its NAFTA partners has soared since the agreement entered into force.

U.S. goods and services trade with NAFTA totaled $1.1 trillion in 2008 (latest data available for Goods and Services trade). Exports totaled $482 billion; Imports totaled $596 billion. The U.S. goods and services trade deficit with NAFTA was $114 billion in 2008.

The United States has $735 billion in total (two ways) goods trade with NAFTA countries (Canada and Mexico) during 2009. Goods exports totaled $334 billion; Goods imports totaled $401 billion. The U.S. goods trade deficit with NAFTA was $68 billion in 2009.

Trade in services with NAFTA (exports and imports) totaled $110 billion in 2008 (latest data available). Services exports were $69.8 billion; Services imports were $40.2 billion. The U.S. services trade surplus with NAFTA was $29.6 billion in 2008.

9.4.2 Exports

The NAFTA countries (Canada and Mexico), were the top two purchasers of U.S. exports in 2009. (Canada $204.7 billion and Mexico $129.0 billion).

U.S. goods exports to NAFTA in 2009 were $333.7 billion, down 19.1% ($79 billion) from 2008, but 102% from 1994 (the year prior to Uruguay Round) and up 135% from 1993 (the year prior to NAFTA). U.S. exports to NAFTA accounted for 31.6% of overall U.S. exports in 2009, down slightly from 32.2% in 1994.

The top export categories (2-digit HS) in 2009 were: Machinery ($52.0 billion), Electrical Machinery ($44.2 billion), Vehicles (parts) ($41.4 billion), Plastic ($18.5 billion), and Mineral Fuel and Oil ($17.4 billion).

U.S. exports of agricultural products to NAFTA countries totaled $28.6 billion in 2009. Leading categories include: red meats, fresh/chilled/frozen ($2.5 billion), coarse grains ($2.1 million), fresh fruit ($1.7 billion), snack foods (excluding nuts) ($1.7 billion), and fresh vegetables ($1.7 billion).

U.S. exports of private commercial services* (i.e., excluding military and government) to NAFTA were $69.8 billion in 2008 (latest data available), up 5.6% ($3.7 billion) from 2007, and up 146% since 1994.

9.4.3 Imports

The NAFTA countries were the second and third largest suppliers of goods imports to the United States in 2009. (Canada $224.9 billon, and Mexico $176.5 billion).

U.S. goods imports from NAFTA totaled $401.4 billion in 2009, down 27.7% ($154 billion), from 2008, but 126% from 1994, and up 166% from 1993. U.S. imports from NAFTA accounted for 25.8% of overall U.S. imports in 2009, down from 26.9% in 1994.

The five largest categories in 2009 were Mineral Fuel and Oil (crude oil) ($89.0 billion), Vehicles ($58.5 billion), Electrical Machinery ($54.1 billion), Machinery ($37.8 billion), and Special Other (returns) ($12.2 billion).

U.S. imports of agricultural products from NAFTA countries totaled $26.1 billion in 2009. Leading categories include: fresh vegetable ($3.7 billion), snack foods, (including chocolate) ($3.4 billion), fresh fruit (excluding bananas) ($2.1 billion), processed fruit and vegetables ($1.9 billion), and wine and beer ($1.7 billion).

U.S. imports of private commercial services* (i.e., excluding military and government) were $40.2 billion in 2008 (latest data available), up 0.5% ($207 million) from 2007, and up 127% since 1994.

9.4.4 Trade Balances

The U.S. goods trade deficit with NAFTA was $67.7 billion in 2009, a 52.7% decrease (75 billion) over 2008. The U.S. goods trade deficit with NAFTA accounted for 13.5% of the overall U.S. goods trade deficit in 2009, up from 8.7% in 1994.

The United States had a services trade surplus of $29.6 billion with NAFTA countries in 2008 (latest data available).

9.4.5 Investment

U.S. foreign direct investment (FDI) in NAFTA Countries (stock) was $322.9 billion in 2008 (latest data available), down 0.7% from 2007.

U.S. direct investment in NAFTA Countries is in the finance/insurance, nonbank holding companies, manufacturing and mining sectors.

NAFTA Countries FDI in the United States (stock) was $229.8 billion in 2008, up 7.3% from 2007 (latest data available).

NAFTA countries direct investment in the U.S. is in the finance/insurance, manufacturing, and banking sectors.

9.4.6 India's Trade with NAFTA

After the formation of NAFTA (North American Free Trade Agreement) in 1994,USA's imports of textiles and clothing items have clearly shown a trend in favor of the Latin American suppliers, particularly Mexico, which is a member of NAFTA. Though India maintains a very low share in the global textiles trade (3%), it is one of the major items in India's export basket. However, India's position as a major supplier of textiles and clothing items to USA market has been sliding since 1994. It was at 7th position in 1995 and came down to 11th position in 2001. On the other hand, Mexico has improved its position from 7th in 1993 to 2nd just after China, in 2001. The direction of trade reveals that India has been losing much of its share due to USA's specific arrangements with countries under CBI (Caribbean Basin Initiative) and NAFTA. The decline of exports to USA is a warning signal of increasing competition from NAFTA-empowered Mexico. There are particularly two categories, i.e., cotton yarn and woven apparel group, where India has been affected, and this may be a result of the trade diversionary effects due to Mexico.

Although the global trade growth during most of 2003 did not display much dynamism as the industrial world posted only anaemic recovery, India's trade with North Atlantic Free Trade Agreement (NAFTA) countries comprising the US, Mexico and Canada maintained positive growth through most of 2003.

According to the Department of Commerce, India's exports to the US from January to October 2003 had grown by 11.5 per cent as compared with the corresponding period in 2002. While global imports to Canada showed a decline of 3.28 per cent during the first 10 months of 2003, India's exports to Canada saw a growth of 9.10 per cent during Jan–Oct, 2003, as compared with the comparable months of 2002. India's exports also marked a healthy trend of 22 per cent to Mexico from January to September, 2003 as compared with the corresponding months of 2002.

By far, the US remains India's largest trading partner and export destination, accounting for about 22 per cent of the country's exports. Substantial increases have been registered in the export of pharmaceutical products (85.14 per cent), electrical machinery (55 per cent), organic chemicals (37 per cent), miscellaneous textile articles (19 per cent), fish and seafood (13 per cent), while negative growth occurred in knit apparels, leather articles, iron and steel and edible fruits and nuts.

Exports from the US to India too displayed a robust trend, registering an increase of 25.36 per cent to reach $4.15 billion with several sectors such as electrical machinery, other machinery, chemical products, aircraft and parts, cotton yarn and fabrics, plastics and mineral oils registering positive trends.

At a time when Canada's imports have declined by 3.2 per cent during the first ten months of 2003, nine out of top 10 export products of India to Canada have shown a growth of 35.67 per cent. Organic chemicals have shown a growth of 35.67 per cent, closely followed by iron and steel products. Preserved foods, plastics and man-made filament yarn also registered salutary trends during this period. India's exports to Canada are currently valued at $1222 million. On the other hand, exports of Canada to India too marked a growth of 7.5 per cent during Jan–Oct, 2003, even as Canada's exports have declined overall by 3 per cent. Paper and paperboard displayed a massive growth of 136 per cent followed by aircraft and inorganic chemicals in Canada's exports to India.

India's exports to Mexico for the period Jan–Sept, 2003 are valued at $398 million, showing a positive growth of 22 per cent, against the global Mexican import growth rate of 0.4 per cent. Among the top 30 exporting countries to Mexico, only 8 have registered a growth of over 20 per cent in their exports, and India is one of them. Mexican exports to India too grew by 83 per cent during the period under review, which is estimated at $318 million.

9.5 ASSOCIATION OF SOUTH EAST ASIAN NATIONS (ASEAN)

9.5.1 Establishment

The Association of South East Asian Nations or ASEAN was established on 8 August, 1967 in Bangkok by the five original Member Countries, namely, Indonesia, Malaysia, Philippines, Singapore, and Thailand. Brunei Darussalam joined on 8 January, 1984, Vietnam on 28 July, 1995, Lao PDR and Myanmar on 23 July, 1997, and Cambodia on 30 April, 1999. As of 2006, the ASEAN region has a population of about 560 million, a total area of 4.5 million square kilometers, a combined gross domestic product of almost US$ 1,100 billion, and a total trade of about US$ 1,400 billion.

Objectives

The ASEAN Declaration states that the aims and purposes of the Association are: (1) to accelerate economic growth, social progress and cultural development in the region and (2) to promote regional peace and stability through abiding respect for justice and the rule of law in the relationship among countries in the region and adherence to the principles of the United Nations Charter.

The ASEAN Vision 2020, adopted by the ASEAN Leaders on the 30th Anniversary of ASEAN, agreed on a shared vision of ASEAN as a concert of Southeast Asian nations, outward looking, living in peace, stability and prosperity, bonded together in partnership in dynamic development and in a community of caring societies.

In 2003, the ASEAN Leaders resolved that an ASEAN Community shall be established comprising three pillars, namely, ASEAN Security Community, ASEAN Economic Community and ASEAN Socio-Cultural Community.

Fundamental Principles

ASEAN Member Countries have adopted the following fundamental principles in their relations with one another, as contained in the Treaty of Amity and Cooperation in Southeast Asia (TAC):

- mutual respect for the independence, sovereignty, equality, territorial integrity, and national identity of all nations;
- the right of every State to lead its national existence free from external interference, subversion or coercion;
- non-interference in the internal affairs of one another;
- settlement of differences or disputes by peaceful manner;
- renunciation of the threat or use of force and
- effective cooperation among themselves.

ASEAN Security Community

Through political dialogue and confidence building, no tension has escalated into armed confrontation among ASEAN Member Countries since its establishment more than three decades ago.

To build on what has been constructed over the years in the field of political and security cooperation, the ASEAN Leaders have agreed to establish the ASEAN Security Community (ASC). The ASC shall aim to ensure that countries in the region live at peace with one another and with the world in a just, democratic and harmonious environment.

The members of the Community pledge to rely exclusively on peaceful processes in the settlement of intra-regional differences and regard their security as fundamentally linked to one another and bound by geographic location, common vision and objectives. It has the following components; political development; shaping and sharing of norms; conflict prevention; conflict resolution; post-conflict peace building; and implementing mechanisms. It will be built on the strong foundation of ASEAN processes, principles, agreements, and structures, which evolved over the years and are contained in the following major political agreements:

- ASEAN Declaration, Bangkok, 8 August, 1967;
- Zone of Peace, Freedom and Neutrality Declaration, Kuala Lumpur, 27 November, 1971;
- Declaration of ASEAN Concord, Bali, 24 February, 1976;
- Treaty of Amity and Cooperation in Southeast Asia, Bali, 24 February, 1976;

- ASEAN Declaration on the South China Sea, Manila, 22 July, 1992;
- Treaty on the Southeast Asia Nuclear Weapon-Free Zone, Bangkok, 15 December, 1997;
- ASEAN Vision 2020, Kuala Lumpur, 15 December, 1997 and
- Declaration of ASEAN Concord II, Bali, 7 October, 2003.

In recognition of security interdependence in the Asia-Pacific region, ASEAN established the ASEAN Regional Forum (ARF) in 1994. The ARF's agenda aims to evolve in three broad stages, namely the promotion of confidence building, development of preventive diplomacy and elaboration of approaches to conflicts.

The present participants in the ARF include: Australia, Brunei Darussalam, Cambodia, Canada, China, European Union, India, Indonesia, Japan, Democratic Republic of Korea, Republic of Korea (ROK), Lao PDR, Malaysia, Mongolia, Myanmar, New Zealand, Pakistan, Papua New Guinea, the Philippines, the Russian Federation, Singapore, Thailand, the United States, and Viet Nam.

The ARF discusses major regional security issues in the region, including the relationship amongst the major powers, non-proliferation, counter-terrorism, transnational crime, South China Sea and the Korean Peninsula, among others.

ASEAN Economic Community

The ASEAN Economic Community shall be the end-goal of economic integration measures as outlined in the ASEAN Vision 2020. Its goal is to create a stable, prosperous and highly competitive ASEAN economic region in which there is a free flow of goods, services, investment and a freer flow of capital, equitable economic development and reduced poverty and socio-economic disparities in year 2020.

The ASEAN Economic Community shall establish ASEAN as a single market and production base, turning the diversity that characterises the region into opportunities for business complementation and making the ASEAN a more dynamic and stronger segment of the global supply chain. ASEAN's strategy shall consist of the integration of ASEAN and enhancing ASEAN's economic competitiveness.

- in moving towards the ASEAN Economic Community, ASEAN has agreed on the following: institute new mechanisms and measures to strengthen the implementation of its existing economic initiatives including the ASEAN Free Trade Area (AFTA), ASEAN Framework Agreement on Services (AFAS) and ASEAN Investment Area (AIA);
- accelerate regional integration in the following priority sectors by 2010: air travel, agro-based products, automotives, e-commerce, electronics, fisheries, healthcare, rubber-based products, textiles and apparels, tourism, and wood-based products.
- facilitate movement of business persons, skilled labour and talents; and
- strengthen the institutional mechanisms of ASEAN, including the improvement of the existing ASEAN Dispute Settlement Mechanism to

ensure expeditious and legally-binding resolution of any economic disputes.

Launched in 1992, the ASEAN Free Trade Area (AFTA) is now in place. It aims to promote the region's competitive advantage as a single production unit. The elimination of tariff and non-tariff barriers among Member Countries is expected to promote greater economic efficiency, productivity, and competitiveness.

As of 1 January, 2005, tariffs on almost 99 per cent of the products in the Inclusion List of the ASEAN-6 (Brunei Darussalam, Indonesia, Malaysia, the Philippines, Singapore, and Thailand) have been reduced to no more than 5 per cent. More than 60 per cent of these products have zero tariffs. The average tariff for ASEAN-6 has brought down from more than 12 per cent when AFTA started to 2 per cent today. For the newer Member Countries, namely, Cambodia, Lao PDR, Myanmar, and Viet Nam (CLMV), tariffs on about 81 per cent of their Inclusion List have brought down to within the 0–5 per cent range.

Other major integration-related economic activities of ASEAN include the following:

- Roadmap for Financial and Monetary Integration of ASEAN in four areas, namely, capital market development, capital account liberalisation, liberalisation of financial services and currency cooperation;
- Trans-ASEAN transportation network consisting of major inter-state highway and railway networks, including the Singapore to Kunming Rail-Link, principal ports, and sea lanes for maritime traffic, inland waterway transport, and major civil aviation links;
- Roadmap for Integration of Air Travel Sector;
- Interoperability and interconnectivity of national telecommunications equipment and services, including the ASEAN Telecommunications Regulators Council Sectoral Mutual Recognition Arrangement (ATRC-MRA) on Conformity Assessment for Telecommunications Equipment;
- Trans-ASEAN energy networks, which consist of the ASEAN Power Grid and the Trans-ASEAN Gas Pipeline Projects;
- Initiative for ASEAN Integration (IAI) focusing on infrastructure, human resource development, information and communications technology, and regional economic integration primarily in the CLMV countries;
- Visit ASEAN Campaign and the private sector-led ASEAN Hip-Hop Pass to promote intra-ASEAN tourism; and Agreement on the ASEAN Food Security Reserve.

ASEAN Socio-Cultural Community

The ASEAN Socio-Cultural Community, in consonance with the goal set by ASEAN Vision 2020, envisages a Southeast Asia bonded together in partnership as a community of caring societies and founded on a common regional identity.

The Community shall foster cooperation in social development aimed at raising the standard of living of disadvantaged groups and the rural population, and shall seek the active involvement of all sectors of society, in particular women, youth, and local communities.

ASEAN shall ensure that its work force shall be prepared for, and benefit from, economic integration by investing more resources for basic and higher education, training, science and technology development, job creation, and social protection.

ASEAN shall further intensify cooperation in the area of public health, including in the prevention and control of infectious and communicable diseases.

The development and enhancement of human resources is a key strategy for employment generation, alleviating poverty and socio-economic disparities, and ensuring economic growth with equity.

Among the on-going activities of ASEAN in this area include the following:

- ASEAN Work Programme for Social Welfare, Family, and Population;
- ASEAN Work Programme on HIV/AIDS;
- ASEAN Work Programme on Community-Based Care for the Elderly;
- ASEAN Occupational Safety and Health Network;
- ASEAN Work Programme on Preparing ASEAN Youth for Sustainable Employment and Other Challenges of Globalisation;
- ASEAN University Network (AUN) promoting collaboration among seventeen member universities ASEAN;
- ASEAN Students Exchange Programme, Youth Cultural Forum, and the ASEAN Young Speakers Forum;
- The Annual ASEAN Culture Week, ASEAN Youth Camp and ASEAN Quiz;
- ASEAN Media Exchange Programme and
- Framework for Environmentally Sustainable Cities (ESC) and ASEAN Agreement on Transboundary Haze Pollution.

External Relations

The ASEAN Vision, 2020 affirmed an outward-looking ASEAN playing a pivotal role in the international community and advancing ASEAN's common interests.

Building on the Joint Statement on East Asia Cooperation of 1999, cooperation between the Southeast and Northeast Asian countries has accelerated with the holding of an annual summit among the leaders of ASEAN, China, Japan, and the Republic of Korea (ROK) within the ASEAN plus Three processes.

ASEAN Plus Three relations continue to expand and deepen in the areas of security dialogue and cooperation, transnational crime, trade and investment, environment, finance and monetary, agriculture and forestry, energy, tourism, health, labour, culture and the arts, science and technology, information and communication technology, social welfare and development, youth, and rural development and poverty eradication. There are now thirteen ministerial-level meetings under the ASEAN Plus Three process.

Bilateral trading arrangements have been or are being forged between ASEAN Member Countries and China, Japan, and the ROK. These arrangements will serve as the building blocks of an East Asian Free Trade Area as a long term goal.

ASEAN continues to develop cooperative relations with its Dialogue Partners, namely, Australia, Canada, China, the European Union, India, Japan, the ROK, New Zealand, the Russian Federation, the United States of America, and the United Nations Development Programme. ASEAN also promotes cooperation with Pakistan in some areas of mutual interest.

Consistent with its resolve to enhance cooperation with other developing regions, ASEAN maintains contact with other inter-governmental organisations, namely, the Economic Cooperation Organisation, the Gulf Cooperation Council, the Rio Group, the South Asian Association for Regional Cooperation, the South Pacific Forum, and through the recently established Asian-African Sub-Regional Organisation Conference.

Most ASEAN Member Countries also participate actively in the activities of the Asia-Pacific Economic Cooperation (APEC), the Asia-Europe Meeting (ASEM), and the East Asia-Latin America Forum (EALAF).

Structures and Mechanisms

The highest decision-making organ of ASEAN is the Meeting of the ASEAN Heads of State and Government. The ASEAN Summit is convened every year. The ASEAN Ministerial Meeting (Foreign Ministers) is held annually.

Ministerial meetings on the following sectors are also held regularly: agriculture and forestry, economics (trade), energy, environment, finance, health, information, investment, labour, law, regional haze, rural development and poverty alleviation, science and technology, social welfare, telecommunications, transnational crime, transportation, tourism, youth. Supporting these ministerial bodies are committees of senior officials, technical working groups and task forces.

To support the conduct of ASEAN's external relations, ASEAN has established committees composed of heads of diplomatic missions in the following capitals: Beijing, Berlin, Brussels, Canberra, Geneva, Islamabad, London, Moscow, New Delhi, New York, Ottawa, Paris, Riyadh, Seoul, Tokyo, Washington D.C. and Wellington.

The Secretary-General of ASEAN is appointed on merit and accorded ministerial status. The Secretary-General of ASEAN, who has a five-year term, is mandated to initiate, advise, coordinate, and implement ASEAN activities. The members of the professional staff of the ASEAN Secretariat are appointed on the principle of open recruitment and region-wide competition.

ASEAN has several specialized bodies and arrangements promoting inter-governmental cooperation in various fields including the following: ASEAN Agricultural Development Planning Centre, ASEAN-EC Management Centre, ASEAN Centre for Energy, ASEAN Earthquake Information Centre, ASEAN Foundation, ASEAN Poultry Research and Training Centre, ASEAN Regional Centre for Biodiversity Conservation, ASEAN Rural Youth Development Centre, ASEAN Specialized Meteorological Centre, ASEAN Timber Technology Centre, ASEAN Tourism Information Centre, and the ASEAN University Network.

In addition, ASEAN promotes dialogue and consultations with professional and business organisations with related aims and purposes, such as the ASEAN-Chambers of Commerce and Industry, ASEAN Business Forum, ASEAN Tourism Association, ASEAN Council on Petroleum, ASEAN Ports Association, Federation of ASEAN Shipowners, ASEAN Confederation of Employers, ASEAN Fisheries Federation, ASEAN Vegetable Oils Club, ASEAN Intellectual Property Association, and the ASEAN-Institutes for Strategic and International Studies. Furthermore, there are 58 Non-Governmental Organizations (NGOs), which have formal affiliations with ASEAN.

India and ASEAN

Since its beginning about a decade ago, the partnership between India and the Association of South East Asian Nations (ASEAN) comprising Brunei, Cambodia, Indonesia, Laos, Malaysia, Myanmar, the Philippines, Singapore, Thailand and Vietnam has been developing at quite a fast pace.

India became a sectoral dialogue partner of ASEAN in 1992. Mutual interest led ASEAN to invite India to become its full dialogue partner during the fifth ASEAN summit in Bangkok in 1995. India also became a member of the ASEAN Regional Forum (ARF) in 1996. India and ASEAN have been holding summit level meetings on an annual basis since 2002.

The Free Trade Agreement (FTA) in goods is expected to be signed between India and the 10 member ASEAN during the India-ASEAN summit in July 2009 in Bangkok. Although, the agreement will pave way to eliminate tariffs on about 4,000 items being traded between the two, India will be able to protect its interests in the agriculture sector by keeping 489 items, mostly farm products, out of the trade pact. Some of the other products included in India's negative lists in the proposed FTA, under which no tariff concessions would be exchanged, include processed food and fruit juices, natural rubber, textile and textile products, chemical and petro-chemical products and auto products.

"All the differences have been resolved and the FTA would be signed either on the sidelines of ASEAN trade ministers meet in October or at the ASEAN Summit in October," a senior commerce ministry official stated recently. He said that signing trade-opening agreements with the Association of South East Asian Nations (ASEAN) is on the 100-day agenda of the new government for restoring high growth to the economy. New Union Commerce and Industry Minister, Mr Anand Sharma plans to present the draft of the FTA to the Cabinet soon for approval.

The FTA is expected to eliminate tariffs on 80 per cent of the items traded between the sides in a phased manner by 2015. However, tariffs will not be eliminated for about 10 per cent of additional items on the sensitive track, instead would be brought down to 5 per cent.

It is expected that ASEAN and India will gradually turn their free-trade agreement into a comprehensive economic cooperation agreement that will also include services and investment.

The agreement has a potential to create a huge market for services like banking, information technology, telecom, education and tourism. The investment agreement is expected to attract foreign direct investment (FDI) from ASEAN members, especially Singapore and Malaysia, and provide opportunity for Indian companies to invest in the ASEAN region in sectors such as pharmaceuticals, coal mining and automobiles.

Trade

The deepening of ties between India and ASEAN is reflected in the continued buoyancy in the trade figures. The trade grew by 13 per cent during April–September, 2007–08 to US$ 17.02 billion as against US$ 15.06 billion during the same period in 2006–07. ASEAN is India's fourth-largest trading partner after the EU, US and China. Indo-ASEAN trade, which has been growing at a compounded annual growth rate (CAGR) of 27 per cent since 2000, stood at US$ 38.37 billion in 2007–08. Projections stood at US$ 48 billion in 2008–09.

The trade momentum is likely to continue further with India and ASEAN planning to implement the FTA.

Further, the major irritant to the FTA—market access for palm oil products—has also been resolved. India has agreed to cut import duties on crude palm oil by 37.5 per cent and on refined palm oil by 45 per cent by 2018.

With the signing of the agreement, India-ASEAN trade is likely to surpass US$ 50 billion by 2010.

South Asian Association for Regional Cooperation (SAARC)

The South Asian Association for Regional Cooperation (SAARC) was established when its Charter was formally adopted on 8 December, 1985 by the Heads of State or Government of Bangladesh, Bhutan, India, Maldives, Nepal, Pakistan and Sri Lanka.

The Association provides a platform for the peoples of South Asia to work together in a spirit of friendship, trust and understanding. It aims to promote the welfare of the peoples of South Asia and to improve their quality of life through accelerated economic growth, social progress and cultural development in the region.

Cooperation in the SAARC is based on respect for the principles of sovereign equality, territorial integrity, political independence, non-interference in internal affairs of the Member States and mutual benefit.

Regional cooperation is seen as a complement to the bilateral and multilateral relations of SAARC Member States.

Decisions are taken based on unanimity. Bilateral and contentious issues are excluded from the deliberations of SAARC.

The SAARC Secretariat

Established in Kathmandu on 16 January, 1987, the SAARC Secretariat is responsible to coordinate and monitor the implementation of SAARC activities, service the meetings of the Association and serve as the channel of communication between SAARC and other international organizations.

The Secretariat comprises of the Secretary-General, a Director from each member state and the General Services Staff. The Secretary-General is appointed by the Council of Ministers upon nomination by a member state, on the principle of rotation in alphabetical order, for a period of two years. The List of Secretary Generals is as follows:

1. Mr. Abul Ahsan, from Bangladesh (16 January, 1987–15 October, 1989)
2. Mr. Kant Kishore Bhargava, from India (17 October, 1989–31 December, 1991)
3. Mr. Ibrahim Hussain Zaki, from the Maldives (1 January, 1992–31 December, 1993)
4. Mr. Yadab Kant Silwal, from Nepal, (1 January, 1994–31 December, 1995)
5. Mr. Naeemuddin Hasan, from Pakistan (1 January, 1996–31 December, 1998)
6. Mr. Nihal Rodrigo, from Sri Lanka (1 January, 1999–10 January, 2002)
7. Mr. Q.A.M.A. Rahim, from Bangladesh (11 January, 2002–28 February, 2005)
8. Mr. Chenkyab Dorji, from Bhutan (1 March, 2005–29 February, 2008)
9. Mr. Dr. Sheel Kant Sharma, from India (1 March, 2008–)

Directors are appointed by the Secretary-General, upon nomination by member states for a period of three years, which, in special circumstances, may be extended by the Secretary-General for a period not exceeding another full term, in consultation with the member state concerned. Following are the Directors presently serving in the Secretariat:

1. Nepal: Rishi Ram Ghimire (2 May, 2006 –)
2. India: Vinay Mohan Kwatra (1 September, 2006 –)
3. Maldives: Hassan Shifau (31 October, 2007 –)
4. Pakistan: Ghulam Dastgir (18 September, 2006 –)
5. Bangladesh: M. Riaz Hamidullah (1 February, 2008 –)
6. Bhutan: Pema L. Dorji (1 June, 2005 –)
7. Sri Lanka: R. D. Rajapakse (21 June, 2005 –)
8. Afganistan: Azizuddin Ahmadzada (18 December, 2007 –)

SAARC Member States

1. India
2. Pakistan

3. Bangladesh
4. Afganistan
5. Nepal
6. Sri Lanka
7. Bhutan
8. Maldives

SAARC International Relations

Cooperation with International and Regional Organisations

1. **UNCTAD:** SAARC-UNCTAD Memorandum of Understanding on the Trade Analysis and Information System (TRAINS) was signed in February, 1993. The global aim of TRAINS is to increase transparency in international trading conditions and thus facilitate trade. This was the first Agreement of cooperation to be signed by SAARC with an international organization. Under this Agreement, UNCTAD provides the SAARC Secretariat, on a regular basis, an updated copy of TRAINS CD-ROM containing latest data on trade control measures prevailing in developed and developing countries. The SAARC Secretariat in turn updates trade control measures prevailing in the SAARC member states on a regular basis and forwards the same to UNCTAD Secretariat, on computer floppies for incorporation in the updated versions of TRAINS CD-ROM.

   SAARC Secretariat has now data on trade control measures prevailing in 50 countries including most of the SAARC member countries. The target of UNCTAD is to include latest trade control measures of 100 countries of the world in this PC-based information system. This information is available to SAARC member states on request.

2. **ESCAP:** A Framework Agreement for cooperation between SAARC and ESCAP was signed in February, 1994. The Agreement provides for cooperation on development issues through joint studies, workshops and seminars and exchange of information and documentation in poverty alleviation, human resource development, trade promotion, foreign direct investment, environmental protection and prevention of drug trafficking, infrastructure development etc.

   SAARC Secretary-General has attended two Consultative Meetings of the Executive Heads of Subregional Organizations in Asia and the Pacific and ESCAP (Bangkok 1994 and Jakarta 1995). The Secretary-General also participated in the Meeting of Eminent Persons on Human Resources Development organized by ESCAP Secretariat in Bangkok (November, 1994).

3. **UNICEF:** A Cooperation Agreement between SAARC and UNICEF, was signed on 10 December, 1993. The Agreement envisages cooperation in implementing the relevant SAARC decisions relating to Children through an annual agenda which include joint studies, exchange of documentation and monitoring of implementation.

In pursuance of the Cooperation Agreement, the SAARC Secretariat and the UNICEF Regional Office for South Asia have been holding regular consultations, which have covered progress in the implementation of Summit directives on Children and the recommendations of the Council of Ministers, Standing Committee and the relevant Technical Committees. The consultations focus on all child related issues including the Annual Review of the Situation of Children in the SAARC Countries; implementation of the Colombo Resolution on Children; Plan of Action to mark 1991–2000 A.D. as the SAARC Decade of the Girl Child; the serious threat faced by Girl Children in Especially Difficult Circumstances (GCEDC); mid-decade goals on Children emanating from the World Summit for Children (1990) and certain aspects of the United Nations Convention on the Rights of the Child. The regular interaction between SAARC and UNICEF has facilitated better understanding of problems faced by Children in South Asia and regional policies and strategies to meet these challenges.

4. **APT:** A Memorandum of Understanding (MOU) was signed by SAARC Secretary-General and Executive Director of Asia Pacific Telecommunity (APT) on February 4, 1994. The MOU envisages cooperation between the two organizations to promote the growth of telecommunications in order to accelerate economic and social development in the region. SAARC and APT will exchange information, publications and documents on their respective activities in this field. They will also exchange technical and operational details of plans for improvement of national, regional and international telecommunications network. Collaboration is also envisaged in planning and development of networks, transfer of technology, promoting international standards, development of human resources and application of telecommunications in sectors such as health, education, environment, transport, and tourism.
5. **UNDP:** A Memorandum of Understanding (MOU) between SAARC and UNDP was signed by the SAARC Secretary-General and Administrator of UNDP in July, 1995. The MOU embodies a general agreement for broad-based collaboration with the aims and purposes of promoting sustainable human development for attaining poverty elimination, preservation and protection of environment, regeneration of natural resources, employment creation, and the goals of women in development; undertakes periodic consultation for joint activities; publishing studies on priority concerns and exchanging relevant reports.
6. **UNDCP:** SAARC Secretary-General and United Nations International Drug Control Programme (UNDCP) Executive Director signed an MOU on 18 August, 1995 to coordinate their efforts in combating drug trafficking and drug abuse in the region. The Memorandum envisages mutual consultation and exchange of information between the two

organizations. In addition, the two organizations have agreed to seek each other's technical cooperation in pursuing their respective drug control activities in areas of drug supply and demand reduction to assist in the development and implementation of such activities as human resource development; improving regional cooperation on drug intelligence through the SAARC Drug Offences Monitoring Desk; legislation; financial investigation; money laundering; precursor control; the establishment of a networking arrangement among existing institutions in drug abuse prevention etc.

7. **Colombo Plan:** SAARC has also entered into cooperation arrangement with the Colombo Plan Bureau for promotion on the Role of SAARC NGOs in anti-narcotic activities. In this context, representative of NGOs from seven countries attended a meeting of the SAARC Forum on the role of NGOs in Drug Demand Reducation in Dhaka on 10–13 April, 1995.

   Efforts are also underway to establish a working relationship between the SAARC Secretariat and the Colombo Plan Bureau on training facilities in the region.

8. **ITU:** The Memorandum of Understanding (MOU) between SAARC and International Telecommunications Union (ITU) has been finalized and is to be signed shortly.

Areas of Cooperation

At the inception of the Association, the Integrated Programme of Action (IPA) consisting of a number of Technical Committees (TCs) was identified as the core areas of cooperation. Over the period of years, the number of TCs was change as per the requirement. The current areas of cooperation under the reconstituted Regional Integrated Programme of Action, which is pursue through the Technical Committees cover:

1. Agriculture and Rural Development;
2. Health and Population Activities;
3. Women, Youth and Children;
4. Environment and Forestry;
5. Science and Technology and Meteorology;
6. Human Resources Development; and
7. Transport.

Recently, high level Working Groups have also been established to strengthen cooperation in the areas of Information and Communications Technology, Biotechnology, Intellectual Property Rights, Tourism, and Energy.

Given the emphasis laid down at successive Summits on the need to expand the areas of cooperation and strengthen the regional cooperation, a number of other areas have been included in the SAARC agenda. Several Ministerial level meetings have taken place to give due emphasis in various fields. The details of work programme under each agreed areas of cooperation can be viewed by clicking the respective links.

SAARC Regional Centres

The SAARC Secretariat is supported by Regional Centres established in Member Countries to promote regional cooperation. These Centres are managed by Governing Boards comprising representatives from Member States, SAARC Secretary-General and the Ministry of Foreign/External Affairs of the host government. The Director of the Centre acts as Member Secretary to the Governing Board which reports to the Standing Committee. Established Centres:

1. SAARC Agricultural Information Centre (SAIC), Dhaka
2. SAARC Meteorological Research Centre (SMRC), Dhaka
3. SAARC Tuberculosis Centre (STC), Kathmandu
4. SAARC Documentation Centre (SDC), New Delhi
5. SAARC Disaster Management Centre (SDMC), New Delhi
6. SAARC Human Resources Development Centre (SHRDC), Islamabad
7. SAARC Coastal Zone Management Centre, Maldives
8. SAARC Information Centre, Nepal
9. SAARC Energy Centre, Pakistan

Centres Being Established.

The following Regional Centres are in the process of establishment:

1. SAARC Cultural Centre, Sri Lanka
2. SAARC Forestry Centre, Bhutan

SAARC Summits

The Heads of State or Government signed a Charter of the South Asian Association for Regional Cooperation on 8 December, 1985. They also adopted the Dhaka Declaration. They approved that the Standing Committee should set up a Study Group to examine the problem of terrorism as it affects the security and stability of Member States of SAARC. They further directed the Council of Ministers to consider the report of this Study Group and submit recommendations to them as to how best the Member States could cooperate among themselves to solve this. They also approved that a similar exercise be carried out with regard to the problem of drug trafficking and abuse. They decided that the Member Governments should concert their views on the ongoing discussions on New International Economic Order and the improvement of the World Trading System through GATT taking particularly into account the interest of the least developed among the developing countries. For this purpose, it was decided to convene a Ministerial level meeting. The Standing Committee should convene a meeting to prepare for it. The Heads of State or Government emphasized that women should increasingly participate in activities at the regional level within the framework of SAARC and that Programmes and Projects should be devised to ensure their active participation in the development process. They therefore directed the Standing Committee to convene a Ministerial Level Conference on the subject to identify the areas of activities and plan a Programme of Action. The Heads of State or Government decided that the Association shall have a Secretariat directed the Foreign Ministers to consider details regarding its location, structure, functions and financing and submit those for the consideration of Heads of State or Government.

Summits	Date	Place
1st SAARC Summit	7 – 8 December, 1985	Dhaka
2nd SAARC Summit	16 – 17 November, 1986	Bangalore
3rd SAARC Summit	2 – 4 November, 1987	Kathmandu
4th SAARC Summit	29 – 31 December, 1988	Islamabad
5th SAARC Summit	21 – 23 November, 1990	Malé
6th SAARC Summit	21 December, 1991	Colombo
7th SAARC Summit	10 – 11 April, 1993	Dhaka
8th SAARC Summit	2 – 4 May, 1995	New Delhi
9th SAARC Summit	12 – 14 May, 1997	Malé
10th SAARC Summit	29 – 31 July, 1998	Colombo
11th SAARC Summit	4 – 6 January, 2002	Kathmandu
12th SAARC Summit	2 – 6 January, 2004	Islamabad
13th SAARC Summit	12 – 13 November, 2005	Dhaka
14th SAARC Summit	3 – 4 April, 2007	New Delhi
15th SAARC Summit	27 Jul – 3 Aug, 2008	Colombo

Source: *www.saarc.com*

9.6 FIRST SAARC SUMMIT DHAKA

Introduction

The Heads of State or Government underscored the historic significance of their first ever South Asian Summit meeting. They considered it a tangible manifestation of their determination to cooperate regionally, to work together towards finding solutions towards their common problems in a spirit of friendship, trust and mutual understanding, to the creation of an order based on mutual respect, equity, and shared benefits.

Main Objectives of the Summit

- They recognized that periodic meetings at their level were central to the promotion of mutual trust, confidence and cooperation among their countries.
- To accelerate the process of economic and social development in their respective countries through the optimum utilization of human and material resources.

- To promote the welfare and prosperity of the peoples and to improve their quality of life.
- The principles governing sovereign equality of States, peaceful settlement of disputes, non-interference in internal affairs and non-use or threat of use of force against the territorial integrity and political independence of other States.
- They also reaffirmed their deep conviction in the continuing validity and relevance of the objectives of the non-Aligned movement as an important force in international relations.
- To make optimum use of these capacities for the benefit of their peoples, accelerate the pace of their economic development and enhance their national and collective self-reliance.
- They emphasized that strengthening of regional cooperation in South Asia required greater involvement of their peoples. They agreed to increase interaction and further promote people-to-people contacts at various levels among their countries.

The Dhaka Summit would place regional cooperation on a firm foundation, play an important role in accelerating the pace of economic and social development of the SAARC countries, promote the objectives of individual and collective self-reliance and further the cause of peace, progress and stability in their region and the world.

9.7 SECOND SAARC SUMMIT BANGALORE

Introduction

The second SAARC Summit was held in Bangalore on 16 and 17 November, 1986.

The Heads of State or Government reiterated their desire of promoting peace, stability, amity and progress in the region through strict adherence to the principles of the United Nations Charter and Non-alignment. Particularly in respect of the principles of sovereign equality, territorial integrity, national independence, non-use of force and non-interference in the internal affairs of other States and peaceful settlement of disputes among the SAARC countries.

Main Objectives of the Summit

- It was enormously accepted to work together in accordance with the SAARC Charter to devise common policies and approaches for finding common solutions to the shared problems that all of them face and stressed that mutual trust, goodwill and understanding must animate their cooperative effort under SAARC.
- Progress and prosperity in each country would redound to the benefit of others. This was what constituted the SAARC spirit.
- To promote the welfare of the peoples of South Asia, to improve their quality of life, to accelerate economic growth, social programmes and cultural development in the region and to provide all individuals the opportunity to live in dignity and to realize their full potential.

- The countries of the region had large, rich and varied human and natural resources. They expressed their determination to achieve the optimum utilization of these resources by intensifying their cooperation, bearing in mind the immense present and potential complementarities among their economies.
- They emphasized the need for promoting greater contacts among the peoples of the region through such action as regular and frequent interchange of scholars, academics, artists, authors, professionals and businessmen as well as facilitation of tourism.
- They agreed that a progressive movement towards more concrete and action-oriented projects and programmes was essential to ensure more tangible benefits from SAARC to the peoples of the region.
- The Heads of State or Government welcomed the signing of the Memorandum of Understanding on the establishment of the SAARC Secretariat by the Council of Ministers and their decision to locate the Secretariat in Kathmandu and appoint Ambassador Abul Ahsan of Bangladesh as the first Secretary-General of SAARC.
- They recognized the needs of all children for the principal means of human resources development. Children should be given the highest priority in national development planning.
- The SAARC countries underlined the importance of enhancing public consciousness and building a national political consensus on the rights of the children.
- The SAARC States were agreed for preventing and eliminating the terrorism from the region.
- They unequivocally condemned all acts, methods and practices of terrorism as criminal and deplored their impact on life and property, social economic development, political stability, regional and international peace and co-operation.
- The SAARC countries were convinced that an environment of peace, security and respect for international law was essential for their growth and stability.
- The SAARC countries were deeply concerned that the world economy continued to be in the throes of crisis, with particularly harsh and severe consequences for the economies and development prospects and aspirations of the developing countries.
- The SAARC countries noted that the rates of growth in the developed countries had turned out to be much lower than what was earlier projected and that the projection for future growth in these countries was not at all encouraging. They expressed their concern at the implications of these trends for the development prospects of the developing countries.
- The SAARC countries expressed their conviction that the Bangalore Summit had helped in consolidating the gains of regional co-operation

activities so far undertaken by SAARC while, at the same time, exploring new avenues and possibilities for such co-operation.

The Bangalore Summit had made a significant contribution to strengthening and streamlining the institutional basis for such co-operation. The SAARC countries reiterated their determination and will to expand and strengthen their co-operation under SAARC. They underlined their belief that SAARC reflected a resurgence of the South Asian consciousness, which had inspired the peoples of this region over several millenia. The leaders expressed their deep conviction that South Asian regional co-operation would not only have a salutary effect on bilateral relations between the countries of the region, but also impart strength and stability to these relations.

The Foreign Ministers of the SAARC countries signed a Memorandum of Understanding on the Establishment of the SAARC Secretariat in their presence. They welcomed the announcement by His Majesty's Government of Nepal that the Secretariat would be inaugurated in Kathmandu on 16 January, 1987. They decided that the first Secretary-General of the SAARC Secretariat, His Excellency Mr. Abul Ahsan, would assume charge of this office from that date.

The SAARC countries decided that the next Meeting of the Council of Ministers would held in India in May, 1987. They directed that this Meeting should undertake a detailed review of the proposals for the establishment of regional institutions. The member countries, which have undertaken to prepare concept papers, pre-feasibility, or feasibility studies on these proposals, should complete them well before the convening of the Meeting. The SAARC Secretariat should establish and submit to the Ministers, an order of priority among these proposals having regard to their costs, benefits, and readiness for implementation, and other relevant factors.

The Heads of State or Government gratefully accepted the offer of the King of Nepal to host the Third SAARC Summit in 1987. They also accepted with gratitude the offer of the President of Sri Lanka to host the Fourth SAARC Summit in Sri Lanka in 1988.

9.8 THIRD SAARC SUMMIT KATHMANDU

Introduction

Third Summit of the South Asian Association for Regional Cooperation (SAARC) in Kathmandu on 2–4 November, 1987. The Members countries of SAARC launch the beginning of a new era of regional cooperation for the promotion of peace and progress mutual trust and goodwill in South Asia. It also underlined the importance of annual meetings at their level, as a prime mover, in consolidating and accelerating the pace and process of overall social, economic and cultural development in the region. They renewed their commitment to the SAARC Charter. They reiterated their desire of promoting peace, stability, amity and progress in the region through strict adherence to the principles of the United Nations Charter and Non-alignment, particularly respect for the principles of sovereign equality, territorial integrity, national independence, non-use of force and non-interference in the internal affairs of other States and peaceful settlement of disputes. The main agenda of this submit was:

- The SAARC nations emphasized about the fundamental goal of SAARC is to promote the welfare of the peoples of South Asia and to provide them with the opportunity to live in dignity and realize their full potential.
- They were conscious of the formidable tasks ahead of eradicating poverty, hunger, disease, illiteracy and unemployment and alleviation of environmental degradation facing South Asia.
- The SAARC nations recognized that the external environment had a critical bearing on the development of the economies of the South Asian Region. They noted with deep concern that growth in the world economy had again slowed down with adverse consequences for South Asia and other developing countries, especially for the least developed and landlocked countries.
- They observed that equitable participation of the developing countries in international trading and economic systems and in arrangements for the coordination of global macro, economic policies were essential for enhancing prospects and performance of the world economy.
- The SAARC nations reiterated the urgent need for resumption of North-South Dialogue. With a view to promoting coordinated actions by developed and developing countries to channel trade surpluses for development, revive growth in flagging economies overcome debt difficulties, expand export access to the developing countries and stabilize commodity prices, regulate capital flows and exchange rates more closely, and provide emergency relief and assistance to the poorest countries.
- The Heads of State or Government expressed concern at the deteriorating international political environment which was due to great power policies and practices of domination and intervention as well as the increased resort to threat or use of force, aggression, occupation, pressure, economic coercion and interference in violation of the principles and purposes of the Charter of the United Nations.
- The SAARC nations expressed their deep concern at the fast and continuing degradation of the environment, including extensive destruction of forests, in the South Asian region. They also noted that South Asia was afflicted with such natural disasters as floods, droughts, landslides, cyclones, tidal waves that have had a particularly severe impact recently, causing immense human suffering. At the same time, they expressed concern over the danger posed by the global sea level rise and its effects on South Asian countries. These natural disasters and the degradation of the environment were severely undermining the development process and prospects of the member countries.
- The SAARC nations reaffirmed their conviction that the region being most populous in the world and having age-old socio-cultural links,

rich and varied human and natural resources, offered immense scope and potential for regional cooperation and that the growing interaction among its people had added stimulus towards this end. They reiterated their determination to pursue their individual and collective efforts for the optimal utilization of the vast human and untapped natural and other material resources.

- The SAARC nations sign the Agreement establishing a South Asian Food Security Reserve and expressed confidence that this will provide a much-needed cushion against food shortages and scarcity situations in the region.
- The SAARC nations expressed happiness at the signing of the SAARC Regional Convention on Suppression of Terrorism and considered it a historic step towards the prevention and elimination of terrorism from the region. In this regard, they also reiterated their unequivocal condemnation of all acts, methods and practice of terrorism as criminal and expressed their abhorrence of their impact on life and property, socio-economic development, political stability, regional peace and cooperation.

The SAARC nations Bangladesh, Bhutan, India, Maldives, Pakistan and Sri Lanka gratefully accepted the offer of the President of Sri Lanka to host the Fourth SAARC Summit in 1988, in Sri Lanka. They also gratefully accepted the offer of the Prime Minister of the Islamic Republic of Pakistan to host the Fifth SAARC Summit in Pakistan in 1989.

9.9 FOURTH SAARC SUMMIT ISLAMABAD

Introduction

The Fourth Summit of the South Asian Association for Regional Cooperation at Islamabad from 29–31 December, 1988. They reiterated their commitment to the SAARC Charter and renewed their determination to cooperate in promoting the welfare of the peoples of South Asia and to improving their quality of life by eradicating poverty, hunger, disease, illiteracy, unemployment and environmental degradation.

- The SAARC Nations recalled that cultural, social and historical ties linked their countries and they had at their disposal substantial human and natural resources.
- The leaders endorsed the decision of the Council of Ministers that any country in the region subscribing to the objectives and principles of the SAARC Charter may be admitted as a member of the Association by a unanimous decision of the Heads of State of Government.
- The SAARC Countries lauded the smooth functioning of the SAARC Audio Visual Exchange (SAVE) Programme which had proved to be a useful medium for promoting a South Asian consciousness amongst the peoples of the region. They decided that SAVE Programmes should also emphasise social, economic and technical themes.

- The Heads of State of Government expressed grave concern over the growing magnitude and the serious effects of drug abuse, particularly among young people, and drug trafficking. They recognised the need for urgent and effective measures to eradicate this evil ad decided to declare the year, 1989 as the "SAARC Year for Combating Drug Abuse and Drug Trafficking.
- They expressed the conviction that identification of measures and programmes as envisaged by the Group of Experts would supplement national, bilateral, regional and global efforts to deal with the increasingly serious problems being faced by the region as a result of the recurrence of natural disasters and the continuing degradation of the environment. They urged that the study should be completed in the shortest period of time so that it could provide a basis for the member countries to draw up an action plan for meaningful cooperation amongst the Member States. They decided that a joint study be undertaken on the "Greenhouse Effect" and its impact on the region.
- The Heads of State or Government reviewed the progress on the Situation of Children in SAARC countries. They decided to declare 1990 as the "SAARC Year of the Girl Child".

Countries to work out modalities for the realization of "SAARC 2000 – A Basic Needs Perspective". The Heads of State or Government welcomed the idea of holding South Asian Festivals from time to time and accepted the offer of India to host the first such festival. The SAARC Countries decided that any country in the region subscribing to the objectives and principles of the Charter might be admit as a member of the Association by a unanimous decision of the Heads of State or Government. The Heads of State or Government gratefully accepted the offer of the Government of Sri Lanka to host the Fifth SAARC Summit in Colombo in 1989.

9.10 FIFTH SAARC SUMMIT MALE

Introduction

The Fifth Summit of the South Asian Association for Regional Cooperation at Malé on 21–23 November, 1990. The SAARC Nations reiterated that cooperation among the countries of South Asia was necessary for improving the quality of life of the peoples of the region. They recalled their conviction that the objectives of peace and stability in South Asia could be best serve by fostering mutual understanding, cooperation and good neighborly relations. They reaffirmed their commitment to the purposes and principles of the South Asian Association for Regional Cooperation and renewed their resolve to intensify cooperation under its aegis in pursuit of their common objectives.

- The SAARC Nations stressed their desire to promote peace, stability, amity and progress in the region through strict adherence to the principles of the United Nations Charter and the Nonaligned Movement, particularly respect for the principles of sovereign equality, territorial integrity, national independence, nonuse of force, non-interference in the internal affairs of other States and peaceful settlement of disputes.

- The SAARC Nations expressed satisfaction that the launching of SAARC in 1985 and the initiatives under the Integrated Programme of Action for strengthening regional cooperation in South Asia had generated much enthusiasm and hope in their peoples, and that the South Asian consciousness necessary for the success of regional cooperation was gradually permeating the region.
- They reiterated their resolve to make optimal use of the positive forces of goodwill, trust and understanding existing among their peoples and to turn SAARC into a dynamic instrument for achieving its objectives and creating an order based on mutual respect, equity, cooperation and shared benefits.
- The SAARC Nations reviewed the status of children in South Asia and noted that the recent World Summit for Children had imparted a new impetus to the ongoing efforts in this field. They believed that relevant recommendations of the World Summit could be usefully incorporate into a Plan of Action in the South Asian context and its implementation should be review annually.
- The SAARC Nations endorsed the recommendations made by the Second SAARC Ministerial Meeting on Women in Development held in Islamabad in June, 1990. They noted with satisfaction the enthusiastic response in all Member States to their collective call for the observance of 1990 as the "SAARC Year of the Girl Child". They decided that in order to maintain focus on the problems of the Girl Child, the years 1991–2000 AD should be observed as the "SAARC Decade of the Girl Child".
- The SAARC Nations satisfied the growing regional cooperation in combating the problems of drug trafficking and drug abuse. They expressed serious concern over the growing linkages between drug trafficking and international arms trade and terrorist activities.
- The SAARC Nations noted with satisfaction that the national studies on Trade, Manufactures and Services had been complete. They underlined the need for expeditious action for completing the Regional Study within the timeframe stipulated by the Council of Ministers. They expressed the hope that it would open new avenues of cooperation for the prosperity of the peoples of the region.
- The SAARC Nations approved the recommendations of the Council of Ministers regarding Special SAARC Travel Document and decided to launch the scheme.

The SAARC Nations reaffirmed their commitment to the principles and objectives of SAARC and reiterated their resolve to intensify cooperation under its aegis. They issued the Malé Declaration. The Heads of State or Government decided to launch the Special SAARC Travel Document, which would exempt its holders from visas for travel within the region. They welcomed the proposal for institutionalized cooperation among the tourist industries of the Member

States with a view to attracting more tourists from outside the region. They satisfaction that all Member States had completed their national studies on Trade, Manufactures and Services. They underlined the need for completing the Regional Study within the stipulated timeframe. The Heads of State or Government gratefully accepted the offer of the Government of Sri Lanka to host the Sixth SAARC Summit in Colombo in 1991.

9.11 SIXTH SAARC SUMMIT COLOMBO

Introduction

The Sixth Summit of the South Asian Association for Regional Cooperation (SAARC) at Colombo, Sri Lanka on 21st December, 1991. The SAARC Nations reaffirmed their commitment to the principles and objectives enshrined in the Charter of SAARC. They resolved to promote regional cooperation for the benefit of their people, in a spirit of mutual accommodation, with full respect for the principles of sovereign equality, independence and territorial integrity of all States and in strict adherence to the principles of nonuse of force, the peaceful settlement of disputes and non-interference in each other's internal affairs. They also reiterated their commitment to the principles of the United Nations Charter and the Nonaligned Movement.

- The SAARC Nations emphasised the vital importance of assessing the nature and extent of international economic interdependence and of the need for reviving the North/South dialogue. They noted the recent developments that had radically transformed the international development relationship deeply affecting the prospects for the economies of the seven SAARC countries.
- The SAARC Nations emphasised the need for vigorously promoting south economic cooperation to offset the negative consequences of international economic developments.
- The SAARC Nations also exchanged views on the priorities of their respective national economies. They identified, for the further development of their economies, the importance of securing less restrictive trading and marketing opportunities for their products, more extensive technology and resource transfers to South Asia, debt relief and access on favourable and on more concessional terms to resources from multilateral financial institutions. They agreed to keep an open dialogue on these aspects through mutual consultations.
- The SAARC Nations assessed current international developments in the political sphere particularly those that affected the lives of the people of South Asia. They noted the changing power structures in international relations and the reduction of confrontations and tensions, particularly among the Super Powers. These have contributed to the receding of the threat of nuclear confrontation and to agreements on disarmament measures.
- The SAARC Nations hoped that these developments would restrain the pursuit of military power in all areas of the world. They expressed the

hope that the peace dividend would be used for promoting further development of developing countries. They welcomed the trend towards popularly based democratic governments in different parts of the world including in South Asia.

- The SAARC Nations observed that civil and political rights on the one hand and economic and social rights on the other are interdependent and of equal importance Human rights issues should not therefore be viewed in narrow and exclusively political terms. In this context they underlined the need to view the efforts of States to guarantee human rights in their full context, through the pursuit of development for all citizens in conditions of stability, which in turn guarantees the enjoyment of human rights of all persons. They also reaffirming their commitment to democracy, human rights and the rule of law, emphasised the need to ensure that development remains at the centre of international attention.
- The SAARC Nations agreed to participate in the ongoing process of revitalising the United Nations as an effective universal instrument for addressing international issues on an equitable and democratic basis, taking full account of the interests and concerns of all states, including those in South Asia. Issues such as the protection and preservation of the environment and the equitable and sustainable management of global resources, economic development and the alleviation of poverty, the suppression of terrorism, drug trafficking and other international crimes required global responses and solutions calling for action by all states.
- The SAARC Nations accorded the highest priority to the alleviation of poverty in all South Asian countries. They affirmed that South Asia's poor could constitute a huge and potential resource, provided their basic needs were met, and they were mobilized to create economic growth. This requires that the poor are empowered and are irreversibly linked to the mainstream of development. It was noted that each South Asian country has had significant success cases of this approach to poverty alleviation. Recognizing that a great majority of these people remain below the poverty line, they evinced keen interest in a "Daal-Bhaat", or assured nutritional standards approach towards the satisfaction of basic needs of the South Asian poor.
- The SAARC Nations deeply conscious that primary education is the cutting edge in the struggle against poverty and the promotion of development, the Heads of State or Government reaffirmed the importance of attaining the target of providing primary education to all children between the ages of 6–14 years by the year, 2000. They agreed to share their respective experiences and technical expertise to achieve this goal.

The SAARC Nations noted with satisfaction that the Scheme in regard to the entitled categories of Members of Parliament, Judges of the Supreme Court, Heads of national academic institutions and the accompanying spouses and dependent children will become operational from 1st March, 1992. They called for expeditious action to implement the scheme as well as to consider other categories eligible for exemption. They were conscious of the vast potential being afforded by current advances in scientific research for the application of science and technology towards the wellbeing of the peoples of South Asia. They agreed that for the South Asian region to derive the maximum benefit, scientific and technological cooperation should transcend national frontiers. The SAARC Nations gratefully accepted the offer of the Government of Bangladesh to host the Seventh SAARC Summit in 1992.

9.12 SEVENTH SAARC SUMMIT DHAKA

Introduction

The Seventh Summit of the South Asian Association for Regional Cooperation (SAARC) at Dhaka, Bangladesh on 10–11 April, 1993. The SAARC Nations reiterated their commitment to the principles and objectives of the South Asian Association for Regional Cooperation (SAARC), to the five principles of peaceful co-existence, the UN Charter and non-alignment. The SAARC Nations noted the progress achieved in regional cooperation under the aegis of SAARC. They felt that time was now opportune for SAARC to provide a further dynamic impetus to activities in the core areas of economic, social and cultural cooperation in the SAARC region. The SAARC Nations welcomed the Report of the Independent South Asian Commission on Poverty Alleviation established at the Colombo Summit. The Report provided valuable insight and illustrative examples of successful poverty alleviation programmes in individual Member States. Acknowledging that the abiding human qualities of dignity, creativity and productive potential are eroded by chronic poverty, the SAARC Nations reiterated their commitment to empowering the poor for enhanced growth, consistent with human development and equity.

- The SAARC Nations reaffirmed the need to liberalize trade as early as possible through a step by step approach. They underscored that this should be done in such a manner that all countries in the region could share the benefits of trade expansion equitably. In this context, they welcomed the finalization of the framework Agreement on SAARC Preferential Trading Arrangement (SAPTA). They expressed their deep satisfaction over the signing of the framework Agreement. The Leaders stressed that all necessary steps should be taken to begin the first round of trade negotiations to exchange trade preferences among Member States under the Arrangement.
- The SAARC Nations further underlined the critical importance of urgently promoting intra-regional cooperation, particularly in the area of manufactures in order to enhance the productive capacity of the Member Countries, and to promote sustained growth and development to prevent the marginalization of South Asia's trade interest in the larger global context.

- The SAARC Nations expressed their deep concern at the unabated degradation of the environment and recurrence of devastating natural disasters. They also underscored the risks and dangers involved in overlooking the challenge posed by these problems. They expressed their commitment to implementing at all levels — national, bilateral, regional and global — programmes for the protection and preservation of the environment and prevention of its degradation. They also recognized that the completion of the Regional Study on the "Greenhouse Effect and its Impact on the Region" was a significant step forward in promoting regional cooperation in this vital area. They also stressed the importance of continuing the ongoing SAARC activities in the field of environment.
- The SAARC Nations Recognizing the sovereign right of all countries to promote, adopt and implement their population policies and mindful of their cultures, values and traditions, stressed the need to integrate demographic objectives and population strategies in the formulation of the development strategies of Member Countries. In this context, they also noted the importance of adequate investment in the health and education sectors for the success of their population programmes. They agreed that cooperation among Member States should be strengthened, both through sharing experiences and in other practical ways, to enhance their capacity to deal with the population problem.
- The SAARC Nations Reaffirming their commitment to accord the highest priority to child survival, protection and development, they noted with satisfaction that all Member States had completed their National Plans of Action on Children. They reiterated their call at the Colombo Summit to continue to ensure coordinated follow-up action by Member States on their respective plans.
- The SAARC Nations endorsed the "Colombo Resolution on Children" adopted by the Second SAARC Ministerial Conference on Children held at Colombo in September, 1992 and urged Member States to implement programmes as appropriate in their respective national contexts, to achieve the illustrative goals embodied in the Resolution, and the goals of the SAARC Plan of Action on Children.
- The SAARC Nations worried that the youth of South Asia faced a number of serious problems requiring urgent attention and remedial measures. They welcomed the offer of the Maldives to host a Ministerial Conference on Youth in South Asia in 1994 to address the problems of the Youth and focus on the broad theme of youth and development. They also agreed to designate 1994 as the "SAARC Year of the Youth".
- On reviewing the situation of women in the region, it was noted with satisfaction that over a period of time, the content of regional cooperation which addresses the issue of development, gender and equality for women has steadily grown in SAARC. The SAARC Nations hoped that the cooperation thus developed will enable Member States to achieve the ultimate goal of bringing women into the mainstream of development with independence and equality.

- The SAARC Nations emphasized that cooperation in the field of Science and Technology was of utmost importance in order to accelerate the process of development in South Asia. They called for further intensification of efforts by Member States in this important area, particularly to facilitate research and exchange of information through networking arrangements in the field of bio-technology, genetic engineering, energy modeling techniques and other identified areas of cooperation. The SAARC Nations reiterated their unequivocal condemnation of all acts, methods and practices of terrorism as criminal. They strongly deplored the adverse consequences of terrorism.
- The Leaders of the SAARC nations reiterated the need to give high priority to the enactment of enabling legislation at the national level to give effect to the SAARC Regional Convention on Suppression of Terrorism, while urging the Member States which had not yet done so, to make every effort to finalize this matter before the Eighth SAARC Summit.
- The SAARC Nations reiterated their grave concern at the growing menace of drug trafficking in the region and the aggravation of the problem of drug abuse among the South Asian population, particularly the youth. They recognized the devastating impact of drug abuse on the very fabric of society and the serious threat to security and stability posed by drug trafficking through its growing linkages with organized crime, illicit arms trade and terrorism.
- The SAARC Nations reaffirmed their commitment to pay special attention to the monitoring of the security of small States and underscored the need to consider special measures of support to preserve their sovereign independence, territorial integrity and the well-being of their people. They further noted that real protection of small and weaker States should be firmly rooted in the Rule of Law and strict adherence to universally accepted principles and norms relating to the sovereign rights and territorial integrity of all States — big or small. This, they stressed, should be ensured by all countries either severally or collectively through the pursuit of appropriate actions.
- The SAARC Nations endorsed the recommendation of the Council of Ministers for the establishment of an Inter-Governmental Group (IGG) on South Asian Development Fund (SADF) on an ad-hoc basis. They directed that the IGG define in clear terms the size, structure, resources and operational modalities of the proposed Fund. They also directed the IGG to examine the complementarities between the SAARC Fund for Regional Projects (SFRP) and SADF, and their relationship, including the possibility of their merger. They welcomed the offer of the Maldives to host the meeting of IGG.
- The SAARC Nations had wide-ranging discussions on the current global political trends and future prospects, particularly those issues that affect South Asia. In this context, they reiterated their deep commitment to the purposes and principles of the United Nations

Charter and reaffirmed their resolve to strengthen the United Nations as the central instrument for peace, security, disarmament, development and cooperation among the nations of the world. To this end, the Leaders supported all constructive initiatives aimed at strengthening the United Nations. They, however, underscored that any move to adapt or reform the United Nations must be undertaken with the sole objective of rendering the United Nations more democratic, efficient and effective and not to limit the focus of its attention to a narrow and isolated range of objectives.

- The SAARC Nations noted that while it was important to build peace and create conditions of stability in the world, it was equally important to promote economic and social development. They underscored that international cooperation for development and eradication of poverty were inextricably linked with the preservation of international peace and security and hence needed to be treated on an equal footing and pursued with equal vigour. The SAARC Nations expressed their grave concern over the continuing deterioration in economic situation in the majority of developing countries. The economies of developing countries, they observed, continued to suffer as a result of limited market access for their exports, dwindling resource flows, absence of adequate foreign investment, mounting external indebtedness, inadequate transfer of technology and the inequities in the global monetary, financial and trading systems. The Heads of State or Government noted that although the developing countries themselves had the primary responsibility for their economic development, the role of developed countries remained central to the revival of the growth of the world economy — in particular the economies of the developing countries.

The SAARC Nations expressed their deep satisfaction over the positive outcome of the Seventh SAARC Summit and expressed their conviction that this Summit would greatly contribute towards strengthening the policies and cooperative actions of the Member States in response to the challenges of the 1990s and beyond in areas where SAARC has a distinct contribution to make. They also reiterated once again their determination to strengthen and enrich SAARC as an instrument — endowing it with a clear set of forward looking goals and objectives as well as all the requisite institutional capacities — so that it can continue to work to enrich not only the lives of its own members but also promote peace, progress and stability in South Asia in a larger context. The Heads of State or Government gratefully accepted the offer of India to host the Eighth SAARC Summit in 1994.

9.13 EIGHTH SAARC SUMMIT NEW DELHI

Introduction

The Eighth Summit of the South Asian Association for Regional Cooperation (SAARC) at New Delhi, India on 2–4 May, 1995. The SAARC Nations expressed their satisfaction on the achievements of the First Decade of SAARC and resolved to celebrate its completion of the First Decade both in the individual Member States and collectively. They endorsed the proposal of the Council of Ministers to convene a Commemorative Session of the Council on the theme "SAARC — Vision for the Second Decade" to identify the areas on which SAARC should focus in its Second Decade. The SAARC Nations reaffirmed their resolve to intensify regional cooperation in order to accelerate the process of promoting the welfare and improving the quality of life of the peoples of South Asia. They reiterated their commitment to the principles and objectives enshrined in the SAARC Charter, particularly, to the principles of sovereign equality, territorial integrity, national independence, non-use of force and non-interference in each other's internal affairs. They recalled their conviction that in an increasingly interdependent world, regional cooperation was a dynamic instrument for promoting economic prosperity, mutual understanding and good neighbourly relations to achieve the objectives of peace and stability in South Asia. In this context, a climate of peace and stability would contribute to the economic growth.

SAARC Nations decided to declare 1995 as the "SAARC Year of Poverty Eradication". Acknowledging that the abiding human qualities of dignity, creativity and productive potential are eroded by chronic poverty, the Heads of State or Government reiterated their commitment to empowering the poor for enhanced growth consistent with human development and equity. Recognizing that poverty is a complex multi-dimensional problem with origins in both national and international domains, country-specific programmes to tackle poverty and international efforts supporting national efforts and the parallel process of creating a supportive international environment conducive to economic growth and social development of developing countries, are crucial for a solution to this problem. The World Summit for Social Development recognized the need for focusing the attention of the international community on and supports the special needs of countries and regions in which there are substantial concentrations of people living in poverty, in particular those in South Asia and which face serious difficulties in achieving social and economic development.

- The SAARC Nations reiterated their commitment to eradicate poverty and noted with appreciation the outcome of the World Summit for Social Development. The SAARC Nations committed themselves to addressing the fundamental causes of poverty and to provide for the basic needs of all. They reaffirmed their commitment to work for guaranteeing the realisation of the rights of all, in particular those of the poor, to food, work, shelter, health, education, resources and information. The SAARC Nations reaffirmed their commitment to provide expanded opportunities to the poor to enhance their overall capacities and improve living conditions and to adequate economic and social protection during unemployment, disability and old age. While recognising the need to improve, expand and deregulate markets to promote sustained economic growth they felt it was essential to mitigate any negative features created by the market forces and make all efforts to make the markets friendly to the poor.

- The SAARC Nations noted with satisfaction that subsequent to the signing of the Framework Agreement on SAARC Preferential Trading Arrangement (SAPTA) during their Seventh Summit in Dhaka in April 1993, the first round of trade negotiations to exchange trade concessions among Member States has been completed. They directed that all necessary steps should be taken to facilitate ratification by all Member States and operationalise SAPTA by the end of 1995 as mandated. The Leaders reiterated their firm belief that the operationalisation of SAPTA will herald the beginning of a new and significant process of regional cooperation and would lend strength to SAARC as an institution for promoting the welfare of the peoples of South Asia.
- The SAARC Nations endorsed the "Kathmandu Resolution on Women and Family Health", adopted by the Ministerial Conference on Women and Family Health in Kathmandu in November 1993, and expressed satisfaction that appropriate programmes were being undertaken to implement the Resolution at the national level by the Member States. The Leaders of SAARC Nations noted the progress in the implementation of the Plan of Action to mark 1991–2000 as the 'SAARC Decade of the Girl-Child', and requested the Council of Ministers to conduct a comprehensive mid-decade review for presentation to the Ninth SAARC Summit.
- The SAARC Nations noted that illiteracy is one of the major causes of poverty, backwardness and social injustices and called on the Member States to initiate more concrete programmes aimed at eradicating illiteracy in the region preferably by the year 2000 A.D. They decided to observe 1996 as the "SAARC Year of Literacy".
- The SAARC Nations Reaffirming the need for a concerted action for the protection and preservation of the environment, they also expressed their satisfaction over the formulation of a common position by Member States prior to the World Conference on Natural Disaster Reduction and the presentation of the collective position at the Yokohama Conference. They recognised that international cooperation is vital for building up national capabilities, transfer of appropriate technology and promotion of multilateral projects and research efforts in natural disaster reduction.
- The SAARC Nations expressed their deep concern at the unabated degradation of the environment and recurrence of devastating natural disasters. They also underscored the risks and dangers involved in overlooking the challenge posed by these problems. They expressed their commitment to implementing at all levels—national, bilateral, regional and global—programmes for the protection and preservation of the environment and prevention of its degradation.
- The SAARC Nations noted that although some work has been carried out in the area of disseminating information on the problems of environmental degradation and their impact on the region, progress in the implementation of the recommendations of the SAARC Regional

Study on the Causes and Consequences of Natural Disasters and the Protection and Preservation of the Environment and the Regional Study on Greenhouse Effect and its Impact on the Region, which were completed in 1992, had been slow. They stressed the importance of effective and speedy implementation of the recommendations of the two Studies and requested Member States to take all necessary steps without further delay in vital areas such as sharing and developing scientific capabilities to protect and manage the environment.

- The SAARC Nations recalled the decisions expressed in the Dhaka Declaration of April, 1993 on the outcome of the United Nations Conference on Environment and Development (UNCED) of June, 1992 and reiterated the urgent need to ensure the flow of new and additional resources that are adequate and predictable to successfully implement the programmes of Agenda 21. They also recalled the United Nations minimum target for developed countries of 0.7 per cent of GNP as Official Development Assistance, a target which is yet to be approximated by most developed countries. The SAARC Nations also noted that international actions in the area of environment protection should be based on partnership and collective endeavours and should reflect the principle enunciated in the UNCED, of common but differentiated responsibilities. Integral to such actions is the promotion of economic growth in developing countries, that is both sustained and sustainable and direct action in eradicating poverty.
- The SAARC Nations expressed serious concern on the spread of terrorism in and outside the region and reiterated their unequivocal condemnation of all acts, methods and practices of terrorism as criminal. They deplored all such acts for their ruinous impact on life, property, socio-economic development and political stability as well as on regional and international peace and cooperation.
- The Leaders of SAARC Nations welcomed the ratification of the SAARC Convention on Narcotic Drugs and Psychotropic Substances by all Member States and entry into force of the Convention in September, 1993. They urged all Member States to take necessary follow-up action for effective implementation of the Convention.
- The Leaders of SAARC Nations noted with satisfaction that the SAARC Chamber of Commerce and Industry (SCCI) have been functioning satisfactorily. They expressed hope that the SAARC Chamber and its constituent units in the Member States will do their utmost to promote trade and economic cooperation in the SAARC region. The Leaders commended the SAARC Chamber for disseminating information on the scope, content and potentials of SAARC Preferential Trading Arrangement (SAPTA) among the business community in the region.
- The SAARC Nations endorsed the establishment of a three-window South Asian Development Fund with the merger of SAARC Fund for Regional Projects and the SAARC Regional Fund and a third window for social development and infrastructure development.

- The SAARC Nations noted that the end of the Cold War had resulted in fundamental changes in the political landscape. It was therefore important that a new idiom be found to address new concerns. The disappearance of the confrontation between the two power blocs presented an opportunity towards building a genuine consensus for a new international order.
- The SAARC Nations had wide ranging discussions on the current global political trends and future prospects, particularly those issues that concern South Asia. In this context, they reiterated their deep commitment to the purposes and principles of the UN Charter and reaffirmed their resolve to strengthen the United Nations as the central instrument for peace, security, disarmament, development and cooperation among the nations of the world. While pledging their support to all constructive initiatives aimed at strengthening the United Nations, the Leaders emphasised that such initiatives must be undertaken with the sole objective of rendering the United Nations and all its organs more democratic, efficient and effective and not to limit the focus of its attention to a narrow and isolated range of objectives.
- The SAARC Nations welcomed the successful conclusion of the Uruguay Round of multilateral trade negotiations and reaffirmed their commitment to implement fully and as scheduled, the Final Act of the Uruguay Round of multilateral trade negotiations. They also welcomed the coming into existence of the WTO and expressed the hope that it would help to expand international trade, particularly that of the developing countries. They reaffirmed the immediate need to elaborate policies to enable developing countries, to take advantage of expanded international trading opportunities, in the context of the full implementation of the Round. They called on all countries to refrain from any unilateral measure not in accordance with international law, the Charter of the United Nations and enlightened regionalism and globalism that creates obstacles to trade relations among States and thereby impedes the full realisation of social and economic development.
- Recognizing that the promotion of mutually reinforcing broad-based sustained economic growth on a global scale, as well as a non-discriminatory, and multilateral rule-based international trading system, provided a basis for social development, SAARC Nations called for the establishment of an open, equitable, cooperative and mutually beneficial international economic environment. They also called for a reduction of trade barriers and promotion of expanded access to global markets.
- The SAARC Nations their commitment to safeguard the basic interests of workers. They called upon countries to refrain from erecting trade barriers in the guise of promotion and protection of workers' rights. They deplored the tendency to impose any conditionalities on international trade, whether as a "social clause" or as the "environmental clause", while reiterating their commitment to ensuring workers' rights as well as protection of the environment.

The SAARC Nations noted with deep concern that economic growth in the Least Developed Countries and Land-Locked Countries is not satisfactory and emphasized the need to take special measures for accelerating the process of development. They reiterated the need to fulfill the internationally agreed aid targets for the developing countries and the Least Developed Countries. They emphasized on the need for exceptional finance to facilitate implementation of economic reform programmes in SAARC Countries. The SAARC Nations gratefully accepted the offer of the Government of Maldives to host the Ninth SAARC Summit.

9.14 NINTH SAARC SUMMIT MALE

Introduction

The Ninth Summit of the South Asian Association for Regional Cooperation (SAARC) at Malé, Maldives on 12–14 May, 1997. The SAARC Nations reiterated their commitment to SAARC and resolved to accelerate regional cooperation in order to realise the aims and objectives of the Association. They reaffirmed their commitment to the principles enshrined in the SAARC Charter, especially to the principles of sovereign equality, territorial integrity, national independence, non-use of force and non-interference in each others' internal affairs. They were convinced that regional cooperation was indispensable in an interdependent world for the realisation of the full potential of the South Asian region. The SAARC Nations welcomed the holding of the Commemorative Session of the Council of Ministers in New Delhi in December, 1995 to mark the First Decade, on the theme "SAARC—Vision for the Second Decade". They observed that over the past decade SAARC has matured as an institution and the scope and volume of cooperative activities have expanded. They expressed satisfaction that in addition to continued cooperation in agreed areas, SAARC has now moved into the core areas of economic cooperation.

- The SAARC Nations noted that, in the twelve years of its existence, SAARC has seen progress in various fields of its endeavour. They directed that a Group of Eminent Persons (GEP) be constituted, with distinguished backgrounds in activities pertaining to regional cooperation, comprising of one representative from each Member State, with the discretion of each Member State to appoint an additional representative. This Group, to which the SAARC Secretary-General will be invited, will undertake a comprehensive appraisal of SAARC, and identify measures including mechanisms to further vitalise and enhance the effectiveness of the Association in achieving its objectives. They further decided that the Group may develop a long-range vision and formulate a perspective plan of action including a SAARC Agenda for 2000 and Beyond which will spell out the target that can and must be achieved by the year, 2020.
- The SAARC Nations reiterated their determination to reinforce the unity and cohesion of SAARC. With the objective of enhancing regional solidarity and promoting overall development within SAARC, the

SAARC Nations encouraged, under the provisions of Articles VII and X of the Charter, the development of specific projects relevant to the special individual needs of three or more Member States.

- The SAARC Nations recalled their commitment to the promotion of mutual trust and understanding and, recognising that the aims of promoting peace, stability and amity and accelerated socio-economic cooperation may best be achieved by fostering good neighbourly relations, relieving tensions and building confidence, agreed that a process of informal political consultations would prove useful in this regard.
- SAARC Nations agreed that effective implementation of poverty eradication programmes required a focus on greater participation of target groups in the formulation and implementation of such programmes through social mobilization. They, therefore, decided to designate 1997 as the "SAARC Year of Participatory Governance".
- The SAARC Nations welcomed the successful holding of the Micro-credit Summit in Washington, D.C. in February, 1997 and its Declaration of support to launch a global campaign to reach 100 million of the world's poorest families, especially women, with credit for self-employment and other financial and business services, by the year, 2005 A.D. Recognizing that micro-credit programmes have successfully demonstrated their usefulness toward achieving many goals of socio-economic upliftment, including the eradication of poverty and empowerment of women, the Leaders agreed to intensify endeavours in their respective countries so that the outreach of these programmes becomes widespread.
- The SAARC Nations were convinced that an enabling international environment to support poverty eradication efforts of the SAARC countries is an essential element in attaining success for these efforts. They urged all donor countries, international institutions and other bodies engaged in eradication of poverty to increase their support and assistance to these efforts.
- The SAARC Nations noted with satisfaction the entry into force of the Agreement on SAARC Preferential Trading Arrangement (SAPTA) on 7 December, 1995. They recognised the importance of achieving a free trade area by the year 2001 A.D. and reiterated that steps towards trade liberalisation must take into account the special needs of the smaller and the Least Developed Countries and that benefit must accrue equitably. While expressing satisfaction at the conclusion of the two Rounds of Trade Negotiations under SAPTA, the SAARC Nations welcomed the decision to launch the Third Round of Trade Negotiations shortly. They agreed that preferential tariff concessions should cover products which are being actively traded amongst Member States. They further agreed that the Third Round should deepen tariff concessions along with the removal of non-tariff barriers and structural impediments in order to move speedily towards the goal of SAFTA.

- The Leaders of SAARC Nations welcomed the holding of the First Meeting of the Commerce Ministers and the First SAARC Trade Fair in New Delhi in 1996 and noted the decision of the Commerce Ministers to meet annually. They further welcomed the offer of Pakistan to host the second SAARC Trade Fair to coincide with the SAARC Commerce Ministers' Meeting.
- The SAARC Nations agreed that the efforts to enhance trade and economic co-operation in the region would be further strengthened by initiating specific steps to promote and protect investment, increase complementarities in economic activities of Member States and other measures supportive of promotion of SAARC joint ventures. They also welcomed the offer of India to host a meeting on promotion and protection of investment and the offer of Pakistan to host a meeting on avoidance of double taxation. They also welcomed measures of cooperation in the areas of customs standardization, arbitration and enhancing industrial economy and management. They also agreed for the intensifying economic cooperation of the interests of smaller countries, especially the least developed among them, should be taken into account through the implementation of special measures in their favour.
- The SAARC Nations expressed satisfaction that the annual reviews of the situation of children in SAARC countries for the years 1995 and 1996 revealed significant progress in reducing infant mortality and in enhancing the coverage of immunisation in the region. They stressed that sustained efforts should be made by Member States to consolidate the gains in these areas. In this regard, they welcomed the decision to designate Seventh December, 1997 and Eighteenth January, 1998 as "SAARC Polio Immunisation Days". They reaffirmed their commitment to improve the status of children in disadvantaged circumstances in the SAARC region. They recognised that the problems of these children are inextricably linked to the prevailing socio-economic conditions and problems of the region, and therefore, called for a holistic approach to address them. They expressed the need to formulate a Convention on Regional Arrangements on the Promotion of Child Welfare in South Asia in launching the SAARC Decade of the Rights of the Child, from the year 2001 A.D. to 2010 A.D.
- The SAARC Nations agreed to launch an Initiative on Nutrition aimed at promotion of availability of food of essential nutritional value to individual household and evolving policies for supplementing and fortifying essential micro-nutrients, deficiencies of which have affected the well being of the most vulnerable sections of the population, particularly women and children.
- The SAARC Nations recognised that illiteracy is one of the major causes impeding the development of the vast human resource potential of the region and a major factor contributing to the region's economic backwardness and social imbalance. They noted that the Member States had observed "1996 as the SAARC Year of Literacy" and reiterated

their commitment to continue endeavours to eradicate illiteracy from the region. Recognising the resource, manpower and infrastructural constraints to the promotion of vocational and higher education in the region, the Leaders agreed that new and innovative methods like Open Learning and Distance Education can play an effective role in meeting regional needs in a cost effective and flexible manner. Accordingly, they agreed that the institutional facilities in such education available in the region should be utilised on a regional scale. The possibility of the creation of a Consortium of Open Universities in the region should also be explored.

- The SAARC Nations emphasized the need to continue cooperation in the field of Science and Technology was imperative in ensuring the acceleration of the process of development in the region and recognizing the progress made in this field, especially in facilitating research and exchange of information in the fields of bio-technology, genetic engineering, energy modeling techniques and low-cost housing and building technologies.
- The SAARC Nations Emphasising that tourism plays an important role in promoting people to people contact in the region stressed the importance of strengthening cooperation with the aim of realizing its full potential in the region. They were convinced that greater cooperation in this area would contribute to the enhancement of people-to-people contact within the region as well as to the economic development of Member States.

The SAARC Nations noted that current trends of globalisation and liberalisation were imposing a heavy burden on developing economies, in particular, the least developed countries (LDCs) which are becoming marginalized from the mainstream of the world economy. They also expressed concern over trends to erect new protectionist barriers by linking imports from developing countries to politically motivated social and environmental values and concerns, such as human rights. They observed that the impact of these trends is compounded by new challenges relating to issues of access to markets, capital and new technologies. They also noted with regret the overall decline in the Official Development Assistance (ODA) over the years which have contributed to the aggravation of the condition of the LDCs. They affirmed the promotion of a non-discriminatory and multilateral rule-based global system of economic relations in order to engage the developing countries constructively and on the basis of reciprocal shared benefits in the process of liberalisation, as well as to assist them integrate into the global economy. The SAARC Nations called on the developed countries to assist the developing countries through the creation of a favourable and supportive global economic environment, in particular, through domestic action in their countries for purposes of accelerating investment flows to developing countries thereby generating a positive impact on the developmental efforts of developing countries as well as assisting their integration into the multilateral trading system. They also called on the developed countries to substantially reduce tariff and non-tariff barriers and desist from restrictive trade practices, which would negatively affect the access of developing countries to global markets. The SAARC Nations accepted with deep appreciation the offer of the Government of Sri Lanka to host the Tenth SAARC Summit. They further decided that the Eleventh and Twelfth Summits will be held in Nepal and Pakistan, respectively.

9.15 TENTH SAARC SUMMIT COLOMBO

Introduction

The Tenth Summit of the South Asian Association for Regional Cooperation (SAARC) at Colombo from July 29 to 31, 1998, in the year of the Golden Jubilee of the Independence of Sri Lanka. The SAARC Nations re-affirmed their firm commitment to the objectives, principles and provisions of the Charter of the South Asian Association for Regional Cooperation (SAARC) and to the pursuit of regional cooperation on the basis of their acceptance of the principles of sovereign equality, territorial integrity of States, political independence, non-interference in each others internal affairs, non-use of force, the peaceful settlement of all disputes and mutuality of benefit. The SAARC Nations recognised that the rich potential for productive, equitable regional cooperation among the Governments and people of South Asia which accounts for a fifth of humanity should be fully realised. The SAARC Nations recognized that South Asia, while reflecting a rich, complex and varied plurality of cultural and religious traditions, was heir to a profound common civilizational continuum of great antiquity which constitutes a historical basis for sustaining harmonious relations among the people of the region. They acknowledged that the SAARC process could draw more deeply from the vitality and strength of South Asia's shared cultural heritage as a source influencing and enhancing creative energies in all fields.

- The SAARC Nations welcomed the offer of Sri Lanka to host a meeting of the Ministers of Cultural Affairs of SAARC to prepare a practical Action Plan to network the national institutes of cultural relations and to establish a South Asian Cultural Center to promote the distinctive arts of South Asia. They requested the Government of Sri Lanka to circulate a concept paper on the issues to be addressed by the meeting including financing arrangements for the proposed institute.
- The SAARC Nations reiterated their commitment to the promotion of mutual trust and understanding and, recognising that the aims of promoting peace, stability and amity and accelerated socio-economic cooperation may best be achieved by fostering good neighbourly relations, relieving tensions and building confidence, agreed that a process of informal political consultations would prove useful in this regard. The Heads of State or Government further recognized that this process would contribute to the appreciation of each other's problems and perceptions as well as for decisive action in agreed areas of regional cooperation.

- The SAARC Nations continued their review of the nature, extent, and effectiveness of the cooperative activities of SAARC. They considered the Report and Recommendations of the Group of Eminent Persons mandated by the Ninth Summit in Malé to undertake a comprehensive appraisal of SAARC and to develop an Agenda for 2000 and beyond.
- The SAARC Nations assessed the implications of current global economic developments on the economies of South Asia and other developing countries. They noted the profundity of the wide-spread changes being effected in the economic, technological, social and information fields and their apparent unpredictability. They expressed serious concern over the severe distortions produced by the process of unrestrained globalisation as has been evidenced in the downturn of economies of several Asian States. The challenges and opportunities inherent in these fast evolving developments could best be met and the full potential of South Asia realized through effective practical regional and bilateral cooperation among Member States.
- The SAARC Nations observed that following the WTO Ministerial Conference in Geneva, a process has been initiated at the WTO where implementation issues, built in agenda issues, issues arising out of the WTO Ministerial Conference and other multi-lateral trade issues will be considered with a view to making recommendations to the next Ministerial Conference of the WTO in 1999. These issues and the decisions arising from this process will have far-reaching consequences for our development strategies and prospects. The SAARC Nations, therefore, resolved that SAARC countries would endeavour to coordinate their decisions on these issues in areas of common concern so as to protect and promote the interest of the developing countries. They expressed concern about the erection of protectionist barriers and the tendency to impose arbitrary "norms" relating to labour conditions, environmental regulations, governance and other extraneous issues to regulate trade exchanges, which would amount to additional non-tariff barriers, that would have the effect of restricting market access for developing countries including preferential access by Least Developed Countries (LDCs) into markets of developed countries. They agreed on the need for collective strategies to promote a rule-based, non-discriminatory and equitable international trading system in which the interests and concerns of developing countries would be fully safeguarded and served.
- The SAARC Nations noted that emerging issues relating to copyright, patents and marketing franchises including on foodgrains, plants and herbs indigenous to South Asia require firm collective responses to preserve these bio-resources from unregulated commercial exploitation by extra-regional interests. They emphasized in this regard, the principle of sustainable development of bio-resources and the provisions of the UN Convention on Bio-diversity which provided for regulated access to such resources on terms and conditions to be agreed upon with the State in which such resources are located.

- The SAARC Nations cautioned that potential efforts to formulate a new Multilateral Investment Agreement should not overlook the need to ensure the continued independence of developing countries and Least Developed Countries (LDCs) to formulate specific investment policies appropriate to their stage of development.
- The SAARC Nations While reviewing the beneficial effects of globalization stressed the fact that systemic crises are becoming unpredictable with increased globalization. They expressed their concern about the shortcomings of the international monetary and financial system, and its tardiness in anticipating impending financial market crises sufficiently in advance, so that pre-emptive remedial action be adopted. They noted that the problem is systemic, and not unique to Asia, nor confined to emerging economies, and that it can have global ramifications, unless more fundamental reforms are put in place.
- They recognized the risk that ad-hoc approaches, however prompt, once crises supervene, may lead to excessive social costs in the attempt to restore financial discipline. More effective social safety nets would, therefore, need to be devised for protecting vulnerable groups and a more appropriate balance between financing and adjustment found in a reformed international system or architecture, if both the economic and social aspirations of SAARC countries are to be realized. They acknowledged the need to strengthen the individual financial systems of SAARC countries through enhancing institutional capacity, surveillance mechanisms as well as through closer consultations on, and coordination of macro-economic policies where appropriate.
- The SAARC Nations assessed progress made in the two rounds of negotiations already undertaken under SAPTA. They decided that the third round should be concluded well before the Twenty-first Session of the Council of Ministers. The SAARC Nations decided that to accelerate progress in the next round of SAPTA negotiations, deeper preferential tariff concessions should be extended to products which are being actively traded, or are likely to be traded, among Members; that discriminatory practices and non-tariff barriers should be simultaneously removed on items in respect of which tariff concessions are granted or have been granted earlier. Measures to remove structural impediments should also be taken in order to move speedily towards the goal of SAFTA. They also directed that domestic content requirements under SAPTA Rules of Origin should be reduced and that the SAPTA Committee of Participants should meet by mid-October '98 in Colombo to finalise the extent of reduction in keeping with the decision of the Second SAARC Commerce Ministers' Meeting. The Heads of State or Government reaffirmed that measures to enable smaller and Least Developed Countries to benefit equitably from economic liberalization were especially important.
- The SAARC Nations reiterated the importance of achieving SAFTA as mandated by the Ninth SAARC Summit. To this end they decided that

a Committee of Experts, in consultation with Member States, be constituted with specific Terms of Reference (TOR) to work on drafting a comprehensive treaty regime for creating a free trade area. The Heads of State or Government expressed the view that such a treaty must incorporate, among other things, binding time-frames for freeing trade, measures to facilitate trade, and provisions to ensure an equitable distribution of benefits of trade to all states, especially for smaller and least developed countries, including mechanisms for compensation of revenue loss. They emphasised the importance of finalising the text of the regulatory framework by the year 2001.

- The SAARC Nations noted links initiated between SAARC and other international and regional organizations. They considered the prospects for the development of SAARC projects and programmes in association with such organizations with which SAARC has cooperative arrangements as well as through other forms of cooperation. The Heads of State or Government were of the view that priority needs to be given in establishing contact with those regional groupings which have experience in economic cooperation and functional regional cooperation.
- The SAARC Nations urged the Forum, to spearhead the development of distance education outside the Open University System as well, drawing on the advances in Information Technology, to reach out to the remote and under-privileged sections. They welcomed the offer of Sri Lanka to host a meeting of Vice-Chancellors of SAARC Open Universities during the last quarter of 1998 to discuss the modalities for the establishment of the Forum and to draw up a programme to achieve the objectives identified by the SAARC Nations. They requested the Forum to report to the Standing Committee on a continuous basis on its programmes.
- The SAARC Nations reiterated the commitment of SAARC to the eradication of poverty in the Region at the earliest possible, preferably by the year 2002. They emphasised the need to encourage maximum participation by target groups in the formulation and implementation of poverty eradication programmes. The Heads of State or Government were of the view that such participation is essential for success of efforts in this field. They stressed the need for effective utilisation of the SAARC Three-Tier Mechanism on Poverty Eradication and in that context welcomed the offer of the Government of Pakistan to host the next meeting of the SAARC Finance/Planning Ministers under the Mechanism in October, 1998.
- The SAARC Nations noted that Human Resource Development is a key element in any poverty eradication programme. The Heads of State or Government, therefore, agreed that once the SAARC Centre for Human Resource Development in Islamabad is established, it could look in to the possibility of its contributing to the strengthening of the human resource development components of the regional poverty eradication programmes.

- The SAARC Nations welcomed the results of the First Conference of SAARC Communication Ministers held in Colombo in May, 1998. They noted that technological advances were making telecommunications an important medium for socio-economic development and developing commercial and business relations as well as promotion of people-to-people contact. They called for the speedy implementation of the Plan of Action adopted by the First Meeting of the SAARC Communication Ministers.
- The SAARC Nations expressed their deep satisfaction at the positive outcome of the Environment Ministers' Conference held in Malé in October 1997, and called for the effective and early implementation of the SAARC Environment Action Plan. In this context, they welcomed the offer of Maldives to prepare a feasibility study on the establishment of a Coastal Zone Management Centre. The Heads of State or Government also committed their governments to prepare National Environment Action Plans and State of the Environment Reports before the end of 1998.
- The SAARC Nations expressed their satisfaction over the adoption of a common position by Member States prior to the Third Session of the Conference of the Parties to the United Nations Framework Convention on Climate Change, held in Kyoto, Japan and welcomed the adoption of the Kyoto Protocol to the United Nations Framework Convention on Climate Change in December 1997, and underscored the importance of the Protocol for the protection of the climate system. They urged all industrial countries to ratify the Protocol and to undertake urgent and effective steps to implement the commitments undertaken by them to reduce their emissions of green-house gases.
- The SAARC Nations condemned the exploitation of children by terrorist groups in hostilities and called for special measures for the psychological, physical and social rehabilitation of child victims. In this respect, the SAARC Nations noted the initiative taken by Maldives in pursuance of their directive at the Ninth SAARC Summit in drafting the Convention on Regional Arrangements for the Promotion of Child Welfare in South Asia. They welcomed the offer of Maldives to hold an Expert Group Meeting to finalise the draft Convention for its adoption at the Eleventh SAARC Summit.
- The SAARC Nations noted that many groups of women and girl children in South Asia continue to be in disadvantaged positions and lack equal opportunities for economic and social development. They were of the view that sustained efforts and practical affirmative action was required to offset the effects of discriminatory, social and psychological perceptions and to empower women through affirmative action, including where necessary, legislative measures. The SAARC Nations condemned in particular violence against women and acts of discrimination and humiliation which tend to depress the status of women. They also expressed concern over the plight of women and girl

children in situations of conflict. Equal opportunities in education, health facilities and nutrition were vital for the integration of women in the mainstream of national development. They agreed to work in close association, where possible, with professional and other women's groups in the region to ameliorate their conditions.

- The SAARC Nations welcomed the recommendations of the First Meeting of SAARC Information Ministers held in Dhaka in April, 1998 and the offer of Pakistan to host the Second Meeting of Information Ministers of SAARC Countries. The SAARC Nations called for concerted endeavours for the promotion of practical programmes among South Asian countries, including through professional organizations, in the field of information and media exchanges benefitting from technological advances. Such action would help promote deeper understanding of issues common to the region, as well as to project a more balanced view of developments in the region. They welcomed the offer of India to host the First Meeting of SAARC Editors and Journalists.

The SAARC Nations taking note of the 50th Anniversary of the Universal Declaration of Human Rights reaffirmed their commitment to the further promotion of human rights and fundamental freedoms by strengthening the respective national institutions in South Asia in this field. The Leaders agreed that tolerance and mutual accommodation, combined with the strengthening of participatory governance, constituted the foundation for the sustainable economic and social development of the SAARC region. The SAARC Nations called for intensification of efforts for promoting peace and stability at the global and regional levels for realising universal progress and prosperity. The SAARC Nations accepted with deep appreciation the offer of His Majesty's Government of Nepal to host the Eleventh SAARC Summit in the second half of 1999.

9.16 ELEVENTH SAARC SUMMIT KATHMANDU

Introduction

The Eleventh Summit meeting of the South Asian Association for Regional Cooperation (SAARC) in Kathmandu, Nepal from 4 to 6 January, 2002. The SAARC Nations reaffirmed their commitment to regional cooperation through SAARC and underscored the importance of annual Summit meetings in charting common strategies for the realization of the objectives and principles set out in the Charter of the Association. Meeting for the first time at the dawn of the new millennium, they solemnly renewed their pledge to strengthen the Association and make it more cohesive, result oriented, and forward looking, by adopting clearly defined programs and effective implementation strategies in line with popular expectations. To give effect to the shared aspirations for a more prosperous South Asia, the Leaders agreed to the vision of a phased and planned process eventually leading to a South Asian Economic Union. The SAARC Nations stressed that equitable sharing of the benefits of regional cooperation is essential to achieve and maintain a minimum acceptable level of economic and social development in each Member State. To this end, they expressed their commitment to a speedier process of harmonizing their policies and practices and imbibing regional goals and strategies in their national development programs.

- The SAARC Nations expressed their firm determination to fully benefit from the wealth of traditional wisdom, creativity and enterprise in the region. They also pledged to enhance transparency and accountability in governance and to encourage effective participation of the peoples and civil societies in the formulation as well as implementation of the programs of cooperation. Reiterating their resolve to promote South Asian regional identity and to strengthen cooperation at the international level, the SAARC Nations also reemphasized the need to evolve common positions on issues of shared interest at the international forum.
- The SAARC Nations agreed to accelerate cooperation in the core areas of trade, finance and investment to realize the goal of an integrated South Asian economy in a step-by-step manner. They expressed their determination to make full use of regional synergy to maximize the benefits of globalisation and liberalization and to minimize their negative impacts on the region. While recognizing that trade and economic expansion is closely inter-linked, the Leaders made a commitment to widen and deepen the scope of regional networks of activities in trade and financial matters.
- The SAARC Nations vernment noted with satisfaction the outcomes of the successive meetings of the SAARC Commerce Ministers aimed at enlarging the scope of cooperation in the core areas. They recognized the importance of achieving a free trade area and reaffirmed that the treaty regime for creating a free trade area must incorporate, inter alia, binding timeframes for freeing trade, measures to facilitate trade and provisions to ensure an equitable distribution of benefits of trade to all states, especially for small and least developed countries, including mechanisms for compensation of revenue loss.
- Recognising the need to move quickly towards a South Asian Free Trade Area, the SAARC Nations directed the Council of Ministers to finalize the text of the Draft Treaty Framework by the end of 2002. They also directed that in moving towards the goal of SAFTA, the Member States expedite action to remove tariff and non-tariff barriers and structural impediments to free trade. They also instructed to conclude the meeting of the Inter Governmental Group on Trade Liberalization for the Fourth Round of Trade Negotiations under SAPTA as early as possible as per the decision of the Tenth SAARC Summit in Colombo.
- The SAARC Nations renewed their commitment to encourage the participation of the private sector and assured their full support for their socially responsible economic initiatives. While welcoming the practice of holding trade fairs in cooperation with the private sector at the regional level, they appreciated the efforts of the SAARC Chamber

of Commerce and Industry to promote regional economic cooperation in the spirit of public and private sector partnership.

- The SAARC Nations recognized the immense tourism potential of South Asia and underlined the need to take measures to promote South Asia as a common tourist destination through joint efforts in areas such as upgrading of infrastructure, air linkages, simplification and harmonization of administrative procedures and training and joint marketing.
- The SAARC Nations acknowledged that investment in poverty alleviation programs contributes to social stability, economic progress and overall prosperity. They were of the view that widespread and debilitating poverty continued to be the most formidable developmental challenge for the region. Conscious of the magnitude of poverty in the region, and recalling also the decision of the UN Millennium Summit 2000 to reduce world poverty in half by 2015, and also recalling the commitments made at the five year review of the World Summit for Social Development to reduce poverty through enhanced social mobilization, the Heads of State or Government made a review of the SAARC activities aimed at poverty alleviation and decided to reinvigorate them in the context of the regional and global commitments to poverty reduction.
- The SAARC Nations expressed their firm resolve to combat the problem of poverty with a new sense of urgency by actively promoting the synergetic partnership among national governments, international agencies, the private sector, and the civil society. They reaffirmed their pledge to undertake effective and sustained poverty alleviation programs through pro-poor growth strategies and social as well as other policy interventions with specific sectoral targets. The Leaders also agreed to take immediate steps for the effective implementation of the programs for social mobilization and decentralization, and for strengthening institution building and support mechanisms to ensure participation of the poor, both as stake-holder and beneficiary, in governance and the development process.
- The SAARC Nations decided to undertake sustained measures to extend rural micro-credit programs with focus on women and the disadvantaged sections of society. They also stressed the need for widening the opportunities for gainful employment. While highlighting the importance of promoting agriculture, indigenous skills and small scale and cottage industries to address the incidence of rural poverty, they decided to enhance cooperation in agricultural research, extension and adoption. They specifically instructed that the Technical Committees should identify programmes and activities that impact on poverty alleviation. They urged the need to create gainful employment and promote cooperation in vocational training.
- The SAARC Nations emphasized the need to promote sharing of the best practices and experiences among the Member States and to this end, instructed the Secretary-General to disseminate such information

to the Member States on a regular basis. They directed the Council of Ministers to review, on a continuous basis, the regional poverty profile to be prepared by the Secretary-General with the assistance of the related UN agencies, nodal agencies and independent research institutions specialized in the field.

- The SAARC Nations reiterated the need for an early finalisation of the SAARC Social Charter and instructed the Inter Governmental Expert Group to expedite their work on the basis of the draft to be submitted by the Secretary-General, as a working paper for its consideration and to complete the draft framework of the Charter as early as possible for consideration at the next meeting of the Council of Ministers. In drawing up the Charter, they also directed the Council of Ministers to include the important areas of poverty eradication, population stabilization, the empowerment of women, youth mobilization, human resources development, the promotion of health and nutrition and the protection of children as decided at the Tenth Summit.
- The Leaders recognized the debilitating and widespread impact of the HIV/AIDS, TB and other deadly communicable diseases on the population of South Asia and stressed the need for evolving a regional strategy to combat these diseases. The strategy should include, inter alia, culturally appropriate preventive measures, an affordable treatment regime and should specially target the vulnerable groups. In this regard, they felt that SAARC should collaborate with the international organizations and civil society. They also emphasized that the SAARC Tuberculosis Centre in Kathmandu should play a coordinating role in the related areas.
- The SAARC Nations welcomed the signing of the SAARC Convention on Preventing and Combating the Trafficking in Women and Children for Prostitution and expressed their collective resolve to treat the trafficking in women and children for commercial sexual exploitation as a criminal offence of a serious nature. They also welcomed the signing of the SAARC Convention on Regional Arrangements for the Promotion of Child Welfare in South Asia and observed that the Convention reflected their commitment to place the child first in the national and regional programs of the Member States.
- The SAARC Nations agreed to establish, on the basis of recommendations of the Regional Task Force responsible for the implementation of the provisions of the SAARC Convention on Preventing and Combating Trafficking in Women and Children for Prostitution, a voluntary fund with contributions from Member States, individuals, and donor countries and agencies for the rehabilitation and reintegration of the victims of trafficking.
- The SAARC Nations recognized the need to actively pursue and promote social development through empowerment of women and to achieve their full participation in decision making at all levels. They reaffirmed their commitment to uplift the social status of the people, women and children in particular, in the region and expressed their

common resolve to accord the highest priority to promoting social development through specific and targeted programs.

- The SAARC Nations agreed to mobilize the necessary resources and intensify broad based actions to achieve a set of priority goals related to improving the status of children, such as polio eradication by 2005, protection of children from mother-to-child transmission of HIV/AIDS, and quality basic education to the children within a time-bound period.
- The SAARC Nations recognized that access to quality education was an important element for the empowerment of all segments of society, and undertook to develop or strengthen national strategies and action plans to ensure that all children particularly the girl child have access to quality primary education by 2015; and to improve levels of adult literacy by 50 per cent by eliminating gender disparities in access to education as envisaged in the Dakar Framework for Action on Education for All adopted by the World Education Forum held at Dakar in April, 2000.
- The SAARC Nations were of the view that stability, peace and security in South Asia should be promoted together with efforts to improve the global security environment. They underscored their commitment to general and complete disarmament including nuclear disarmament on a universal basis, under effective international control. They agreed that global non-proliferation goals could not be achieved in the absence of progress towards nuclear disarmament and in this context called upon all nuclear weapon states, whether party or non-party to the NPT, to engage constructively through a transparent and credible process of negotiations at the Conference on Disarmament. The Leaders also recognized the linkage between disarmament and development.
- The Leaders emphasized the need to take appropriate measures to make international financial institutions and the global trading regime more responsive to the needs and concerns of the developing countries. They reiterated the call for genuine partnership among the developed and developing countries in international trade and finance and for the reform of the global financial architecture with an enhanced level of resources. The Leaders also called upon the developed countries to facilitate and ensure an unimpeded and enhanced level of market access to products from the developing, the least developed and the land-locked countries.
- The SAARC Nations welcomed the initiative of the donor countries to relieve the external debt burden of the Highly Indebted Poor Countries. They urged the international donor community and financial institutions to widen the scope and extent of debt relief initiatives to cover all those developing and the least developed countries, which are facing developmental difficulties particularly due to the current global recession. In the context of growing global interdependence, they underlined the importance of forging cooperative partnership between the developed and the developing countries to ensure equitable benefits to all.

- The SAARC Nations were convinced that terrorism, in all its forms and manifestations, is a challenge to all states and to all of humanity, and cannot be justified on ideological, political, religious or on any other ground. The Leaders agreed that terrorism violates the fundamental values of the United Nations and the SAARC Charter and constitutes one of the most serious threats to international peace and security in the Twenty-first century.
- The SAARC Nations emphasized the need for the urgent conclusion of a Comprehensive Convention on Combating International Terrorism. They also emphasized that international co-operation to combat terrorism should be conducted in conformity with the UN Charter, international law and relevant international conventions.
- The SAARC Nations were unanimous in recognizing the distinct ominous link between terrorism, drug-trafficking, money laundering and other trans-national crimes and emphasized the need to coordinate efforts at the national and regional levels to strengthen the global response to this serious challenge and threat to international security. They called upon the international community to assist Member States of SAARC to deal effectively with the adverse economic effects of terrorism in general and to meet the rising insurance and security related costs in particular.
- The SAARC Nations reaffirmed their commitment to the promotion of mutual trust and understanding and, recognizing that the aims of promoting peace, stability and amity and accelerated socio-economic cooperation may best be achieved by fostering good neighbourly relations, relieving tensions and building confidence, agreed that a process of informal consultations would prove useful in this regard. The Leaders further recognized that this process would contribute to the appreciation of each other's problems and perceptions as well as for decisive action in agreed areas of regional cooperation. They underlined the importance of informal political consultations in promoting mutual understanding and reinforcing the confidence building process among the Member States.
- The SAARC Nations underlined the urgent need to make the South Asian Development Fund operational by making utilization of the existing funds. They also instructed the Secretary-General to submit a proposal for seeking possible assistance from regional and international sources for the implementation of specific regional poverty alleviation priority projects.
- The SAARC Nations noted with satisfaction the growing public awareness on the need for protecting the environment within the framework of regional cooperation. They reiterated their call for the early and effective implementation of the SAARC Environment Plan of Action as endorsed by the SAARC Environment Ministers. They directed their Environment Ministers to take this into account and come up with an agreed position in their forthcoming meeting.

- The SAARC Nations noted with appreciation the proposal made by Nepal to institute a SAARC Award to honour the outstanding work of individuals and organizations within the region in the fields of peace, development, poverty alleviation and regional cooperation, and requested His Majesty's Government of Nepal to submit a concept paper for consideration by the next session of the Council of Ministers.

The SAARC Nations were in agreement that the Summit and all other meetings of SAARC needed to be made more business-like and result-oriented with focus on programs and activities supported by informed regional inputs from the cross-sections of the society. They directed the Chairman of the Council of Ministers to undertake a review of the functioning and operation of SAARC Secretariat, and to make recommendations to advance the process of rationalisation and to make SAARC more functional and business-like, to the next meeting of the Council of Ministers. The Twelfth Summit Meeting of the SAARC Nations of the South Asian Association for the Regional Cooperation (SAARC) in Pakistan in early 2003.

Question Bank

Short and Long Type Questions

1. What is International Business? Explain the nature of International Business.
2. Why is international business a crucial venture?
3. Why do business firms of a country go to other countries? Explain with suitable examples.
4. What are the competitive advantages of international business?
5. Explain the stages of international business.
6. Explain the different approaches to international business.
7. What is Mercantilism theory of International Trade? Explain the grounds that this was attacked.
8. Discuss the theory of Absolute Cost Advantage Proposed by Adam Smith. What are its assumption and implications? Explain the grounds on which this story was criticized.
9. Discuss the theory comparative Cost Advantage with money. What are its assumption and implications?
10. Explain the Relative Factor Endowment Theory of International Trade.
11. Discuss the Product Life Cycle Theory of International Trade in detail.
12. What are the limitations leveled against product life cycle theory?
13. Explain the Comparative Cost Advantage Theory of International Trade. What are the distinctions of this theory over other theories?
14. Why do firms enter international markets?
15. How do the different kinds of environmental factors enable the domestic firm to global?
16. How do you evaluate the benefits, costs and risk going global?
17. What is Exporting? How do the firms enter international markets through exporting strategy?
18. What is a joint venture? What do the firms prefer joint venture to go global?
19. What is globalization? Explain the features of globalization.
20. What are the different stages of globalization?
21. Discuss the globalization of the markets. What are the features of globalization of markets?

22. How do the companies globalize sourcing of finance?
23. Discuss the advantage and disadvantages of globalization.
24. What are the essential conditions for globalization?
25. Explain the steps taken by government of India to globalize the economy.
26. Explain the factors responsible for globalizing the Indian economy.
27. Describe the organizational structure of the WTO.
28. What do you mean by World Trade Organization?
29. Why is the third ministerial meeting of the WTO regarded as failure?
30. What are the various agenda and issues consider in the Hong-kong ministerial conference of WTO?
31. What are the basis reasons for India and other developing nations to form G-20?
32. Do you think the DOHA ministerial conference is the major success of WTO?
33. Discuss the role of India in the WTO and the WTO's role in Indian Socio-economic development.
34. Discuss in detail, how the GATT is responsible for the establishment of the WTO?
35. What is dumping? What are the impact of dumping by China and East Asian countries on Indian industry and agriculture?
36. Do you feel WTO is the third pillar of global business? Explain.
37. Explain the need for formulating International trade policy.
38. What are the various instrument of international trade policy?
39. Explain the following (1) Tariff (2) Quotas (3) Subsidies.
40. Define the term International relations. How does it affect international business?
41. What is economics integration? Explain the different kinds of economics integration.
42. State the objectives of EEC. Explain the achievements of EU in integrating its member countries.
43. What are the advantages and disadvantages of economics integration?
44. What are the distinct issues involved in international business agreements?
45. How do you determine exchange rates?
46. What are the advantages and disadvantages of fixed exchange rate system?
47. What are the implications of convertibility of the rupee on Indian economy?
48. Explain the functions and activities of the International Bank for Reconstruction and Development. How far has it been successful in achieving them?
49. Explain briefly the working of the World Bank. What contributions has it made for the economic development of India?
50. What do you mean by SWAP? Explain the Interest Rate Swap and its function to eliminate the exchange rate risk.
51. Describe the term currency SWAP. How it work in eliminating the exchange rate risk?

Objective Questions

State whether True (T) or False (F).

1. Globalisation work to a country when there is free trade. ☐
2. Globalisation help in developing the domestic industry of the home country. ☐
3. The comparative cost theory is propounded by David Recardo. ☐
4. "No country is self-sufficient" is said by prof. Haberler. ☐
5. Special Drawing Rights (SDRs) are international reserves asset created by the IMF. ☐
6. The Bid rate of foreign exchange is the synonyms of selling rate. ☐
7. The Ask rate and selling rate carry the same meaning. ☐
8. The basic objective of arbitrage is to eliminate exchange rate risk. ☐
9. The exchange differ from one exchange market to another. ☐
10. The settlement in spot market transaction falls after 10 days. ☐
11. One currency have same exchange rate in every market. ☐
12. The future contract of a currency is done under forward contract. ☐
13. Options are exercised when they are–in–the money. ☐
14. In a call option, the option buyer buys the underlying currency. ☐
15. Is the change in present cashflow involves in transaction exposure. ☐
16. Translation exposure, is also known as Accounting Exposure. ☐
17. Leading and laggis are practised between two dependent firms. ☐
18. The World Bank is a combined of IDA, IFC and IBRD. ☐
19. The World Bank provide loans for the long-term projects only to its member countries. ☐
20. The Uruguay round of GATT is responsible for establishing ASEAN. ☐
21. The fourth ministerial conference was held in Cancun. ☐

ANSWER

1. (T)	2. (F)	3. (T)	4. (F)	5. (T)	6. (F)
7. (T)	8. (T)	9. (T)	10. (F)	11. (F)	12. (T)
13. (T)	14. (T)	15. (T)	16. (T)	17. (F)	18. (T)
19. (T)	20. (F)	21. (F)			

Multiple Choice Questions

1. International business is doing business
   (i) Inside the national boundaries
   (ii) Across national political boundaries
   (iii) (i) and (ii) both
   (iv) None of these

Ans. (ii)

2. Which is not the difference between domestic and International business?
   (i) National Boundaries
   (ii) Difference in customs and language
   (iii) Currency and interest rates differs
   (iv) Both countries have restriction on trade to across the border.

Ans. (iv)

3. Globalisation of business means
   (i) Business across the border
   (ii) Production base across the globe
   (iii) Product presence in different market of the world
   (iv) Above all

Ans. (iv)

4. Benefit of the globalisation include
   (i) Change in the political system
   (ii) Profits to the small scale industries
   (iii) Protect the national boundaries from International Trade
   (iv) Expansion and growth in the economy.

Ans. (iv)

5. Essential conditions for globalisation
   (i) Restriction on the freedom of business and industry.
   (ii) Removal of Quotas and Tariffs
   (iii) Providing infrastructural facilities
   (iv) Liberalising the rules and regulation of control.

Ans. (i)

6. Disadvantages of globalisation
   (*i*) Free flow of technology (*ii*) Increase in Industrialisation
   (*iii*) Exploits Human Resources (*iv*) Increase in production and consumption.

Ans. (*iii*)

7. Modes of globalisation of investment
   (*i*) Acquisition of foreign companies (*ii*) Domestic money lendering
   (*iii*) Joint ventures (*iv*) Issuing equity shares, debentures, bonds.

Ans. (*ii*)

8. Among these economist who had propounded 'Absolute cost Advantage theory of International trade
   (*i*) Prof. Marshall (*ii*) J.B. Say
   (*iii*) Adam Smith (*iv*) David Recardo

Ans. (*iii*)

9. Which is the not the assumption of the theory comparative cost Advantage Theory?
   (*i*) Trade is free from cost of production
   (*ii*) There are no trade barriers
   (*iii*) Labour and capital are the factors of production
   (*iv*) Two country and two goods are involved in trade.

Ans. (*iii*)

10. "International trade is nothing but extension it is inter-regional or inter-local trade" who said these words
    (*i*) Prof. Haberler (*ii*) David Recando
    (*iii*) Prof. Marshall (*iv*) Bertil Ohlin

Ans. (*iv*)

11. According to Hechscher–Ohlin, the International Trade is based on
    (*i*) Labour–capital relationship (*ii*) Countries comparative advantage
    (*iii*) Relative factor cost (*iv*) Free Trade

Ans. (*iii*)

12. Which is not the phase of International Product life cycle?
    (*i*) Introduction (*ii*) Growth
    (*iii*) Saturation (*iv*) Maturity

Ans. (*iii*)

13. The Tariff is a price-based measure, it restricts the
    (*i*) Volume of export (*ii*) Volume of Imports
    (*iii*) Effective demand (*iv*) None of these

Ans. (*ii*)

14. Which is not the instrument of restricting import by a country
    (*i*) Import Quota (*ii*) Custom Union
    (*iii*) Voluntary Export Restraints (*iv*) Trading Blocks

Ans. (*iv*)

15. If the demand for foreign currency increase it means the home country's

(*i*) Export increases (*ii*) Import increases

(*iii*) Export decreases (*iv*) Import decreases

Ans. (*ii*)

16. The Exchange Rate determination is held When

(*i*) Demand for foreign currency increase over supply for foreign currency

(*ii*) Demand for foreign currency decrease over supply for foreign currency

(*iii*) Demand and supply for foreign currency is equal

(*iv*) Both demand and supply for foreign currency decreases

Ans. (*iii*)

17. International monetary fund favour

(*i*) Floating rate of exchange (*ii*) Forward rate of exchange

(*iii*) Fixed rate of exchange (*iv*) None of these

Ans. (*iii*)

18. The Purchashing Power Parity theory is given by

(*i*) Gustav Cassel (*ii*) Fisher

(*iii*) Hick (*iv*) Sweezy.

Ans. (*i*)

19. Which is not the Hedging Techniques of Exchange Rate Risk?

(*i*) Currency option (*ii*) Netting

(*iii*) Currency swap (*iv*) Interest rate Swap

Ans. (*i*)

20. Which is not the Derivative Techniques of Exchange Rate Risk?

(*i*) Currency option (*ii*) Interest rate swap

(*iii*) Future contract market (iv) None of these

Ans. (*ii*)

21. The WTO came into existence on

(*i*) 13 January, 1994 (*ii*) 21 July, 1991

(*iii*) 1 January, 1995 (*iv*) 19 April, 1999

Ans. (*iii*)

22. International Monetary Funds looks after the .... of the member countries.

(*i*) Balance of payment (*ii*) Project Appraisal

(*iii*) International Trade (*iv*) International Intellectual Rights.

Ans. (*i*)

23. Euro-dollar was introduced in

(*i*) 17 December 1995 (*ii*) 14 August 1992

(*iii*) 1 January 2001 (*iv*) 1 January 2002

Ans. (*iv*)

24. NAFTA is the free trade association among

(*i*) USA, Argentina and Mexico (*ii*) USA, Mexico and Canada

(*iii*) USA, Canada and Brazil (*iv*) Canada, Mexico, Brazil

Ans. (*ii*)

25. SAARC Association have .... member countries.

(*i*) 7 (*ii*) 9

(*iii*) 8 (*iv*) 12

Ans. (*iii*)

26. The headquarters of SAARC is situated at

(*i*) Colombo (*ii*) New Delhi

(*iii*) Kathmandu (*iv*) Dhaka

Ans. (*iii*)

27. Which Trading Block is considered as best custom union?

(*i*) SAARC (*ii*) European Union

(*iii*) NAFTA (*iv*) ASEAN

Ans. (*ii*)

28. SDRs are

(*i*) International Reserves Assets (*ii*) US Currency

(*iii*) Sterling Area (*iv*) None of these

Ans. (*i*)

29. Domestic currency tends to depreciate owing to

(*i*) Due to low inflation rate (*ii*) High inflation rate

(*iii*) No change in inflation rate (*iv*) None of these

Ans. (*ii*)

30. Speculators will buy a foreign currency through a forward market deal if

(*i*) Future spot rate of that currency is expected to be lower than the forward rate

(*ii*) Future spot rate of that currency is expected to be higher than the forward rate

(*iii*) If future spot rate is expected to be equal to the forward rate

(*iv*) None of these

Ans. (*ii*)